A
Bicentennial
Portrait of
the American
People

A
Bicentennial
Portrait of
the American
People

U.S.NEWS
&WORLD
REPORT
BOOKS

U.S.News & World Report Books
A Division of U.S.News & World Report, Inc.

Directing Editor
Joseph Newman

Art Director
Donald McCarten

Text Editor
Linda Glisson

Picture Editor
Ruth Adams

Editorial Consultant
Russell Bourne

Assistant Picture Editor
Judith Gersten

Researcher
Christine Bowie

Writers

Russell Bourne (Chapter 1) H. Brandt Ayers (2)
Walter McQuade and Ann Aikman (3) Walter Havighurst (4)
Virginia Weisel Johnson (5) Lon Tinkle (6)
Neil Morgan (7—West Coast) Gavan Daws (7—Hawaii)
Booton Herndon (7—Alaska)

Copyright © 1975 by U.S.News & World Report, Inc.
2300 N Street, N.W., Washington, D.C. 20037

Trade distribution by Simon and Schuster
ISBN 0-89193-220-8 (Deluxe Edition)
ISBN 0-89193-221-6 (Regular Edition)

Library of Congress Catalogue Card Number 75-18902
Printed in the United States of America

Contents

Old Salem, North Carolina

The National Ancient Muster of Fife and Drum Corps, Washington, D.C.

Memorial Day, Grafton, Vermont

Bunker Hill, Boston, Massachusetts

Constitution Day, Washington, D.C.

July Fourth, Stockbridge, Massachusetts

Introduction

The changes that have come over our land since our day of independence are breathtaking. The vast surface between two mighty oceans has been converted into the most productive region of industry and agriculture to be found on earth.

The land, of course, has left its mark on those who settled it and became attached to it. Differences of soil and climate are reflected in the faces you can see in different parts of the country. We go from the extremes of the whiplashing cold of Alaska, with temperatures falling to 70 degrees below zero, to the idyllic clime of Hawaii. And the differences are expressed in the tough, rugged character of the Alaskan oil rigger, on the one hand, as compared with the easygoing, sunny nature of the Hawaiian pineapple picker, on the other.

Different racial antecedents have also made their mark on the different regions of the country. Thus along and behind the Atlantic Coast, the imprint of our English heritage pervades the entire region, with racial undercurrents stemming from all parts of Europe—from Spain, France, Italy, Germany, Scandinavia, all the way to Russia; and more recently from Puerto Rico and other Spanish speaking areas of the New World. These elements—race and climate—fashioned by economic circumstance have produced distinctive lifestyles. And these, in turn, have given the country a number of peculiarly unique regions, each different from the other, and each commanding the loyalty, in varying measure, of those born into it and those who have adopted it. With the growing threat of homogenization, the distinctive quality of our nation's various regions, described in this volume in words and pictures, sustains our greatest chance of escaping the sterilization of uniformity.

The town meetinghouse, the common, and the immaculate white church, with its slender steeple pointing heavenwards, remind all and sundry of the persistent presence of the Puritan ethic and Yankee traditions. They are the hallmark of a culture running through and uniting the fishing villages of New England and the farms and factory towns of its valleys.

As the output of America's farms and factories multiplied, the expanding wealth of the country produced an extraordinary phenomenon along the Atlantic coast: a megalopolis of 400 miles running from Boston, in the north, through New York, Philadelphia, and Baltimore to Washington, in the south. These great urban centers proved to be a mixed blessing. While raising millions of immigrants into the comfort of middle class life, on the one hand, they multiplied pockets of poverty and decay, on the other. The magnetism of the metropolis attracted more immigrants than it could cope with. The result was rising crime, congestion, and oppressive pollution. And flight to the suburbs.

The advance of industrialization and urbanization is also threatening to disturb the soft quality of life in the South. And questions are being raised whether the southerner would be wise to trade his culture, based on traditions of courtesy, civility, friendliness, and an easy way of life, for the promise of more money through more mechanization and standardization. The industrialized city is seen as the ugly product of the Yankee. Having been defeated by him once before, many southerners hardly relish this second advance from the North.

An extraordinary combination of Yankees, Irish, Germans, Poles, Scandinavians, and other racial groups, looking for greater opportunities than those offered in the East, moved toward the fertile plains of the West and eventually produced what they can rightly claim to be the nation's Heartland. They turn out nearly half of the total amount of industrial goods produced in the United States. And a good deal of its foodstuffs. This miracle of productivity comes from a people with traditions of hard work, sober habits, and thrift. Mascoutah, "a nice little town" in Illinois (and incidentally the population center of the country), has no movie house.

20

Instead, it offers a variety of community activities including turkey shoots, picnics, pancake and sausage breakfasts, and bingo. This may not be to the taste of urbanites, but Mascoutans seem quite pleased with their lot.

Nor is the life in the six states of the Rocky Mountain West likely to appeal to those accustomed to the amenities of the city. The soil in general is poor; the climate is cold in winter, lasting about ten months of the year, and hot in summer. The tough, weather-beaten rancher, working from dawn to dusk, barely ekes out a livelihood. Yet the area has a magnetic force which continues to pull people from distant cities and other parts of the country. The magnetism is in the air, clear as spring water, and in the sky, which is infinite. These breathe new life into people who feel oppressed and exploited by the city and who, seeking refuge in the Rockies, follow the trail of earlier settlers.

The Southwest, product of three contrasting and concurrent cultures—Indian, Spanish and "Anglo"—was revolutionized by the latter's thirst for action. The "Anglo," searching for profit, struck it rich when he struck oil. He then went on to create the base from which man was guided to the moon.

No less venturesome were those Americans who, propelled by a hunger for more money, more pleasure, and more freedom, went west in the tradition of earlier pioneers to seek their fortune in California. While farther north Seattle became a haven for Scandinavian homebodies and San Francisco devoted itself to becoming "the most civilized city in America," Los Angeles mushroomed into a megalopolis, dedicated to the twin gods of technology and pleasure. But in their frenetic pursuit of change and innovation, Los Angelinos became trapped in the urban smog and congestion of their own making—a Pacific counterpart of what was happening on the Atlantic side of the country. To make matters worse, they lived as unrelated strangers, vagrants moving too fast and too furiously to put down any roots. That is now being changed by the California-born children of the settlers. The young are attaching themselves to the land and looking to correct the imbalance created by their unbalanced forebears.

Both young and older Americans, in the cities and in the towns menaced by the cities, are giving thought to what has been described as the "imperative issues" of our time. They go beyond the problem of urban decay into the broader economic aspects of unemployment, poverty, and the nature of our economic structure itself; into the social question of racial and sexual inequality, and into the political question of corruption among those who govern us.

Extremists of the left and the right are ready with easy solutions. They would take us along the Soviet path or show us their belatedly rediscovered panaceas of Nazi Germany and Fascist Japan. They have had little success. The majority of Americans have made it quite clear that they prefer to seek solutions to our problems within the framework of the fundamental principles on which our nation was built. They are mindful of the priceless principle of equality and the promise of its progressive fulfillment as the threads which bound the many races of our people into a purposeful union. They therefore recognized the existence of inequality among our races—an essential step toward correcting it—and the process of reparation is now evident throughout the country, dramatically so in the transfer of power to successful black candidates for political office.

The portrait of our multiracial society, as drawn by our writers and photographers, leaves us with the impression that the American people, the product of more than 200 years of history, have been well prepared and well equipped to cope with the critical problems facing them as they enter their third century as an independent nation.

—JOSEPH NEWMAN

New England – Enduring Values

obert Frost had a way of describing what New England means to every American family sprung from that rocky soil. He called it Home. And in the memorable poem, *The Death of the Hired Man*, he defined it even more poignantly:

> Home is the place where, when
> you have to go there,
> They have to take you in.

So, for many Americans in the Bicentennial year when thoughts turn to places of origin, New England will be the point of returning. New England will be the land of rediscovery and reunion. They'll have to take us in.

But who are they? How has the Yankee character weathered the storms of the scores of years since Concord and Lexington? In an era when some believe we live in a look-alike, sound-alike, think-alike country, it's reassuring (and even startling) to go back to New England and find that the crags of the Yankee spirit stand firm. Neither eroded nor leached out, they still cast shadows across the entire American social scene.

The regional accent remains indomitable. The ability to tinker remains superior to any inert mass of wood or metal; a man wouldn't be regarded as a rightful member of the region if he couldn't "turn his hand" to anything that needed fixing.

One recent visitor's car was solidly frozen in ice when he came out the morning after skidding into a Vermont snowdrift; the engine merely whimpered when he turned the key and leaned on the starter. He got out in chilled helplessness and walked across the ringing snow to the ski lodge to call the garage in the village. A boy arrived in his own good time, powering his father's truck up through drifts and gullies with gusto bordering on arrogance. Here he connected the cables, there he attached the sling, then he presented the restored car with a self-deprecating shrug. "Bring huh down to the gay-rahge in the mahnin'; I'll fix the cahbratuh so she'll staht fine and dandy."

Besides the accent and the itch to tinker, there's tradition. As you drive past the solid, clapboard houses standing squarely beneath their protective elms, you suspect they'd rather not give themselves to new owners with the coming of successive generations or latter-day immigrations. And you're right. A conspicuous example: the farm that spreads out around a 1780 house in Dover Point, New Hampshire, has been in the hands of one family, the Tuttles, ever since 1633. It's surely the oldest, still-operating, single-family farm in the country.

But why? Why hasn't the family sold out long since, having realized (in the words of son Bill) that "the only way to get rich from farming is to sell the farm?" Mostly because of tradition. Bill and his sister, having surveyed the alternatives, intend to stay on—prudently selling the farm's seventy-five varieties of vegetables from the stand in the old barn along the road. The ethic of hard work and the practice of canny agricultural principles have helped make the farm a paying proposition; but the family determination to hang in there has been the vital element that's kept the farm going and going.

Then there's ethnic awareness and community concern. These two "social" Yankee qualities usually get along pretty well together, most buoyantly on St. Patrick's Day or other special saints' days when the entire community wears the colors, joins the parade, and feels vicariously ethnic. And more significantly at election time, when such breakthroughs as the election of Edward Brooke to the U.S. Senate (the first black to attain that office from any state in the Union since Reconstruction) may come forth from New England's ballot boxes. But occasionally the two qualities don't harmonize, as in Boston's "Southie" district where to be Irish and to play on or support one of South Boston's athletic teams is an exclusive situation. There, in the taverns among the rows of triple-tiered houses, you hear a discordant song:

> We have Biff Mahoneys
> And Buff Maloneys
> And clowns who know how to clown.
> So if you want to stay healthy
> Stay the hell out of Southie
> Cause Southie is my home town.

Even in disharmony, they're all Yankees. From the accent, the traditional ways, the pride, and the political thrust, you could spot one, though he'd moved "West of Worcester" (the central Massachusetts town where civilization was once thought to end). Perhaps a craggy nose, or what Southerners used to call "that lean, yellow-bellied look," would help you spot him too. But whatever his shape or coloration, his spirit would be unmistakable.

You can tell Yankees by their peculiar institutions too.

Around the common of a typical New England town cluster the white and classically columned church whose steeple strikes the conscience of nearly everyone in town, the elementary school with its basic principles and its granite stoop, the library which serves as a vital public information center, the town meetinghouse whose clock will never go again for want of an adequate municipal budget.

Inside the church, whether it be Congregational, Presbyterian, or Unitarian—all offshoots of seventeenth-century English and Scottish Puritanism—a plain and clear-shining beauty recalls the stern Protestantism of New England's first settlers. Of them Don Marquis wrote in *archy & mehitabel*:

> that stern and rockbound coast
> felt like an amateur
> when it saw how grim the puritans
> who landed on it were.

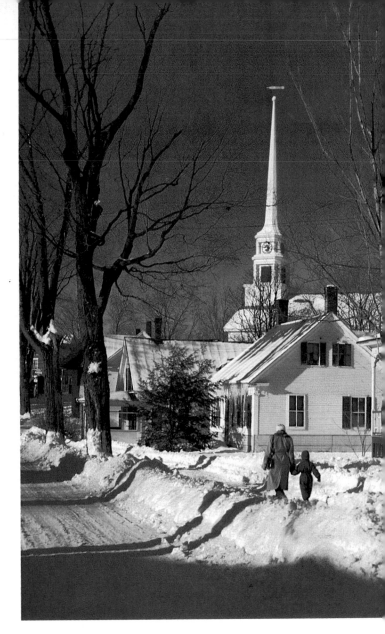

Radically determined to cut through the heavy growth of ecclesiastical convention back to the original root of Christianity in scriptural times, they cleared away the priestly connections. Instead they instituted a direct link between man and God, by which the individual was held personally responsible for his behavior—that link being his mind and conscience. Like St. Augustine, they found their text in Romans xiii (a verse often proclaimed from the Yankee pulpit today):

> The night is far spent, the day is at hand; let us put on the armour of light. Let us walk honestly, as in the day; not in carousing and drunkenness, not in debauchery and lust, not in strife and jealousy.
> But put ye on the Lord Jesus Christ, and make no provision for the flesh, to fulfill the lusts thereof.

A second corollary of the Puritan ethic was democ-

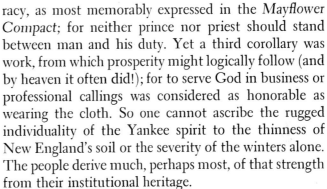

In the small towns of New England, winter mornings often begin with a shovel. The man clearing the roof (above) actually lives in Florida—Florida, Mass.

The streets of Stowe, Vt., (at left) are plowed by truck, but in tiny Waits River, Vt., (below) people often have to dig themselves out by hand. Two-thirds of all Vermonters still live in towns which, like these two, have populations of 2,500 or less.

racy, as most memorably expressed in the *Mayflower Compact*; for neither prince nor priest should stand between man and his duty. Yet a third corollary was work, from which prosperity might logically follow (and by heaven it often did!); for to serve God in business or professional callings was considered as honorable as wearing the cloth. So one cannot ascribe the rugged individuality of the Yankee spirit to the thinness of New England's soil or the severity of the winters alone. The people derive much, perhaps most, of that strength from their institutional heritage.

The common itself is an institution. Green and coolly shadowed, it represents the contradictory fact that, for all their vaunted individuality, Yankees live and think in a community manner. Indeed the community of believers was what it was all about when the Separatists and Puritans sailed off to this new world. And as historic New England grew, new communities spun off from the original settlements. The new leaders and their followers perennially sought more favorable sites—a valley with copper or potash, a hillside of rich timber—plus a different kind of freedom, removed from the tyranny of the parent. The newly planted town established its green, its common property for cow-grazing, as a manifestation of its coherence.

The grieving Civil War statue we see on most commons today, the forage-cap-wearing lad with his rifle pointed muzzle down, isn't really what the common is about. The statue is too sentimental and nonfunctional. Yet it does serve as a reminder that there have been a lot of group experiences and tribal memories. Memorial Days and Fourths of July come and go, bunting or wreaths are hung on the bandstand as the seasons pass, and the common asserts *itself* as the Yankee ideal: to be naturally green, socially concerned, and totally private. Each can keep his cow (or car) there, but no one need speak to anyone else, except for a noncommittal "Evenin'."

25

When asked about a recently departed neighbor who had lived across the common from him, a Yankee replied, "He know'd me and I know'd him. But we didn't know each other." The community exists by subtle and mutual assumption.

Less subtle are the outbursts in town meeting. "Question! Question!" chorus the voices from the back of the room as the moderator seems to take an excessive amount of time in pressing the matter forward. At issue is whether certain roads in the town should be deemed *abandoned* (meaning forever closed) or *closed* (meaning reopenable); the great virtue of the former solution being that the town will be freed from the cost of maintaining them. This all may be known, formally, as "Article Two" on the Warrant, a lengthy and legalistic docu-

Beacon Hill overlooks the Charles River and turns its back on the steel and glass towers of downtown Boston. The ancient bricks and cobbles of this lovely residential area are protected by state law.

ment which is read through in its entirety at the start of the meeting. On their respective sides of the hall the knitting women and the gallused men discuss the items among themselves, then demand recognition from the moderator to declaim their views. Finally the vote

The monthly Waltz Evenings in the ballroom of the Copley Plaza are a Boston tradition. Subscribers to the October-May series dress formally, and family groups often include three generations.

The Festival of Saint Anthony, another Boston tradition, is held in August in an Italian-American, working-class neighborhood. The saint's statue, accompanied by crowds, bands, and blizzards of confetti, is carried through the North End from 1 pm until nearly midnight.

comes: with but one dissent, the road is *abandoned*.

The town meeting usually takes place at the end of the winter, when the meetinghouse is banked around by muddy March snow. By then tempers have been stretched to snapping point by the length of winter; cantankerous and critical minds have been sharpened by the press of other people's needs. The budget and the taxes are honed down to the leanest necessities. But still every household may be heard from; everyone's right to speak to the issue is maintained no matter how late the hour or how cold the night. And in an odd way, after all the rancors have been voiced and all the dissents noted, a new kind of concord descends on the citizenry. As coats are donned, backs are slapped.

"I didn't think she'd make it over the March hill" is a phrase one hears in New England of a sickly oldster. And it's the same way with town affairs—once over the hassle of the town meeting, it's relatively smooth sailing for the rest of the year. Then the selectmen are left to run things with minimal interference from their peers (but they'd better not forget that peers they are). Yet with the growth of the towns and the weight of many complex decisions—traffic control, sewage disposal, regional high schools—there's some question whether the town meeting form of government may

not be too limited and amateurish. In an increasing number of towns, professional managers and trained staffs are providing the solid base for town or city affairs, leaving the meeting and the selectmen as rather vestigial reminders of another, simpler age. But get rid of the town meeting? "No, sir," answered a Yankee spokesman. "And I wouldn't shoot the old mare either. They've both got their place."

Making-do is another Yankee institution that's a recognizable aspect of the individual character. If you go to the symphony in Boston in anticipation of seeing high society, you will indeed be rewarded—but not with plumage. The gentlemen's shoes look like GI Joe's; the ladies' hats appear to have been brought down from the attic. A perennial remark: "In Boston you don't ask where women buy their hats. They *have* their hats." And when walking down such a fashionable road as Chestnut Street on Beacon Hill, one may be startled, upon glancing into a richly paneled room, to spy the lady of the house reknitting a tattered sweater's arm or darning the darns on a veteran sock.

For outsiders moving to New England, the mix of these Puritan traditions and folkways may seem a bit thick. But the remarkable thing is how soon and how thoroughly new New Englanders become old Yanks.

27

Playing on the ball team, sharing in the community clambake, and marching in the tercentennial parade make neighbors out of strangers. Immigration from abroad, begun with the Puritan influx (when, between 1630 and 1634, some 10,000 Englishmen settled in the Massachusetts Bay Colony), continues strongly today, bringing in a great variety of ethnic strains. In the last decade alone, some 100,000 Portuguese have come to New England's shores.

Indeed, one of the pleasurable surprises of visiting a small Yankee town is finding out who owns the local country store. DiCrocco? Miller? Kazin? Giftopolous? Whatever his or her name or place of origin, the running of that crowded, flavorful store remains a thoroughly Yankee enterprise. And the dialogue is timeless.

> "Got any stove blackin'?"
> "Yup. You want two cans?"
> "Nope. Only got one stove."

The pungent aroma of steamed clams attracts every self-respecting Yankee in town to the Annual Grange Clambake at Exeter, R.I.

Perhaps that's the best definition of a Yankee town, a definition drawn from the memory of a Maine native: "Our town was like a general store. Very self-sufficient."

When you head east from New York on the bankrupt New Haven railroad, the Yankee character of the land immediately asserts itself—the tight valleys with the little industrialized cities, the harbors spotted with "character boats," the steep-roofed houses crowded along narrow streets. The six-state territory is divided into distinctly different quarters by a north-south route (the Connecticut River) and an east-west line (Massachusetts's northern border). The two southern quarters provide major cities, fertile fields, sandy shores. North of the line lie cold woodlands, lofty mountains, and the proverbial rockbound coast. In each quarter the accents are peculiar (in southern Connecticut the letter "R" is heard with almost as much regularity as it is in Ohio), and in each section the native architecture is uncommon (though wanderers may claim they've seen "Cape Cod" cottages in the North, not knowing that the northerners have their own, equally snug version). But in whichever portion you travel, you will discover that the Yankee spirit thrives in all of its individuality and ingenuity.

"Bet you didn't know that Connecticut still milks enough cows for all the state's milk drinkers," challenged a farmer in the northwestern corner. There, where dairies and truck farms take advantage of loamed meadows tilting down from the rounded tops of the southern Berkshires, man and nature seem to have worked out a marriage of convenience. Farmers produce enough from the land to fill the needs of the tightly packed manufacturing cities, many of which were organized at mine sites for the making of such metallic gadgets as clocks, radiators, and—more recently—precision instruments.

Upon this natural scene is imposed the pattern of big

Making money seems as old a trade as farming in Connecticut—indeed the insurance business came into being in the last century as a direct result of canny Yankees' desire to hedge their bets when investing in perilous ship voyages. Thus it's perhaps to be expected that above each humble mill town, with its clutter of workers' houses, stands the grand home of the mill owner; outside such depressed cities as Bridgeport (where blacks and Puerto Ricans contend with each other to get what jobs exist for untrained workers) sprawl the golf clubs and yacht clubs of those doctors, lawyers, and businessmen who no longer contribute taxes or talents to the destiny of the city. "Bridgeport has its own style of life and I have mine," explained one lawyer. "Why should I live there just because I have to work there?"

Slicing through the region from the north (where it divides Vermont from New Hampshire and threads Massachusetts) is the broad Connecticut River, a river which nurtures learning and the arts. Portrayed by both primitive and romantic painters, the river valley offers a home today for such disparate artistic geniuses as Alexander Calder and Roger Tory Peterson. Peterson, who rues the passing of ospreys from the river scene, recently remarked, "We pay a price for population and progress in the disappearance of wildlife. But there's a way of winning it back: we can become more intensely aware of the birds and fish and mammals that remain." Upstream from his studio stand the scholastic towers of Trinity and Smith and Dartmouth, colleges which have enlightened Yankee minds ever since the early settlers determined to perpetuate their investigation of the scriptures unto new generations and to spread the Word to the heathen Indians (precious few of whom remain in Connecticut or other New England states).

Living in the valley near Wesleyan University, where he taught for many years, aged poet and politician Wilbert Snow mused back over his career, including

business and the commuter "rat race" that goes with it. Fairfield County, Connecticut, one of the highest per capita income counties in the country, luxuriates in two-acre developments and so many pools that author John Cheever fantasized in "The Swimmer" that one could Australian crawl one's way across it. But increasingly the county's executives with their leather brief cases and camel's hair coats commute not to New York City but to relocated, exurban corporate headquarters in Greenwich and Stamford.

Around Hartford cluster other splendid suburbs where dwell tycoons from such nationwide insurance firms as Travelers and Phoenix. Farmington is one of these richly endowed towns: a quiet main street on which front discreetly restored eighteenth-century houses, beyond which spread the shopping centers and porticoed would-be mansions of the newly arrived.

his youth in Maine, for an interview with Audrey and Woody Klein for *Connecticut Magazine*:

Why am I ninety years old? Because I lobstered from the age of fourteen to seventeen, with no gasoline engine, just my oars. I had sixty pots, hauled them in during the early hours, spent all afternoon catching enough bait to bait the pots the next day and then came home after it was dark. I was outdoors eighteen hours a day. I don't know how I did it, but I think it was that more than anything else that has helped me. There are no secrets: I do physical work for half an hour each morning; in the winter, I saw three armfuls of wood for my stove; in spring and summer, I work in my rose garden.

I discovered poetry in my teens when I found *Swinton's Sixth Reader* in my father's attic. I fell in love with the poets—Emerson, Longfellow, Edgar Allan Poe. I used to stay up in the attic and read them. That really set me on fire. . . .

Wesleyan offered me a job because they had lost thirteen straight debates and my specialty was argumentation. They offered me $2,500 to come here as an assistant professor of English and debating. That's how my career in Connecticut got started. But you know I was practically kicked out before I got here. I had given a speech on May 30 and I said we had to have the League of Nations. It's either anarchy or internationalism. The newspaper headline said, "Snow is a nut." When I arrived for my interview, though, I wore my American Legion pin in my lapel—and I told them I was no bolshevik. I got the job and taught here for thirty-five years. I was almost fired twice—once for swearing on the tennis courts and once for swearing in debating class.

Yankees find salty memories of their seafaring ances-

tors in the reconstructed seaport of Mystic, Connecticut. They also find employment at certain crafts—sail making, harness work, blacksmithing—which the young regard with particular respect today. "Orders Taken" is the sign that hangs above the youthful shipcarver's work bench. And as this eighth-generation Yankee chisels and gilds eagles and Indians for boats or dens, he gives a running course on the virtues of manual labor. "The mind moves when the fingers work," he says, looking up for a moment over his glasses. "And when you're makin' something like this [sweeping his hand down the line of the brilliantly painted figureheads in his shop] you don't want to make two the same way. Reminds me of what my grandmother used to say about the flowers she raised on the farm: 'They're never twice alike, you know!' "

Keen and daring, the Yankee businessman continues to find ways of existing in the valleys of southern New England. The tiny Providence & Worcester Railroad (fifty workers, seventy-five miles of track) offers an example of individual grit in the face of corporate immensity. From Rhode Island's capital city north into Massachusetts the line hauls freight—and defies the efforts of the gigantic Penn Central to put it out of business. President Robert Eder has committed the industrial heresies of cementing a friendship with the local United Transportation Union leader and guaranteeing an annual wage ($16,460) to each of his trainmen. As a result of these innovations, Eder has been able to cut train crews nearly in half compared to those the Penn Central and other deficit-ridden lines are forced to maintain. Through such efficiencies and the loyalty of his well-served employees, Eder and his Providence & Worcester are operating in the black—the little engine that could.

"*Bom dia, Senhor*" greets a newcomer to one of New England's Portuguese enclaves. Pawtucket, Rhode Island, and Fall River, Massachusetts, are two such communities. From the emotional saints' days and the

states of Our Lady of Fatima on the lawns, a visitor might conclude that these towns have been transported intact from the old country (whether from Portugal itself or from the Azores or other mid-Atlantic islands). But there are signs that these Portuguese-Americans have become thoroughly converted Yankees. For six years after his ship reached these shores, Raul Benevides painted houses to support his wife and two children. Then he branched out like any Yankee with a better product and developed an automobile sales line. After that, a weekly radio show. "The show is all in Portuguese," he explains. "I rent the station and sell ads for the program. I'm independent." That magical word.

But unemployment remains high (upwards of 10 percent) among Benevides's compatriots who knock without response on the locked gates of the huge, dead, red brick factories that dominate the area. Fishing is therefore the usual calling of Portuguese Yankees, whether by talent, choice, or lack of other alternatives. Along with Yankees from other homelands, they pursue this livelihood with the ancient tools of net and line, transported by trawler, seiner, or outboard-driven skiff.

From New Bedford, the famous whaling port, and other harbors south and north of Cape Cod, Yankee fishermen surge out to sea in their rust-streaked vessels, a swarm of gulls streaming astern of their spars. The tides, the shoals, the powerful and cranky machinery make it a hazardous way of life. The rewards: glimmering but uncertain. Hauled up with the trawler's net, a slimy, silvery cascade of fish, mud, sand, and shells demands the deft fingers of men who know the good from the bad. Sole, flounder, haddock, and cod are the most marketable fish; the rest feed the seagulls. "I eat fish every day too," one of the hardy trawlermen admitted. "On Sunday, I eat it for breakfast. That's why I'm so healthy."

From Provincetown, the original landing place of the Pilgrims, fishermen journey out to Georges Bank, a wrecker's delight which stretches 200 miles out to sea from the Cape's crooked elbow. Or they sail on to the Grand Banks off Newfoundland, where they vie with boats from Gloucester for the big catches of the North Atlantic. On return and after tying up to the bulkhead, they contend with "water rats" of various kinds, including the amateur painters. Ships and shacks and nets

hung in the sunset are their particular prey. In both
Gloucester and Provincetown, the apartment over the
chandlery at the head of the pier is as likely to be occupied by an art teacher as by a fisherman.

For all of them, the death of the fishing industry—a
death after years of slow decline in the face of foreign
competition—would be a catastrophe. But Yankees
have a way of wriggling out of the net at the last minute.
For example, it appeared for a time that the entire salty,
sandy Cape Cod area was doomed. Avid landowners
seemed determined to sell it, dunes and all, to real estate
developers, fried clam stand operators, and anyone else
who had the price. But regional planning and the subsequent declaration of certain portions as preserved National Seashore salvaged major sections of the territory.
Almost despite themselves, Yankees repossessed some
of their precious natural heritage.

Between Provincetown and Gloucester rise the steel

*Historic Faneuil Hall in Boston's Haymarket Square (above)
was named the "Cradle of Liberty" by John Adams because
the meetings held in the town hall (at left) upstairs lit the spark
that started the Revolution. There has always been a public
market on the ground floor.*

and glass towers of Boston, "The Hub" of New England
—and, to hear Yankees tell it, the world. Once a hilly
peninsula connected to the mainland by little more than
a causeway, the land has now been leveled and filled to
the point that midtown office workers are barely aware
of the harbor. And yet a sense of the past remains. This
is, after all, the home of Paul Revere and *the* Tea Party,
the city of Harvard and MIT (which are actually situ-
ated across the Charles River in Cambridge), and the

headquarters of financial firms that have sent clippers to the Orient and railroads across the United States.

> And this is good old Boston
> The home of the bean and the cod
> Where the Lowells talk only to Cabots
> And the Cabots talk only to God.

So goes the unforgettable rhyme. It's unforgettable in large part because it's true: the Boston Brahmin remains in residence, living his private, aristocratic life, controlling the tone (if no longer the politics) of New England's capital.

In the declining years of Godfrey Lowell Cabot's life, the early 1960s when he had reached his hundredth year, one of his nurses took some notes as he reminisced: "He said that when he went to the engagement party of his friend, Will Putnam, they were having a fine time until the father of the fiancée took Mr. Cabot into the library and said, 'You know, Godfrey, I have another daughter.' Mr. Cabot laughed and said, 'I got my hat and stick and got out of there as fast as I could because the other daughter was Amy Lowell.'"

Surrounded by the maxims of Emerson and the teachings of Thoreau during his youth, Cabot retained a peculiar relationship to literature. Though recognized for his robber-baron-era success in founding a dynasty secured by millions of Yankee dollars (the carbon black industry being the goods he hustled across the land), he is more widely remembered for his fostering of Boston's "Watch and Ward Society." Cabot's bluenosed group, which delighted in banning books and breaking up alleged vice rings, has its comical aspect; yet in a serious way it reveals how the Puritan conscience, though sublimated and subordinated in modern times, keeps perking.

Godfrey Cabot read novels not for the sake of literature but in order to discern the shocking sentiments they contained—from such lewdness he felt he must

The Union Oyster House has served Bostonians since 1826.

protect the masses. As early as his Harvard years, Cabot was condemning *The Three Musketeers* as "coarse and immoral"; in 1919 his Society invited the directors to attend "a private exhibition of motion picture reels, incorporating the parts cut out of the pictures by [another censor's] Board." Appointed by his caste and position to

33

the role of arbiter, he exercised that function self-consciously and rigorously. Yet he was neither a fool nor a fraud: his educational benefactions were numerous, his patriotism courageous, and his manhood tough. His son, the distinguished U.S. diplomat John Moors Cabot, who spoke of him with little fondness, wrote, "He never flew in a flock, but always above and lonely."

Other Yankee dynasties, which have served the nation as well as themselves, come readily to mind: the Saltonstalls, the Lodges, the Kennedys. Among the Higginsons, the following story is told:

> Once, when a western brokerage firm had written to the Boston investment bankers Lee, Higginson asking about the qualifications of a young Bostonian who was applying for a job, the venerable Boston house sent a genealogy showing the youth's connections with the first families of Boston. The western firm thanked Lee, Higginson but pointed out that this was not the kind of information they were seeking, since they were not planning to use him for breeding purposes.

Today the youths who flock to Boston are more interested in being together than in participating in the games aristocrats play. Attracted in part by the city's many schools and universities, in part by its congenial livability, they have turned Boston into the San Francisco of the East. Narrow streets, terrible drivers, run-down conditions merely add to the city's charm in their eyes. They feel, these urban Yankees, free of the "big rip-off" that characterizes other major cities.

Journalist James Shapiro recently talked with a number of Boston's single people in an effort to find out what makes the place *the* place they want to be in. He concluded that "Boston is, in many respects, a big city that never got too big . . . its residents retain a relaxed view and style of life that have not yet been eroded by the

34

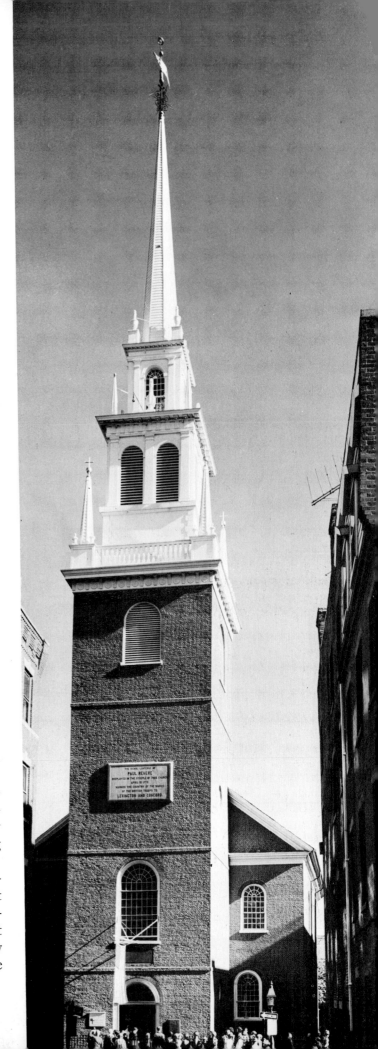

pressure of urban life." He points out that the historic
city is marked by layer upon layer of social overlays:
"Artists, students, working-class people and the middle
class are woven into a crazy quilt pattern of neighborhoods."

Sampling a few of these neighborhoods, he interviewed young people downtown, in Cambridge, and in
the nearby suburbs. Sally Dempsy said, "When I got out
of college, I moved to Cambridge and I haven't left
since, except when I head north to New Hampshire or
Vermont for skiing or camping." Al Keith, a painter,
lives in a huge loft apartment atop a deteriorated downtown building. Local landmarks include a police station,
taverns, and blocks which mix Armenians, Chinese,
blacks, Puerto Ricans, whites, and Jews. "I like Boston
because there's always so much going on," he says.

Near him, in South Boston, the mixture tends to be
100 percent Irish. There live some 40,000 of Boston's
2,750,000 people, the hard and unintegrated core of
Yankeeland's many waves of immigration from the
Emerald Isle. James Michael Curley, the convicted

mayor who spoke up for the Irish against the Brahmins,
used to be their hero. In 1974 it was Louise Day Hicks,
the woman who led fellow "Southies" against the federal order to integrate Boston's schools by means of
busing. "We trust our leaders because they've grown
up with us; we know them," explained one resident.
"And we love them because we know they aren't any
better than we are."

That limited definition of Yankee democracy may
seem in contrast with the concept at large, but South
Boston is a locality where parochial attitudes have been
ground in by decades of looking at the backside of the
Lowells and Cabots. Maids, trashmen, stevedores—
they were the people who lived in that other part of the
city—South Boston. And of course policemen and fire-
men, plus a few teachers. What jobs the Southies could
get, they hung on to; and they kept others out. In 1973
the National Education Association cited Boston as
having the worst record for hiring minority (meaning
nonwhite) teachers of any city in the country, north
or south. Despite the fact that Boston's population is

Harvard men in their
nineties (at right) march
proudly in the 1974 Class
Day Parade. Students sun
themselves (far right) on
the banks of the Charles,
while a Harvard crew bends
to the oars. The college,
founded in 1636, is the
oldest in the U.S. It is also
one of the most distin-
guished—70% of its
faculty hold doctorates and
the faculty-student ratio is
an exceptionally high one
to six.

now 17 percent black, the city's fire department, full to burstin' of Southies, is 99 percent white and the police force nearly 98 percent white. In the words of an NAACP official, Boston is "one of the most racist cities in the country."

The irony of this phenomenon in the heart of an Athens of culture and liberality prompted one local reporter to comment: "Listen, there are no liberals in Boston. That's just a veneer from across the river." Meaning Harvard. Perhaps. But remember Senator Brooke, remember that Massachusetts was the only state to vote for the liberalities urged by presidential candidate George McGovern, and remember most of all the young people who come to Boston because that's where the mix is richest.

North of Boston (which is a book by Robert Frost, just as it is a state of mind), the Post Road soon leaves the big cities. It highs-and-lows its way across the strands of New Hampshire and the glaciated coast of Maine. Soon the Post Road driver finds himself in the land of hand-cranked telephones and people-crowded front porches. The Yankees watch the cars coming and going with nearly the same interest as they watch the tides flow and the seasons change. Laconic and long-memoried, the porch rockers delight in giving few words and little information to bewildered strangers. A favorite piece of advice: "Wall, you cahn't get theya from heeyah."

The Post Road may take the traveler to Port Clyde, a fishing village better known than others because summer resident Andrew Wyeth has portrayed its salty character. One reporter admitted to receiving the following conversational setback at Port Clyde:

Reporter: "Do you own your boat?"
Fisherman: "Yuh."
Reporter: "How big is she?"
Fisherman: "Forty-five footer."

Reporter: "Where is she now?"
Fisherman: "On the bottom. Winter storm."
Reporter: "Do you intend to sail her again?"
Fisherman: "Not where she is."

But the people are by no means hostile—or crushed by the fact that they're out of the economic mainstream. They get along, thank you.

If he's doing well, the fisherman makes about $9,000 or $10,000 a year from harvesting the chill waters off Port Clyde. Fall is the best time for lobstering; hauling up each man's fifty or sixty traps every other day nets a community total of some 600,000 pounds a season. Winter is the time to drag for shrimp, which are processed in one or another of the two plants that face each other across the inlet. Spring is the time to go after ground fish; early summer is the season for whiting, a tasty fish that sells well locally. Though youngsters come and go, enough of them remain to keep Port Clyde a fishing village, just as it's been since the mid-1800s when cobblestones from the Maine islands were no longer needed for America's city streets. That's when the Englishmen, Finns, and Swedes who had come to Port Clyde to become quarrymen became fishermen instead.

old trucks, accustomed to potato sacks, groan under bedsteads and bureaus; they boil over in protest along the turnpike.

Across the state line, in Berlin, New Hampshire, one reads in *Le Petit Journal* that another hiker has been lost on Mt. Washington. Tourists all too seldom believe that the 6,000-foot mountain has an average weather condition worse than Labrador's. On the summit, nakedly exposed above timberline to the elements, there are a few buildings to provide protection against the gale; but all must literally be chained to the rocks lest they be blown to smithereens, as the anemometer frequently is. The Yankees who work at this inhospitable weather station take a scientific view toward nature, an aloof view toward men in the world below, reminiscent of Godfrey Cabot's philosophy. "When my days-off come, I'd rahther go skiing than to Bahston," declared one meteorologist. "I'd rahther sleep," countered the other.

Crossing the white fury of the Connecticut River into Vermont, a visitor may slow down for a peaceful town like Middletown Springs (incorporated in 1784) whose sign proclaims "Rest a While With Us." The sign, which stands on the green at the foot of the Community Church, also gives directions to such near and far places as West Rutland and Bennington. "I gave it to the town," the sign maker said modestly. "Strangers didn't know which way to turn, and putting up a sign seemed the friendly thing to do." What would a Mainer say to that?

Middletown Springs—which once enjoyed a slight boom as a spa because of its mineral waters—was the site of America's first horse-driven treadmill. While other Vermont and Massachusetts localities were bursting forth with water mills to power nineteenth-century industry, Middletown Springs went this inventive route, led by the ingenious A. W. Gray. His idea succeeded for a time, operating farm machinery and sawmills; then

Indeed much of the Maine coast remains in a pattern set generations ago. One gets a sense of prudent recycling, particularly among the buildings: a former church is now used as a library; a former railroad station has been turned into a shopping center; a former ship captain's mansion has become a town hall. There's no need to throw anything away.

For Maine is a poor state. The days of the great lumber and shipbuilding fortunes are gone. The plush life style of the turn-of-the-century millionaires with yachts and servants has disappeared at Bar Harbor just as it has at Newport. But traces of the past remain to give perspective to the present.

Driving across the vastness of northern Maine, you realize how underpopulated much of New England is— and what effect this beckoning wilderness must have on the Yankee mind. Roadsigns indicate that this is paper industry country, where French-Canadian names such as Presque Isle abound. It's also potato-growing country, the famous Aroostook giants. And though the papermakers seem to have successfully weathered the angry storms of ecologists' campaigns, the potato farmers are repeatedly swept by waves of poverty. Families continually move out, heading west and south, saying farewell to a land that has barely kept them alive. The

came steam. Yet the town lives on under its sheltering
trees, confident that other ideas and other guiding
spirits will keep it from fading.

But the big industry in Vermont is land development.
Sparked by a new generation of Yankees who originally
came into the state for the magnificence of its fall
color or the excitement of its skiing, and who then decided to stay and buy a second home, the increased land
evaluation has spread into all corners of the granite-
spined state. For many old residents this represents a
final, welcome relief from indebtedness and toil; for
others it means a tragic change in the basic character of
their lives and their country.

In such a hamlet as Whitingham, Vermont, the population has grown 20 percent in the past few years. (The
population increase has been among adults, not children; when one Yankee expressed curiosity about this
at a school board meeting, another asked, "Hain't you
heard about the pill?") A recent reappraisal of the
land has jacked up property values five or six times beyond their previous worth; taxes have soared. Particularly hard hit are retired persons living on Social Security
or other fixed incomes—yet the state has given the
elderly some relief in the form of a partial tax abatement
for those with incomes of less than $4,300 a year. Never-
theless, these modern economic pressures are driving
many Yankees to sell their much-loved homesteads.
They can't afford to do otherwise.

Writes one grief-stricken Yankee woman:

> Should I accept an offer of a substantial sum for
> my 100-acre southern Vermont homestead? To
> sell or not to sell is the question. . . .
> The home of my forefathers has clung to this
> hilltop in Whitingham since the 1790s. Its
> weathered clapboards are brittle with age. Its
> chimneys list and its roofline dips like that of an
> old swayback horse. Yet despite its defects, in
> summer when the lilacs and wild roses bloom,

in the fall when it is drenched in a sea of maple gold, and in winter when the ice-blue sky curves over its loneliness it has a heart-shaking picturesqueness. Five generations of my family have lived and loved within its shelter. I have never felt this house belonged to me. I belong to this house. But I may be the last of my family under this roof. How can my children, with growing families of their own, assume this heavy burden? Like other villagers I face the unanswerable dilemma. Where are the taxes to come from?

Such plaints, for all their worthiness, raise another

Old fashioned wooden rocking chairs still welcome visitors to the block-long porticoes of gracious New England summer hotels like the Equinox (above) in Manchester, Vermont.

question: are Yankees merely looking back and trying to hold their own, or are they striving on with characteristic vigor? Since they can't keep the rest of the country out, or the world either, how are they going to cope with twenty-first century hassles?

One thing is sure, they are armed to defend their landscape much more now than they were when the ecological movement surfaced on Cape Cod in the sixties.

Aiming a shotgun at developers and firing freely has been the reaction of some Vermonters to the assault on their countryside and their traditions. Whereas Yankees had once been opposed to zoning as a bureaucratic threat to their individual freedoms, even conservatives eventually perceived that uncontrolled development was not a blessing. In fighting the developers, they joined forces with a group they had long scorned, the "crazies," the hyperenvironmentalists who had long been struggling against the aesthetic and biological damage caused by building ski area upon housing development upon shopping mall. This strange combination of Vermonters pushed an unprecedented bill through the state legislature—Act 250—which said that no commercial building project could begin until district commissions were satisfied that it would not adversely affect natural resources or municipal services.

There are those who argue that this victory of traditionalists and environmentalists is but a brief reversal of the general trend in New England. They point out that the major backer of Act 250, a conservative in his sixties named Royal Cutts, was defeated in the 1974 election. His opponents were organized by a group of developers known as the Green Mountain Boys, who preached that it was against the Yankee spirit to accept limits on the amount of money one should look to from one's property. But Mr. Cutts may run again, and his law remains on the books.

A strong argument that other Yankees are lining up

39

Fifteen hundred determined runners sprint through suburban Hopkinton (at right) to begin the 77th running of the Boston Marathon. The race ends among the skyscrapers of downtown Boston (at left), where the winner is crowned with a laurel wreath and every finisher gets unlimited helpings of beef stew.

on Mr. Cutts's side came when neighboring New Hampshiremen defeated Aristotle Onassis in 1974. New Hampshire's motto, "Live Free or Die," was invoked many times as citizens of Durham debated whether or not to let Onassis's Olympic Refiners build a 400,000-barrel-per-day facility on the shores of their harbor. Jobs, higher land values, lower gas prices (New England suffers from higher gas bills because it is the only major region in the United States without a refinery)—these were the stated benefits of Onassis's proposal. Backing him, New Hampshire's governor, Meldrim Thomson, Jr., averred that he had promised to keep his Yankee constituents free of sales taxes and income taxes, *but* that he could only deliver on that promise if New Hampshire went along with such money-producing "improvements" as the Durham refinery. Also backing Onassis: the archconservative *Manchester Union Leader*, largest newspaper in the state.

The debate was held in that antiquated vehicle of local government, the town meeting. Clearing their throats, such unaccustomed spokesmen arose as Nancy Sandberg, challenging the power structure. She pointed out that the attempt to thrust the refinery upon Durham was an affront to the Yankee principle of home rule. Phys-ed professor Evelyn Brown then told of the deceitful devices the Onassis forces had used in trying to buy her land; when she'd learned that the land was not to be used for private purposes as promised, she'd struggled free of the signed option, although she was ailing and could use the money. Applause greeted her story; the tide was beginning to turn. Next Representative Dudley Dudley stood up: "Lives are not at stake here; but our seacoast is, our way of life." Foot stamps of approval showed how people felt. The final vote: 144 votes for the refinery; 1,254 against.

Even so, severe economic problems remain in New England, as well as some questions about the capacity of Yankees to deal with the competitive realities of the postindustrial world. Yankees gave America its first industrial revolution. They built the first factories, sent the first product salesmen across the land (who became known, with their flashy gadgets and their occasionally unscrupulous deals, as "Yankee Jonathans"—the first regional stereotype). But with the arrival of the twentieth century and the emergence of other production centers, New England's industrial superiority began to fade. In recent years, industrial unemployment in New England has been worse than anywhere else; Yankees' per capita income has slipped badly in relation to the rest of the United States. To some industrialists, New England began to look like a wasteland; the Yankees themselves seemed to be willful contributors to the blight. Because of high power costs, workmen's unemployment compensation, and state taxes, a company had to pay 60 percent more to operate in Massachusetts than in Texas.

Even when the Boston bankers, Cambridge scientists, and Irish contractors got together in the 1950s to build the new circumferential Route #128 with its dazzling array of science-based light industries, it looked as if an economic resurgence for New England was merely "a big maybe." Many of the companies failed to get off the ground; many others relied excessively on government contracts. Meanwhile the shift of manufacturing and construction industries away from New England continued apace; medium-sized cities like North Adams, Massachusetts, appeared doomed.

But in the place of manufacturing, there sprang up a varied crop of service industries. Yankees, both male and female, rallied to harvest the yield offered by specialized producers. Such giants as IBM saw the opportunity too. Outside Burlington, Vermont, thrives a capital-intensive, high-technology plant. It is IBM's largest facility for assembling computer memories. Says plant manager P. R. Low of the 4,000-man work force: "The Vermont craftsmen and former farm hands have

mastered the subtleties of technology without formal training."

There is reason to believe that Yankees will create for themselves, if not for the rest of mankind, a second industrial revolution. They'll turn their hands to making something special; they'll have better mousetraps to sell once again. This new wave of space-age factories will be relatively small, high-value, high-income service industries rather than big manufacturing units. That is, after all, more in keeping with the way Yankees would structure the universe if they could.

On the Assabet River in Maynard, Massachusetts, where for years the blank brick walls of an abandoned Civil War blanket factory reminded citizens that prosperity and the future had passed them by, there stands today the plant of the Digital Equipment Corporation. It employs 12,000 people, pays them well, and does not pollute their river. And this is by no means an isolated example. By 1970, 18 percent of New England's non-agricultural work force was employed in similar service industries (several percentage points above the national average). The Commerce Department predicts that, because of such trends, Yankees' per capita income will probably exceed the rest of the United States by 1980.

Even downtown Boston has taken heart. A building surge has produced a futuristic blend of government structures, office towers, and urban plazas. But still the distinctive Yankee ways remain—the intellectual vigor, the class snobbery, and the respect for beauty, including old beauty. Says Mayor Kevin White: "Boston is filthy—my God, her appearance is a disgrace. . . . But emotionally she's in great shape, like a beautiful, healthy woman dressed in rags. People want to identify with Boston."

Identify is a thing Yankees have always done down deep. They identify proudly with their landscape, their traditions, their mutual push to succeed.

What you hear when you attend the Boston Marathon—that great, crowded, twenty-six-mile footrace that occurs every April in honor, somehow, of Paul Revere's ride—may be the best indicator of how and with whom Yankees identify today. Near the end of the course awaits an awesome height that has come to be called Heartbreak Hill; it wipes out the pros and convinces the amateurs that they'd rather walk than run. Yankees by the thousands wait by Heartbreak Hill to watch Yankees by the hundreds compete in the event—compete or simply try to finish. The watchers, understanding the ritual, shout encouragement and participate themselves by so doing.

A young collegian jogs by in track uniform, sweating but still game. Then a blind runner, holding the elbow of a fellow marathoner. Next an old man with a leathery face, moving vigorously, essentially walking. A middle-aged woman, ignoring the cut on her leg. An executive, stumbling and holding his side against the pain.

The spectators urge them on, Yankees all, on through life and travail:

> "Come on, you can do it."
> "Don't quit now!"
> "It's all downhill from here."

—RUSSELL BOURNE

41

Yankee Seafarers:
a struggle to survive

Men against the sea have won not wealth but
survival along New England's treacherous coast.
The shoreline is studded with monuments to loved
ones consigned to "Davy Jones's Locker." With
seagulls their companions, small craft their argosies,
Yankee seamen risk the depth's perils, harvesting
$100 million annually. Cod and haddock by
trawler, lobster by trap, menhaden and mackerel
by seiner, fishing calls for specially crafted tools
and all-weather costumes. Both a commercial
industry and a personal preoccupation,
the struggle between man and fish identifies
Yankees today with their salty forebears.

Sentinel of New England, tiny Monhegan rises out of the foggy Atlantic as a front doorstep to the rock-ribbed coast. The island's black and pink granite rocks bristle with dark spruce and pale birches. A painter's delight and a fisherman's harbor, the island was first visited by Capt. George Waymouth in 1605. His party "drew with a small net . . . about thirty very good and great lobsters." Thereby they determined the destiny of the place, now known as the lobster-catching capital of Maine.

Monhegan light, visible for 20 miles, has guided mariners since 1824. At right, lobstermen get together in a fishing shack for a game of cards.

Monhegan Island, 10 miles off the coast of Maine, is a quiet place in the dusk of a winter afternoon. During the season, lobstermen turn in early and row out to their boats before dawn.

Dories take lobster traps out to the
anchored fleet (above) in preparation
for Starting Day, January 1. Mainland
lobstermen, who work the year round,
have learned to stay away from the
two-mile protected zone Monheganers
have staked out as their own.

Bundled up against the piercing cold,
lobsterman (at right) heads for home
in a January snowstorm after a long
day at sea. Only about 55 people—
most of them lobstermen and their
families—live on the island in winter,
but the population swells to nearly
800 in summer.

In the teeth of a winter's storm Monhegan islanders dauntlessly set out to sea. They fish only from January to July, having shortened the season to conserve their resources. Each lobsterman has his specially colored buoys to mark traps moored 1,000 feet beneath the storm-tossed surface. Lobsters must measure about four inches long; all others are tossed overboard to "feed Father Neptune."

Famous port of Gloucester, Massachusetts, today leads all other Yankee harbors in pounds of fish taken. Cod, the state's sacred fish, still fills the holds of ships sailed by men who dare the perils of the coast—though those ships, once a navy, now number less than a hundred because of competition from foreign fleets. Fisherfolk in Gloucester eat frozen fish from European plants at half the price of their own, hard-won catch.

Fishermen row ashore from a trawler at Gloucester, Mass. The town, located on the peninsula of Cape Ann, was originally settled in 1623 by colonists who called themselves the Dorchester Adventurers.

Trawl nets are pulled in, fish are dumped on the deck for sorting (at right), then packed on ice in the hold.

At day's end, baskets of fish are winched to the dock for weighing.

Family Farms: a cherished tradition

Beneath the glory of the hills on rocky fields and in glaciated valleys, Yankee farmers find "slim pickin's" for soil. But it's soil enough for them to pursue their classic ideal: the one-family farm. Its borders set by stone walls and age-old arguments, the average farm contains 200 uphill and downdale acres, yields about $20,000 in produce. Generation after generation, Yankees make each acre count.

Shocks of corn dry on a 150-acre, one-man farm in Norwich, Vt., as farmer Leroy Douglas inspects his pumpkin crop.

Freshly picked corn is shucked on the front porch of a small farm in Pomfret, Vt. The owner milks about a dozen cows and still uses horses to help with the haying.

Well-kept dairy farm prospers near Tunbridge, Vt.

Springtime in the sugarbush finds Yankees tapping giant maples. March sun on a farmer's back and wet snow underfoot tell him to harness horses or oxen to the sledge; now his buckets are brimful with sap from driven spigots. Down at the sugarhouse, water vapor from the boiling vat steams up through the roof; maplesweet fragrance clings to the rafters. About 40 gallons of sap boil down to one of syrup. Neighbors stoke the fires and witness the rite.

When the sap begins to run on the Howes's dairy farm near Cummington, Mass., Stebbins and Raphael make the rounds with their five-barrel sap sled (above). The sap (at right) is poured from buckets hanging on the tapped maples (at left) for transfer to the sled.

Farmer near Bennington, Vt., feeds more wood into his sugarhouse firebox (below). Pure syrup remains after water in the sap has evaporated.

53

The mighty Maine potato must be harvested in the crisp, rainless days of September. Then Aroostook County families and migrant pickers (including Micmac Indians and French-Canadians) separate potatoes from rocks and roots. Kids get a quarter a barrel, can fill maybe 40 barrels a day. The total: $60 million worth of flavorful potatoes for the nation's tables.

Farmer cultivates his potato field (facing page). In the fall, he uses a mechanical digger (above) and relies on family and friends to pick the crop by hand.

Schoolchildren, enjoying lunch at right in a canvas-covered windbreak, get three-to-four-week fall vacations to help pick the crop before winter sets in.

Roadside farm stand in Massachusetts brings
in extra cash for a local farmer.

Family farming keeps kinfolk's
gnarled hands and youthful fingers busy. Apple
and strawberry farmers invite you to come
pick your own. Extra advice for cider-makers:
mix in some tarter varieties along with sweet
McIntoshes. Robert Frost wrote,
 "There were ten thousand thousand fruit to
touch,—Cherish in hand, lift down, and not let
fall." By such enduring techniques, Yankees
harvest 10 million bushels of apples a year.

Three generations of the Stewart Sheppard family in Hartland, Vt., work together to pick and sell the strawberry crop.

Honey provides additional income for many small farmers. The Vermonter above has 25 hives in his apple orchard.

Local farmers in Pomfret, Vt., bring their apples to this hand-operated press (at left), where they work together to produce the fresh cider.

57

At summer's end, the fragrance of full
haybarns rewards farmers for weeks of work.
Fodder for New England's ubiquitous
dairies (which account for a third of the
region's 30,000 farms) comes from small
plots often mowed by the dairyman himself.
Yankee haymakers no longer depend on wooden
hayrakes and horse-drawn wagons. But it's
still a matter of harnessing friends, neighbors,
and small fry to work with small-scale, quixotic
implements against the harsh realities of
terrain and weather.

Vermont farmer bales his hay in August (above).
Farm children help with the haying and thoroughly
enjoy the ride home on the hay wagon (at right).

The more prosperous Yankee
farmers use automatic hay
balers (above).

Young Massachusetts farmer
(at right) takes his son along
to "help" bring in the silage.

Community Life:
fairs, festivals, fellowship

*Holidays on Main Street bring social rhythms to
New England's quiet towns. Individual Yankees fall
into step as drummers parade from town hall to
cemetery on Memorial Day. Locked windows open,
flags fly from severe facades; dignity dares wear a
too-tight veteran's uniform. Townspeople and
summerfolk recognize each other; oldsters find young
ears willing to listen. The Fourth of July brings distant
family members home to stretch the dining-room table
with an extra leaf. Even outsiders are welcome
on the shaded common: it's community time.*

Memorial Day, with a parade featuring the town band (above),
has been celebrated in Grafton, Vt., since 1868. At right,
townspeople gather on the village green to hear a eulogy.

60

"The Horribles Parade," with a prize for the "most horrible" costume, is an annual July 4th event in Marblehead, Mass. Undersized lobsterman (above) uses his wagon to tow a lobster trap, while a young separatist (below) trudges along in his kilts.

The March town meeting at Burke Hollow, Vt., begins with a pledge of allegiance.

Gaveling open the town meeting, the moderator must lead the townspeople through a square dance of opinions, calling the steps with fairness and wit. Sometimes Roberts' Rules give way to local custom; but all are equally—and loudly—heard. Gaffers recall when a jug of cider, kept behind the meeting house, would enliven debates. Today, with growing populations and groaning tax rolls, many communities send representatives to town meetings: more efficient but less fun.

Irate citizen demonstrates what has been described as the Vermonter's "natural aptitude for dissent."

Some votes are cast by a show of hands, others (above) by secret ballot.

Townspeople (at left) listen intently to a debate on the proposed budget.

Auctioneer "Razor"
Crosman (above) donates
his services to the nonprofit
4-H Foundation Auction
held yearly at Maine's
Dover-Foxcroft Fairgrounds.
Auctioneer Willis Hicks
(at right) shows off the
stock at a farm auction
in Eden, Vermont.

Going, going, gone! cries the Yankee auctioneer. Run by churches or 4-H chapters as money-raising events, auctions rely on attic ferrets to find treasures ripe for selling. Tourists heading "down East" (meaning with Southwest winds at their backs like old square-riggers) often spot "AUCTION!" signs and veer off the highway in time to enter the bidding. When they finally turn homeward, stationwagon springs are flattened with the freight of victory.

Weekend auction at Greensboro, Vt., (above) attracts a good crowd. Buyers often face logistical problems like the one confronting the man (below) at the annual church auction in Dennis, Mass.

In Massachusetts, the ladies take their antiques seriously.

65

The pond on Cohasset Common (above) reflects the brightly colored tents erected for the annual South Shore Arts Festival.

Youngsters sell lemonade (below) while adults visit painting exhibit (at right). Festival was inspired some 20 years ago when several local artists simply propped their paintings up against the trees on the common and offered them for sale.

Festivals for craftsmen and artists bring local talents out into the sunshine. Summoned from beach or golf course to bestow blue ribbons, judges must live with the aftereffects of their verdicts (like the painter-plumber who now refuses to fix the pipes). Paintings tend to be titled "Lighthouse Point" or "Seagull I"; displayed crafts run from bayberry candles to modern scrimshaw—all specially priced for today.

Craftsmen (below) sell their wares and demonstrate their skills in outdoor booths.

Farm horses and ferris wheels draw the
crowds to New England's agricultural fairs from July
through October. Visitors marvel at rhubarb pies,
pink-eared shoats, massive bulls, and tuberous begonias.
Muscles bulge, hooves clatter, engines vroom as Yankees
demonstrate industriousness and ingenuity.

Woodchopping contest (above) attracts crowd
at Connecticut's Ledyard Fair. Trotting races
(at left, above) are featured at the Agricultural
Fair in Union, Me. State Fair at Skowhegan,
Me., dominated by its ferris wheel (at right),
has been held for 157 years.

Horse-drawing contest (above)
is a tradition at the Goshen
Fair in Connecticut. Farmers
pass the time of day (at right)
between events at the County
Fair in Barton, Vt.

South-Roots of Change

How many summers has it been since Mrs. Gardner died? Four? Five? No matter, her death was only an incident in a long life, a life which in many ways symbolizes the southern continuum. She carried in her blood that perfectly irrational sense of being southern, a way of seeing and experiencing change but somehow remaining the same.

Mrs. Minnie Bell Gardner was very different from the rootless, disconnected people Vance Packard wrote about in *A Nation of Strangers*. She moved only once. That was when she married Mr. Gardner, at eighteen. She lived the rest of her life in the context of one place, Anniston, Alabama, until she died, much mourned, at the age of ninety-six. At some distance, Mrs. Gardner witnessed her nation at war five times, saw the election of twenty presidents, and lived through almost incomprehensible economic, technological, and social changes.

But, at the funeral, the pastor and pastor emeritus of Parker Memorial Baptist Church didn't talk about presidents or armies or other abstractions; they talked about the fifty-eight years she had taught Sunday school. Those two Southern Baptist preachers had a sense of proportion which put things in their right order because Mrs. Gardner's Sunday school class affected her more directly than technology or elections or even wars. Year after year, every Sunday for nearly six decades, the faces changed in Mrs. Gardner's class but, for her, they were the same. They were sons and daughters of sons and daughters whom she knew and who knew her.

She was rooted, touched by the place she was and the people who lived there. Being connected to people and place, she knew and cared. She knew those changing faces before her, when to worry about them and when not to, in a way that is beyond the skills of academic medicine to teach. It is knowledge that comes only from attending so many baptisms, weddings, and funerals.

There is no record of Mrs. Gardner ever having met the Rev. Dr. D. C. Washington. They could not have met at a social occasion or even at a regular worship service, even though they shared the same faith and lived in the same small town for many years, even though Dr. Washington was one of the town's most prominent citizens. He was, of course, black, pastor of the largest black congregation in town, Seventeenth Street Baptist.

There is no way of finding out whether the two ever met because Dr. Washington is gone now, too. If they ever did, and they well might have, it would have been at a funeral because there have always been some things in the South which ranked above segregation, and death is one of them. Another is that special mixture of feelings about place and people that make us refer to them as "home" and "homefolks" even after we have left.

Dr. Washington left Anniston before the big troubles and before the glory days of the civil rights movement. He went up to Nashville to be executive director of the Sunday School Board of the National Baptist Convention, but he never forgot home. A few years ago when he read in a local paper that a man from Anniston was visiting, he tracked the man to his motel room and insisted that he come by the board's publishing house for a visit. The two men visited and reminisced for a good while. Dr. Washington spoke of good times back home and of good fights—disagreements with men he liked and respected—all told with enormous good humor.

His visitor was white but, in the best tradition of the South, that didn't matter. In the blood of both was knowledge of a people and a place that touched them equally; knowledge not just of Anniston but of the South itself, of two peoples locked together in a history of loving and hating and caring, of enduring through defeat, insult, poverty, and injustice.

It is all of these things, and more, that have made southerners the way they are: a people who have learned to trust their senses and feelings more than ide-

ology because the settled truth of the moment falls like sand on the land and is reformed with every intellectual breeze that blows. Finally, white southerners have begun to trust those feelings more than the ideology of segregation.

Mrs. Gardner was born at a time when water, sewage, and transportation systems were essentially the same as the Assyrians used; she died before the last commuter rocket took off for the moon. Dr. Washington was born before Martin Luther King, and outlived him. Yet, through all the troubles and changes they saw, neither was altered in any essential way.

Change. What *must* the South do about it? What *is* the South doing about it? What is it *doing* to the South? It all depends on what kind of change you are talking about. Racial politics is one thing that the southern people have happily agreed to do without, if every gubernatorial election since 1970 can be trusted as a reliable surface measure of a deeper agreement on that subject.

One of the clearest examples of the South's decision to put racial politics behind it occurred on the afternoon of April 30, 1971, in the ballroom of the Sheraton-Biltmore Hotel in Atlanta. Four of the governors elected the year before appeared on a panel at the second annual meeting of the L.Q.C. Lamar Society, a group that seeks practical answers to urban problems in the South. There was Reubin Askew of Florida, Dale Bumpers of Arkansas, Jimmy Carter of Georgia, and John West of South Carolina. These four governors were to appear together again and again, so often in fact that they began to refer to themselves as "The Dale and Jimmy and Reubin and John Show." What they said, what they stood for, and what those elected after them represented was to add to a growing wave of confidence in the region.

But, at the Biltmore that afternoon, it was their first time out together. Nobody really knew what they would say, although the mood was hopeful because of the kinds of campaigns they had run. The audience was not disappointed. Governor Carter, speaking without notes, put it most directly:

> I think southerners now have realized that the solution of our problems is our own and that we can no longer berate the federal government, the Supreme Court, or any other "outside group" for our own problems, our own needs, our own shortcomings . . . the obstacles we have to overcome.

Never before in this century had so many southern governors come together and said so plainly that the South must turn away from racial rhetoric and begin the serious business of problem-solving. For everyone in that ballroom in the old Biltmore there was a feeling that more is possible for this generation of southerners than had been possible for their fathers and grandfathers. No longer would southerners have to be defensive because they bore the mark of a historic sin. No longer would the South have to starve its talent and imagination by feeding the retarding myths of the past. As Jimmy Carter said three years later in another hotel ballroom, a few blocks from the Biltmore, to many of the same people: "The civil rights movement freed the white people of the South and, incidentally, the black people, too."

By the time Governor Carter made that admission, the last and most significant conversion had taken place, that of George C. Wallace. Perhaps it was the assassination attempt in Maryland in May, 1972, that precipitated the change in George Wallace, although it wasn't noticed until later. He had felt the breath of mortality on his face, so palpably near had it come. Beside the irresistible power of that presence, even views that once were thought to be important seem trivial.

John West of S.C. (far left),
Reubin Askew of Fla. (left),
Dale Bumpers of Ark. (right),
and Jimmy Carter of Ga. (far
right) typify new breed of
moderate southern politicians
who are leading the region
away from racial rhetoric
toward solution of its
other problems.

At any rate, as Wallace began to recover he was seen to move symbolically, to do things he had never done before: crowning a black homecoming queen at the University of Alabama where, a decade before, he had stood in the door to bar the entrance of two black students; attending a black mayors' caucus; exchanging public pleasantries with Ted Kennedy at a July Fourth celebration. For one Alabama newspaper editor, who had been a consistent Wallace foe, the opportunity to see personally how much his old enemy had changed came when the editorial board of his paper was interviewing candidates for statewide office during the 1974 primaries. He later recalled the meeting:

> George Wallace was wheeled into my office on a Thursday afternoon, March 28. The conversation began awkwardly. The gulf that had lain between us was like a presence in the room.
>
> The opportunity to clear the air came through Neal Peirce's book, *The Deep South States of America.* Neal had quoted me at some length on

what George Wallace represents beyond racism. I marked the pages and handed the book to the governor. When he had finished reading, he looked at me warmly and said, "Hell, man, we aren't too far apart." His answer gave me the chance to ask a question which on "Meet the Press" couldn't be asked in the same way.

> "We never have been too far apart, George," I said. "You have always said you were standing up for the little man, and we have too. I inherited my newspaper principles from Dad. He always said, 'It is the duty of a newspaper to become the attorney for the most defenseless among its subscribers.' Our policy, and Dad's

Champion of the little man is the way Gov. George Wallace of Alabama views himself. "I'm a Populist," he told author Neal Peirce. But what else is Wallace? A consummate politician say some; a master of ambiguity say others. Certainly Wallace has skillfully manipulated the race issue to fit the mood of the times: in 1963 he tried to block attempts to integrate the University of Alabama (left); in 1973 he crowned the school's first black homecoming queen (above).

Blacks and whites working together, what author Pat Watters calls "casual desegregation," is a common sight in the South today. At right, South Carolina factory workers bag disposable diapers; at left a seamstress at work in another Carolina factory.

before me, has been to champion the cause of the little man. But, George, it didn't take walking around sense to know who the real 'little man' was in Alabama and the South and the nation: it has always been the black man. So, we tried to give him a voice, to stand up for him because he was the nation's number one underdog. But you never did, George. Why?"

The only answer Governor Wallace gave, the editor recalled, was to look at his useless legs for a moment that seemed to go on and on. There was no quick, slicing debater's point; no sly evasions or overlong explanations; no attempts to hide an ancient wrong under a constitutional camouflage. There was no deceit; neither were there any confessions or apologies. That is not his way. There was only a very long silence. That Alabama editor believes he saw in Wallace's face, and in his wordless answer, an acknowledgment that perhaps his victories had been won at too great a cost and a wish that, some of it at least, had been different.

George Wallace's journey from an older to a newer vision of the South covered a distance of only one city block. In January of 1963, he stood on the State Capitol steps where Jefferson Davis was inaugurated and proclaimed in his own inaugural address: "Segregation today; segregation tomorrow; segregation forever!" In October of 1974, he sat in his wheelchair where Martin Luther King, Jr., had preached and welcomed an audience of blacks to the Dexter Avenue Baptist Church. From the cradle of the Confederacy to the cradle of the civil rights movement. A breathtaking conceptual swoop? Perhaps. But in a region where past and future crowd each other because they are simultaneously occupying the same space, it doesn't seem such a remarkable distance to go. That is why, in most essential ways, George Wallace is unchanged. When he is feeling really good and the conversation turns to politics, he is the same old George—despite his much publicized, and real, change in attitude and action toward blacks.

Like the governor, State Rep. Chris McNair is a symbol of continuity and change. Today he is one of nearly one hundred black legislators elected in the South and serves as chairman of the Jefferson County (Birmingham) delegation, which is two-to-one white. But again, like the governor, Chris McNair knows that no one ever gets to ride the glory train free.

He has paid his dues. His daughter, Denise, would have celebrated her twenty-fifth birthday during the last month of the Bicentennial year if she hadn't been attending Sunday school in Birmingham, at Sixteenth Street Baptist Church, in 1963 when the bomb exploded.

The death of a child is an injury that never heals. It hurts Chris McNair every day but, incredibly, he isn't bitter: "If a man is forever lamenting yesterday, he doesn't give himself time to do anything about today, or plan for the future. In 1963 we were dickering about integration. Today I'm down here in the rotunda of the State Capitol and the problem now is to do something about education, period, what our whole society is based on."

But what does he answer the Atlanta woman, wife of a still-prominent civil rights leader, who says with cold implacable contempt that there is never any reason for any black to cooperate with George Wallace? "If I'm a Christian, I've got to believe in the possibility of redemption," says McNair. "I'm not in love with the George Wallace who stood in the schoolhouse door, but if he's still in power and talking differently, I'm not fighting him; I'm moving with it. What we demonstrated for in the sixties was to get inside. It's a different era but, basically, I don't think I'm any different from where I was all the time."

Chris McNair lives in the present but the past, the relentless hound of memory, pursues him at a distance.

"The past is never dead," said Faulkner. "It's not even past." He didn't mean to say that the South would never experience change. What he was saying is that southerners have collected an attic full of historical instincts and they are not going to throw all of it away just because they have changed from a rigidly segregated society to a relatively free one, or because they have moved from the farm and small town to the big city.

There was a lot of moving and changing going on as the meter prepared to clock off another 100 years of the American experience. Southerners were sure they wanted to move past racial politics; but as they turned off the farm-to-market roads onto the fuming rapids of steel that ring the metropolis, there were some second thoughts about the effects of uncontrolled growth. Ever since Henry Grady, southerners have been hankering after the twin sentinels of Yankee material progress: cities and factories. Urbanization and industrialization meant the South could slice off a bigger chunk of the Gross National Product; southerners could get better jobs, better health care, send the kids to college, fix up the house, and buy that camper.

But there were some second thoughts. . . .

God knows, southerners can't be blamed for wanting a little more of the mass being produced and consumed in other parts of the country. A black co-ed, Class of 1975, confirms the rank of the gods of city and industry in the mind of the South. She understands the virtues of southern life well enough to articulate them clearly, but there is one thing she would leave the South for, even if it meant living in a worn-out industrial city. "For a good-paying job," she smiled, "Sure!"

She is young, rural, black; she wants to feel some pavement under her feet. She will go to the city, but what is she willing to pay as a toll for that journey? After she furnishes her apartment with her own things, puts a little money aside and, more importantly, accumulates a past and memories of her own, she may remember that there are other things she needs.

It is an article of faith among southern people that there are some things they are unwilling to change. It is a matter of soul. Southerners aren't willing to give up their distinctiveness; to say there is no longer any reason for pride in self, in "our kind of folks," and in the place where they live. They are touchy about matters of the spirit, and that isn't a statement only about black people. There is black soul and there is white soul, too, just as there is mountain soul and delta soul.

How do you define southern soul, what the young president of the University of Alabama, Dr. David Mathews, calls "that perfectly irrational sense of being southern?" Maybe it will help to listen to a few southern voices, talking and singing.

First is the reporter, the Arkansas boy who has seen Harvard and Washington and covers half the South for *The New York Times*. He is talking to a bunch of Mississippi reporters and editors:

> One night last week, I was out with a bunch of men in a Louisiana marsh catching alligators. I was sitting in that boat with six or eight alligators hog-tied and piled up around my feet and it occurred to me that this was a *southern* experience. There is no place I know of north of the Mason-Dixon line where a man can hunt alligators. I've heard those stories about the sewers of New York City being full of alligators, but I don't believe it, because if it was true, my friends from

75

Breaux Bridge and Lafayette would be up there right now poaching them "long green boogers" and selling their hides. The fact is, this part of the country is still physically different from the north, and no amount of air conditioning is going to change that. In the long sweep of things, what are a handful of air-conditioned skyscrapers on Canal Street compared to a thousand miles of bayous that are air conditioned by a million live oak trees?

How do you describe the South? One way is to make a list. The reporter's list includes:

> . . . the sugar cane workers of Louisiana and Florida, the gutpullers and gizzard splitters who work in the poultry plants—and the peculiar hill people of the Ozarks and the Blue Ridge Mountains—and the honky-tonkers who walk along the edge of violence every Saturday night in two or three thousand little towns like Wiggins, Tylertown and Poplarville. It includes those thousands of certifiably insane race car drivers, on and off the official tracks. I also include on my list a lot of trivial stuff that only a southerner would even recognize, much less appreciate— things like fried okra and purple hull peas; Coca Cola used as a chaser for whiskey; Merle Haggard perceived as a superb musician and not just a kinky fad who is good for a few laughs at a Washington cocktail party.

Despite the list, the reporter knows intellectually that old Dixie is a goner. He has read the books and articles that say so, even written some himself. And yet, his gut may have the truer vision:

> I'm sure it's silly to fret over these things. The prophets are right—if old Dixie is not dead, it at least has one foot in the grave, and it's just a matter of time now. But I have a small comic

vision of what's going to happen when they finally hold the funeral. The graveside music will turn out to be "Precious Memories" and "Shall We Gather at the River"—and the only people there who will know the words will be the loved ones from Arkansas and Mississippi.

Yes, even the young executives whose community center is the country club know the words. It is Saturday night on Sunset Drive; the house is new but the money old. Inside, the twin guitars are manned by textile and advertising executives. The advertising man, son of a former Republican congressman, strums with his partner and recites a Hank Williams piece about a black child's funeral. The preacher speaks:

> Now, mourners, don't you be weepin'
> For this pretty bit of clay
> For the little boy what lived there
> Is done up and gone away.
> He was doing mighty finely
> And he 'preciates yo' love
> But his sho' nuff daddy wanted him
> In that big house up above.
> He didn't give you that baby
> By no hundred thousand miles
> He jus' think you need some sunshine
> So he lent him for awhile.
> And he let you keep and love it,
> 'Til your hearts was bigger grown
> And them silver tears you're shedding now
> Is just int'rest on the loan.
> So my poor dear mourners
> Creeping 'long on sorrows way
> Why, just think what a blessed picnic

This here baby got today.
Your good fathers and good mothers
Crowd the little fellow 'round
In the angels' tender garden
Of the big plantation ground.
And his eyes they brightly sparkle
At the pretty things he views,
But a tear rolls down his cheek
And he says, "I want my parents, too."
Then the angels' chief musician
Teach dat little boy a song,
Say, "Son, if they be faithful
Well, they soon be coming 'long."
So my poor detached mourners,
Just let your hearts with Jesus rest,
And don't go to criticizing
The one what knows the best.
He has give us many comforts,
He's got the right to take away.
To the lord be praise and glory
Forever, let us pray.

It is an odd scene, one that couldn't be recreated in Newton or Pasadena: young men and women of privilege being moved by a verse written by the poet of blue-collar whites about the funeral of a black child.

People who trust their instincts more than academic models speak a secret language that communicates more fully than the harsh jargon of the social sciences. Few in the South are more fluent in the secret language than the Tuskegee graduate, retired tailor, and civil rights toiler. He is talking about police brutality—one of the most active, ugly phrases of journalism and social science. He is saying that relations with the police have improved but not everyone in the black community is as sure of that as he is:

Let me explain it to y'all this way. You remember the time the dogs had the moratorium on chasin' rabbits. For three months all the dogs agreed they wouldn't chase any rabbits. Well, one day a couple of rabbits was sittin' down by the side of the road, just visitin' with each other, when over the hill come a pack of mean lookin' bird dogs, a-runnin' and a-hollerin'. One rabbit turns to the other and says, "I think we better be movin' out through the woods." But the second rabbit says, "Naw, we don't have nuthin' to worry about; you know about the moratorium." Then, the first rabbit says, "Yeah, I know about the moratorium but from the looks of them dogs, I don't think they heard about it."

One final voice needs to be heard, that of the gentleman, the Rhodes Scholar. He still lives close to the eternal soil in that subregion, the Black Belt. He obeys the patrician's call to *noblesse oblige*; is both honorable and skilled at statecraft. He draws pleasure from the graces, plays in the family string quartet, and honors an older but enduring vision of the South. And yet, and yet, he admits to being baffled at the behavior of those southerners who have not been touched by the refinements which shaped him. He is speaking of the broad sweep of history:

It was necessarily a long process and filled with instances of discrimination, but over the long pull it worked for both races. . . . I think it can be safely said that no race on earth ever advanced more rapidly and on broader fronts than the black man in the Deep South during the forties and fifties—not because of pressure from Washington but from our own doing, and with dignity and understanding.

I said earlier this was done without losing our sense of values. We are still the stronghold of rugged individualism, self-reliance, patriotism, religion, and a belief in the free enterprise system on which this government was founded. This statement, though, carries with it a paradox

which I cannot explain; for with all these virtues, our people continue to elect such populist demagogues as Bibb Graves, Huey Long, Bilbo, Jim Folsom, Lester Maddox, and George Wallace.

What are these voices saying? Do they fully describe why southerners are unique and prideful? Even the Rhodes Scholar cannot fully behold and comprehend his people, so we must go on. . . .

Eventually, anyone who hopes to understand any part of the riddle of the South must ask C. Vann Woodward, the indispensable historian and interpreter of the South. Woodward says that other sections of the United States have been exempt from the burdens of history, but the South's experience has been far closer to the common lot of man: "For southern history, unlike American, includes large components of frustration, failure and defeat. It includes not only an overwhelming military defeat but long decades of defeat in the provinces of economic, social and political life."

The Yale scholar's insight is confirmed by others. Take one southern barber and expatriate businessman now living in New York. Southerners are distinctive, says the barber, "because we come up the hard way; we know what it's all about." This transplanted executive, who in many ways has never really left home, has a one-sentence answer for people who ask what it is like to be a southerner: "It's like being Jewish."

Defeat in war, moral complacency, poverty, protein deficiency, and pellagra are truly un-American experiences. But there is another factor beyond Woodward's litany of southern distinctiveness which is perhaps as important as the others. It helps explain the two faces of southern clannishness: the happy, comfortable lubricant of contact among people known as a sense of community and, on the other hand, the deep suspicion of critical or exotic ideas and people, which southerners are often too quick to label "outside agitators."

Southerners got to be so defensive because the South is the only region of the United States that has suffered the scorn of other Americans, heavy words meant to crush the spirit. Black and white, the people of the South have been called lazy, no 'count, shiftless. There have been names for southerners: niggers, rednecks and crackers, hillbillies and hicks. As a group, they have suffered blows to their self-respect, which is a necessity even more important than material comfort. Self-respect has very little to do with a new car or even an indoor toilet; it has to do with the way southerners take what fate has dealt them and how they are regarded by friends and neighbors.

Black and white, southerners have always been more like each other and more different from other Americans; but it is this human necessity, self-respect, that has been the Catch-22 in their relations with each other and in the South's relations with the rest of the nation. Until recently, white southerners couldn't find words to champion the cause of "the little man" without ignoring or damaging the self-respect of the black man. And, in

the great centers for export of moral concern like Boston, the talent was lacking to champion the cause of the black man without demeaning the average white southerner.

In the opinion of one southern writer: "For a region which values courtesy out of respect for the feelings of others and because it makes human contact pleasant, we are shamed, or ought to be, by the words our white citizens spoke so casually about our black citizens. North and South we are aware, or ought to be, of our sinful disregard for the self-respect of black Americans."

But very few are aware of the sensitivity of the white Chapel Hill taxi driver. He is the paradox which even the Black Belt patrician, the Rhodes Scholar, cannot explain. To the man riding in his cab to the airport, however, he was no abstraction. He was a mass of unhurried good will, a good ole boy.

Passenger and driver got a quick fix on each other, as southerners tend to do, and were communicating free and easy until George Wallace's name entered the conversation. A perplexed look came over the driver's face.

"Explain something to me," he said. "How come the educated people are always raising up the nigger but looking down on folks like me? I've done every kind of nigger work there is: chopped cotton, washed dishes, scrubbed bathrooms. Why are they always taking up for the nigger and don't give folks like me no respect?"

"First of all," said the passenger with a smile, "I've known a lot of niggers in my lifetime, and almost all of them were white." The driver chuckled agreement, knowing full well that sorry folks don't come in just one color. "And, second," continued the passenger, "you never had as much of your self-respect peeled off you as the black folks did. When you put on your Sunday-go-to-meetin' clothes, that was your passport; you were as good as anybody with a little change in his pockets. You went anywhere you damned well pleased: to the movies, hotels and motels, restaurants, and nobody told you to go around to the back—unless he wanted trouble."

It would have been too much to expect the cab driver to be blinded by the light of a new reality, to go through a Saul-like conversion right there behind the wheel on the way to Raleigh-Durham airport. He nodded gravely, indicating he would think about it. From the friendly farewell he gave his passenger, he may really think about it and come to some new understanding about blacks, his own kind of folks, and the "educated people."

He will have to get over some cherished resentments, however, because he and the people like him have long been accustomed to thinking they have gotten the short end of the stick, and with some justice. This is what George Wallace has understood so well—the bruised self-respect of many average white southerners—and evoked as powerfully as he stirred in the minority of true haters an aggressive hostility toward black people. It is what made Wallace, not so much a universal political leader, but an ethnic spokesman. He has soul-knowledge of a people who believe they have earned some respect, too, because they have been the first to fight and the majority to die in the nation's wars; like blacks, they have planted our fields, built cities with their own hands, and been among the first to gauge hard times with supper-table reality.

Attitudes are changing; there aren't as many now as there were who are willing to follow "populist demagogues" like Lester Maddox. Old Lester had his last "phooey" in the Georgia primaries of 1974, getting only 40 percent of the vote. But, does that mean that 40 percent of the Georgia electorate are haters? Isn't it just as plausible to believe that many Georgians saw in Lester Maddox something of themselves, and liked what they saw? He (like them) didn't have much of an education; he clowned around some but didn't do any harm with his harmonica-playing and bicycle-riding. He was friendly and courteous to everyone he met, white and "colored" alike, and he had given his life to Christ.

The Maddox and Wallace people like to think of themselves as good people and ask little more than anyone else, human respect. They are puzzled and hurt when educated people refer to them as "crackers" or "rednecks," but they'd never admit it. And, for the life of them, they can't understand why they can't sing their song, "Dixie."

"Dixie" is a symbol of a place and of the things that happened to a people along the way. To some who sing it, the song means that even though the South has known defeat and hard times it will never accept the final defeat, destruction of the human spirit. To others who harmlessly enjoy the symbols of the Confederacy, the song means simply: "We are southerners, a little bit different, and we're perfectly happy to be what we are." To most, the flag and the song are no more aggressive in intent than the high school colors and fight song. The southern barber's partner, in fact, is hard put to understand why blacks don't like "Dixie." He feels the song is for them, too, because they are southerners just as much as he is.

Blacks, on the other hand, do not understand the barber's innocent belief that the symbols he enjoys are for everyone. Growing up in Selma, for instance, they saw the Confederate flag most frequently as a specially designed license plate on the front of police cars. The symbol was like somebody else's religion, which tended to exclude everybody who was not of that faith and can be fully understood only by living for generations in the skin of another creed. That cannot be done, so each perceives the other in the false half-light of incomplete understanding.

The tricks that symbols play on the eye and the perceptual gaps they create in the mind were discovered by two of the South's new breed of moderate politicians at the 1974 annual meeting of the American Society of Newspaper Editors in Atlanta. Arkansas Governor Dale Bumpers, now a U. S. Senator, and Senator Ernest F. (Fritz) Hollings of South Carolina appeared on a panel entitled, "Has the South Rejoined the Nation?" They were persuasively turning that question around until an editor from Cincinnati, Ohio, asked what he should think of now when he sees the Stars and Bars displayed. Their reactions of defensive pride seemed to come from a time that supposedly is past. Senator Hollings answered first:

> We just do it out of community pride. We believe in our families. We believe in our communities. We have a lot of fun out of it. We get these silly questions like the one you asked. What it is is that it sort of puzzles you. We accept Brown against the Board; we accept it fully. There is no such thing as second-class citizenship. But if somebody comes in and really asks that question, it gives us delight to see them nettled by it. We are proud of our states and sections and we don't think there is anything wrong with it. And many, many blacks have a hell of a good time with it too.

Bumpers agreed with Hollings and expressed his own sense of frustration at the selective gullibility of northerners, a willingness to believe anything bad or bizarre about the South:

> Obviously, one of the lines in what I said earlier went over the heads of some and now I'd like to expand on that by saying I believe the North and the rest of the nation—and especially the political leaders and commentators in the rest of the nation—have often accepted the fiction, the stereotypes, and the pure myths about the South. And some of these questions certainly indicate that that is true.

Later, in a friend's hotel suite, Bumpers talked about the question and his answer. He wasn't happy with what he had said and, in retrospect, thought the question was fair and reasonable. The two men talked it over and decided the best possible answer would have been a short one: "Unfortunately, the symbols of the South are enjoyed more innocently than they are perceived."

Perhaps an even better answer would have been to remind the editor from Cincinnati that southerners were Americans before they ever thought to be southern and to point to the most prideful symbols of the South: Mount Vernon, Monticello, and the Hermitage. After all, it was a southerner whose words Declared our Independence, a southerner who chaired the Constitutional Convention, a southerner who defined the role of the Supreme Court, and a southerner who served as the first President of the United States. In fact, between the Washington and Lincoln administrations southerners dominated the White House, the Congress, the Supreme Court, the diplomatic corps, and the military.

It is these symbols, too, that are part of the continuum of the South, part of the cumulative experience that describes southern soul. Southerners have been nation builders and attempted nation wreckers. Southerners are the blues and bayous, fried okra and purple hull peas, populists and patricians. They have known defeat and, black and white, they have known hard times and even scorn. All of it, taken together, has created a bond among southerners which Governor Reubin Askew of Florida calls "an affinity." Pressed for a sharper definition of that affinity at another caucus of southerners in Atlanta, he said, "I don't know; maybe it's like your faith—if you can understand it completely, then it is too small a thing." Maybe so.

Whatever it is that history has made of southerners, it is a sense of community that preserves them and, therefore, must itself be preserved. Community, with its accompanying philosophy, which values the personal over the abstract, can develop only in places that are made to fit a humane scale. Because most larger cities are built for profit rather than people, there is much to fear from those Yankee inventions, cities and factories, which most southerners have longed for since Henry

Grady's time and a few have dreaded and opposed. The birth of a city does not automatically mean the death of civility, as the people of Savannah and Charleston will confirm. And, in many small towns, conformity is enforced so irresistibly that it narrows the vision and dulls the wits.

But the virtues of neighborliness, community, and courtesy are better nurtured in a small town than they are among the army of strangers in many modern metropolises.

Because people like the small-town feeling of place, there are hundreds of tiny towns all over the South involved in renewal programs. Even without extensive planning staffs and grant specialists, town clerks and housing directors were getting urban renewal funds for their towns. In Alabama, for instance, thirty-six of the forty-nine cities involved in urban renewal programs were small towns like Boaz, Eufaula, Ozark, Roosevelt City and Scottsboro, Tuskegee and Uniontown. Piedmont was one of them and it looks now as if that town will make it.

On the map Piedmont is a dot on the northern border of Calhoun County, Alabama. Five thousand people live there in absolute anonymity as far as the rest of the nation knows or cares. In 1963 Piedmont was indistinguishable from any of thousands of small towns in the South or elsewhere. Its undistinguished past seemed destined to triumph over whatever uncertain future it might have had. "It has been said that Piedmont was at a standstill," Mayor L. H. (Beans) Gunter was to say after the town's revival, "but it wasn't; it was going the other way. It would have died."

Even then, there were advantages to living in Piedmont. At least a person could die there and somebody would notice, somebody would care. "Piedmont is a pretty good place to live," someone once told Mayor Gunter, "but it's the best place I know of to die."

In 1963, the town itself was dying. Today a $2 million urban renewal program has made Piedmont's four-block downtown area one of the most pleasant in America. Shoppers standing in front of the Jefferson Furniture Company experience a sensory illusion, like being in an enclosed shopping mall—only inside-out, or outside-in. Round mercury-vapor globes bathe the sidewalks in light, soft music flows under the arching concrete canopies, and young dogwoods sprout from sidewalk-level planters.

Maybe now the town will be able to attract the doctors and dentists, the right kind of industry. It may even be able to hold more of its high school and college graduates and add these to the other amenities of small-town living. If so, it will be due to the civic imagination and civic energy of just five men: the mayor; Seward Kerr, city housing authority director; W. K. (Billy) Little,

Saucy, swinging Atlanta, the "bumptious, fractious, energetic upstart" of the South, with its ultramodern architecture such as Peachtree Center (right) and its economic vitality, contrasts sharply with proud Charleston, whose old-line aristocracy and historic houses, such as those in Rainbow Row (left), recall an older South.

city clerk; Joe Lively, grocery store owner and former chamber of commerce president; and Lane Weatherbee, who doubles as director of the chamber and editor of the town's weekly paper, *The Piedmont Journal*.

They undertook the hard work and headaches of trying to give their little town a future because, for one thing, they like the good life and they know the difference. "Younger people are better traveled than the older generation was," says thirty-year-old Weatherbee. "We've been to Chicago and New York and seen how they live. It's a rat race. It just tickles us to death to get home."

Will they achieve everything they sought for their town? Who knows? But the important thing is they tried. They tried because they cared, and they cared because they knew the people of their town and were known by them. It is the way of the small town. Everywhere there are familiar faces. Every day there are thousands of accidental encounters at church, high school football games, the market or post office; opportunities for pleasant contact with people and the exchange of trivial news about family and mutual friends. Each insignificant conversation broadens the webbing of community so that a single death is cause for general grief and every birth is broadly noted, and approved.

Even government is reduced to personal dimensions; almost everyone is on a first-name basis with city hall. Take Billy Little, for instance. He has been city clerk as long as most people can remember. He grew up in Piedmont and is one of only five members of Piedmont High's Class of 1945 who still live there. Everybody knows Billy and he knows everybody. Mayors come and go but Billy stays, keeping city government functioning from administration to administration. Consequently, almost everyone has a friend at city hall.

There was a party in Piedmont when the town had its open house to celebrate the near-completion of the urban renewal project. Everyone came, literally—young and old, black and white. The 600 pounds of barbecue the chamber hoped would last all day were gone by 1 p.m. Young Tim (Bo) Lusk, with moves like an All-Pro cornerback, tackled the greased pig before the crowd was ready for the game to end. Hundreds of pounds of watermelon were consumed by the children, their appetite scarcely blunted. That night, Center Avenue was closed off for a street dance. At one end, Country Boy Eddie provided music for round and square dancing and at the other end of the street there was a rock band for the young people. And, when everybody finally went home, they slept the sleep of happy exhaustion.

Now, the shrubs and flowers, and the mini-park, are in place to complement the dogwoods. The project is finished and the time for celebration is over. Seward Kerr, the housing director, set the tone when he was named "Man of the Year" for his central role in the renewal effort. "There is another dream," he said in his acceptance speech. "We have here in Piedmont an area where housing is not fit. It is my dream that we can have decent, safe, and sanitary housing that everyone can afford. Let us forget the accomplishments of the past and reach forth to those endeavors and opportunities before us to make Piedmont a better place for all of Piedmont's citizens."

The big dreams of small towns are possible to achieve—if there is civic and political leadership—because that leadership is validated by the trust of citizens who know them and care about them. But can these softer virtues of a more agrarian South be used to shape the great cities of the South—the Atlantas and Nashvilles, Birminghams and Columbias—on a more humane scale?

A couple of months after Bo Lusk received his prize from the Piedmont Chamber of Commerce for winning the pig chase, Atlanta had an outdoor celebration of its own. The Affirmation Atlanta rally was larger, more sophisticated, and less spontaneous. It was organized by the biracial civic and political leaders of the city as a means of saying, "We're Doing Just Fine, Thanks." They said it with professional dancers, choirs, and speeches.

The public optimism, however, covered a creeping private uncertainty. For the first time Atlantans felt the need to reassure themselves that everything was going to be all right. With crime rising, whites continuing to dribble out of the central city with their taxes, and the city's first black mayor, Maynard Jackson, having a hard time getting his administration organized, there was a growing fear in the minds of city leaders that their city might, after all, become Newark South.

But the beginnings of urban anxiety didn't penetrate the space between 10th and 14th Streets on Peachtree. There, a new urban idea is taking shape out of the oldest instincts of the agrarian South—a small town right in the heart of "bigtown."

Colony Square is twelve acres of urbane small-town living. The population is about the size of Piedmont, if the people who work in the twin office towers, the Fairmont-Colony Square Hotel, the retail shops (eventually fifty in all), and the residents of the apartments, condominiums, and planned town houses are included. While only some of Piedmont's residents can walk to work, every resident of Colony Square can do so—and shop at Rich's, pick up a loaf of bread, or mail a letter on the walk home by the all-weather skating rink or past the Japanese gardens.

It is a town built for people as well as profits, living proof that the nontransferable cultural values of the city can be had without sacrificing the convenience of small-town living. A Colony Square couple can browse at the High Museum of Art across the street; take a five-minute cab ride to the ballet, symphony, theater, to any professional sport, or to a first-run movie; and then come back to their little town for a gourmet meal with live

The Sunshine State

Land of perpetual summer, Florida is like no other state in the Union. Set in the South but in few ways southern, the Sunshine State is a 500-mile-long natural wonderland that has been turned into a vacationer's paradise and a retiree's dream. It is also a fruit grower's heaven; central Florida annually produces a billion dollar's worth of citrus fruit, three-quarters of the nation's total. But it is tourism, bolstered by retirement income, that is prosperous Florida's leading industry. Along the Gold Coast, 24 miles of hotels and apartment buildings extend from Miami Beach (above) north to Fort Lauderdale. Retirement communities, which offer activities ranging from tricycle clubs (below left) to shuffleboard (below right), have attracted so many senior citizens to Florida that it now has a larger percentage (14.5%) of persons 65 and older than any other state.

entertainment and wine or for a beer and ham sandwich.

As impressive as all this may sound, it could be built anywhere with enough money (the development's 1974 value was $100 million). Colony Square's major achievement is the feel of the place—a safe, contained, caring sense of small-town community. Elevator etiquette is an example of the difference. In most large cities, strangers rarely speak in elevators. Not in Colony Square. When the doors open, an attractive young matron smiles brightly: "Good morning," she says. A brief conversation begins and the two passengers are likely to know something about each other by the time they reach their floor and to remember each other when they meet again. Walk through the bank and you can tell who's from Colony Square and who isn't. The people who live or work there speak to each other: "Hi, Emily, when you comin' to see me?" or "Hey, Don, you goin' to the Falcons game Sunday?"

This feeling is not accidental. It comes from Colony Square's developer, Jim Cushman, president of Cushman Corporation, who is also the town's informal mayor (on his way anywhere in his town he is hailing friends, introducing himself to strangers, and asking questions constantly). Cushman is a small-town boy himself and describes Colony Square as "my struggle to regain in the midst of a big city that which I lost when I left a small town in South Carolina (Chester, pop. 7,000)." Only the bankers need marketing studies to confirm what Cushman knows instinctively, that "millions of people living in big cities want to return to the basic small-town values: friendliness and warmth, personal identity . . . simple convenience and accessibility."

Because it's a pretty expensive small town, it isn't the answer to every urban question, although it is surprising that the average age of Colony Square's population is thirty-six. It is, however, a very good and direct answer to one tough urban problem: shoring up the tax base to support schools, garbage collection, and police. The area once contained a nationally ranked density of "hippies" and motorcycle thugs who were beginning to poison the single-family Ansley Park area, hastening the flight of taxes to the suburbs. Then, it produced about $100,000 a year in taxes; in 1974 it yielded the city in excess of $1 million.

What does the future hold? Is Cushman's "micropolis" a way of making southern cities agrarian in values and urban in form? That is a question for the bankers, politicians, and planners.

Bankers are probably the most important part of the trinity. "There was a two-year running battle with lenders regarding Colony—some of whom would finance everything but a hotel—others, everything but apartments—others, everything but retail and parking," said Cushman.

A lot is riding on Colony Square's success as a money-maker for developer and investors because Cushman has plans that can answer some tougher questions about urban life. "The real challenge to Colony is to prove its financial viability and thus attract the kind of support that would allow us to move into the lower and middle income areas," he said. "We already are planning to make the next step down the economic ladder to the middle income group in our next micropolis development."

Nobody will know for some time whether Colony Square will work, whether it or some similar idea can preserve community in the urban South and, thus, preserve the tribe itself. But there are many who wish the idea a long and happy life. It would be good to imagine that in the year 2001 two southerners will share seats on an airplane, ask the inevitable question, and one of them will say, "Oh, I'm from a little ol' town you probably never heard of, Colony Square."

If southerners learn their politics more from life than from books, then the instincts coded into them by his-

tory will set the feet of the region's policy makers on the right road. There is a better than even chance that this will happen because almost every regional leader in the world of opinion and decision is talking about the same thing, in one way or another.

They were all there at the meeting in November, 1974, back in Atlanta again: civic leaders and former diplomats, governors and legislators, writers and editors. All had come to hear the report of the Commission on the Future of the South to the Southern Growth Policies Board. Jim Cushman chaired the commission and, appropriately, the meeting was held at the Fairmont-Colony Square Hotel.

It was the last staging of the "Dale and Jimmy and Reubin and John Show." Dale Bumpers is now in the U.S. Senate and John West's term as governor has expired. Their last appearance together was a traditional southern happening, a family reunion, because it was first cousin to that earlier meeting in April of 1971 a few blocks down Peachtree Street at the old Biltmore.

In 1971 the Lamar Society had asked southern leaders to come to Atlanta with some practical answers to the question, "The Urban South: Northern Mistakes in a Southern Setting?" Terry Sanford, former North Carolina governor and then president of Duke University, came with a warning and an idea. Urban and industrial growth for growth's sake, he said, is the same as the dynamics of the cancer cell. "We need growth, and will get it in any event; but growth cannot be our primary ambition," Sanford said in the 1971 conference's keynote address. "We must learn to control the direction and rate of growth." He proposed creation of a Southern Regional Growth Board.

With Sanford as chairman, a steering committee from Duke and the Lamar Society worked with the governors and their aides. The idea was not to create another planning agency to produce stacks of multicolored reports which no one would read but to channel the work of the staff in a very short, direct line to people with the power to act, southern governors and legislators. By the end of 1971, nine governors had issued executive orders joining their states to the regional compact, newly named the Southern Growth Policies Board.

In 1973, there were fifteen member states, a staff located in North Carolina's Research Triangle Park, and funding by state legislatures. It remained for the board to agree on a set of objectives, and the task of preparing them was given to the Commission on the Future of the South. What will the South make of the future? That's what everyone came to hear at the November, 1974, meeting, the men and women of decision and the rest who had only opinions to offer.

There were many good speeches, fine words spoken by men of purpose: six governors, University of Alabama President David Mathews, and Dean Rusk among others. But the spirit of the gathering was also reflected in the official document itself. In the first column, on the first page, the commission called on the southern states "to preserve and enhance, in meeting the issues of growth and change, the human sense of place and community that is a vital element of the unique quality of southern life."

It was an especially hopeful meeting and report for several reasons. Where but in the South would such a group come together for such a purpose? A Commission on the Future of the Midwest or a Rocky Mountain Regional Growth Board sounds, well, implausible. Is there a Yankee counterpart to the L.Q.C. Lamar Society—a Charles Sumner or Daniel Webster Society? Does the Ivy League have a common market for higher education similar to the Southern Regional Education Board? Could any other region duplicate the Southern Christian Leadership Conference?

Church is still regularly attended by southerners of both races and they rely on their faith to insure their souls' salvation in life after death. But those who also

"Nowhere else, almost surely, is there a Protestant population of equal size so renowned for its piety," wrote historian Kenneth Bailey about the South. Baptist, Methodist, and Pentecostal sects abound in the region's small towns and rural areas. Left, Menlo's churches welcome passers-by to stop in and attend a service. Right, devout churchgoers sing hymns.

believe in a right to life after birth must look to public policy to save the temporal soul of the South, which is rooted in the vast stretches of southern soil that have not yet been given over to cultivation by bulldozers.

There were good reasons for hope as 1975 dawned and we began the final countdown to Bicentennial. Not because any of the commission's recommendations had been crafted into model legislation, incorporated in any southern governor's program, or adopted by the first southern legislature. They hadn't. But among the whole galaxy of regional policy organizations, public and private, there was a kind of corporate communion, a knowledge of who they were, where they came from, and where they wanted to go.

Still, there was no shortage of pallbearers ready to cart off the mortal red clay of Dixie in a pine box. Every generation has produced its professional mourners who prematurely announced the death of Dixie. Back in 1930, the Agrarians up at Vanderbilt predicted in *I'll Take My Stand* that if the South allowed cities and factories to breach the Mason-Dixon Line it would be the death of the region. "So it is gone now, whatever it was we had . . ." wrote Harry Ashmore in *An Epitaph for Dixie* in the late fifties. And there is John Egerton, the reporter of sad countenance and sweet nature, who in 1974 proclaimed *The Americanization of Dixie*.

There are others, but the best symbol of the breed that comes to mind is James Dickey. He is a presence full of booze and poetry, out there in the dark—beyond the mechanical, orange mercury-vapor daylight of his native Atlanta at night—raging at the growth which ruined his Buckhead community and drove him out. Dickey and his brand of soul brothers love the South and despair of the changes they believe are ruining it, have ruined it. But in spite of them, and in large measure because of them, Dixie refuses to die. They have been alone at times but they aren't now. They have al-

lies in high places, even among the city clerks of many small towns.

It is one of the enduring ironies of the South that the death of Dixie has been proclaimed at least as often as the arrival of the New South. In fact, the birth of a New South is just another way of saying the South is dead. Neither has happened although many have said they could see it. The old lady was right when she scolded the speaker who had just given a New South oration: "Young man, you speak as if the South is just beginning."

Yet, the questions persist. Will urbanization and industrialization turn southerners into die-cast Americans? Surely the combined weight of Holiday Inns, new bank buildings, and pennanted filling stations will press out of southerners the last drop of cultural memory. Doesn't the end of racial politics, the emergence of cities, and better paychecks mean that the southerner is doomed? No. As long as there are children born into families with a sense of being southern, Dixie won't die.

History has made southerners what they are and southern history simultaneously flows backward and forward. From that history the South has learned about man's limitations as well as his possibilities, knowledge that is hard to acquire but useful to have. From the same soil sprang the legacies that cast the whole shape of American democracy and those that attempted to destroy it. Are the southern people going to forget that and everything that has happened since; forget to be themselves simply because they are moving to town?

No. There will be no pureed, neuter southerner stepping out of the discarded skin of his old creed. Like his dog who sheds the useless winter coat in summer but remains a dog, the southerner will be talking about different things in a different way—even if he is in a meeting held in a revolving restaurant on top of the new bank building.

—H. BRANDT AYERS

Dixie:
the ever-present past

"There is deep pride in the South,"
Faulkner wrote, "a pride in remembering. . . ."
Memories not only of "courage and honor, pity
and sacrifice," but also of grace and elegance, of
an era when lordly planters lived in luxurious
mansions color the thoughts of many southerners
when they think of the past; memories of crinolined
ladies dancing to the sound of violins, of gentlemen
dashing off to the hunt. With but a few exceptions,
that leisurely life is gone; many mansions are now
museums. But the paradox of the South remains;
as writer Susan Fenwick remarked: What became
of "these men who carved out of a land with the
labor of others a way of life that ended in a
holocaust? . . . there is nothing left but dreams
of what might have been and thanks to God that
it wasn't." Nothing, perhaps, but a gentler pace
of life, a love of civility, a sense of roots.
In memory the Old South lives on.

A cherished Virginia custom, the Blue Ridge Hunt
sets out from Carter Hall estate near Berryville, hounds
and hunters eager for the first glimpse of a fox.

Pride in their heritage has prompted southerners to preserve many of the region's stately old homes, like the Evergreen Plantation (above) in New Orleans and the house at left in St. Augustine. At far left residents of Savannah renovate one of the city's few surviving 18th century mansions.

Southern hospitality, with its
emphasis on comfort and courtesy, is more
than just a ritual; it is a way of life. In the
South, writes author Eugene Walter, "there
is a kind of friendliness and civility that goes
beyond ordinary manners. It is a take-your-time,
sit-down-and-enjoy-yourself attitude that
makes almost every encounter an experience."
Good conversation is expected, but good food
is essential at any southern gathering. From
elegant lawn parties (facing page) to informal
gatherings like Tennessee's Ramp Festival
(at right), the food, be it barbecued chicken
or creamed oysters, sets the tone
of the entertainment.

Café brûlot, a flaming concoction of coffee, brandy,
and spices, served at left at Lamoth House, is but one of the
delights of New Orleans's superb Creole cuisine.

"The Run for the Roses," also known as the Kentucky Derby, is America's favorite horse race and a cherished southern institution. Derby Day, the first Saturday in May, climaxes a week of festivities that includes parades, balls, steamboat races, even a fashion fair. As one author put it, "the horses' run . . . may be the least strenuous aspect of Derby Week." But whatever else takes place, it is the race, held at Churchill Downs (below) near Louisville, that is remembered. Hearts speed up, excitement flares when the band begins to play "My Old Kentucky Home," signaling the start of the long-awaited race. Then the bugle sounds and the horses are off, dust behind them, bettors' dreams riding with them.

Sipping the traditional mint julep, a lady waits for the Derby to begin.

Coming into the homestretch, Cannonade (center) shoots past the leaders of the largest field of horses in Derby history, 23 in all, to win the 1974 race.

With little respect but a lot of goodwill, fans greeted England's Princess Margaret with a banner (above) when she attended the 100th running of the Derby in 1974. "A lovely day of racing," commented the princess (at left) after watching the winner receive the traditional blanket of roses.

A gregarious and warmhearted people, southerners enjoy getting together. The occasions may differ, but the spirit remains the same. Placid porch rockers exchanging the latest gossip (below right), fervent fundamentalists singing gospel songs (below) and listening to "oldtime Bible preaching" (at left), parade watchers and participants (right) —they all have something in common: a deep love of shared experience; a strong desire for human companionship; a need to belong. It's a need felt by most who live in the region and many who have left, a need that finds voice whenever a displaced southerner refers to "home" and "homefolks" in that wistful, wish-I-was-back-there way.

Revelry reigns for weeks on end when Carnival time comes to New Orleans. From Twelfth Night, Jan. 6, to Shrove Tuesday, or Mardi Gras, the city seethes with excitement. More than 60 glittering galas are sponsored by the krewes, the secret Carnival societies that determine not only Mardi Gras events but also the city's social hierarchy. Carnival culminates on Fat Tuesday with rowdy parades, free for all, and regal balls, by invitation only. As Ash Wednesday dawns, church bells toll the end of festival for another year.

From morning to midnight on the last day of Mardi Gras, festive floats fill the streets. The city is given over to Rex, King of the Carnival, and the largest parade is in his honor.

King and queen of the mystic krewe of Comus (right) overlook their ball, the city's most exclusive. The queen is a debutante; the masked king's identity is kept secret.

Black Southerners: the dream and the reality

Cruel reminder of the South's tragic past, constant challenge to
the South's bright future, the rural black southerner lags far behind
the rest of the region's population in obtaining a fair share of life's
essentials. Yearly incomes of less than $3,000 are still the norm
in the Mississippi Delta and Deep South black belts.

Pinewood shanties often house families of twelve; some have electricity, but most lack heat and running water.

Mule-powered plows and ox-drawn carts belie the image of a mechanized South. Near Camden, Alabama, farmer and mule (at left) tend a tiny garden, moving gently, lazily, in the hazy sun. Farm supplies much of family's food, but welfare and odd jobs provide needed cash. Homeward bound on Daufuskie Isle, off the Carolina coast (above), schoolboys relax. Since school ends at 8th grade, children must leave the island or face a bleak future.

Dignity is their distinction. Pride in land, however meager its rewards, sets this Tennessee couple apart from the millions of rural blacks who lost hope and left their native region.

Paul Bray, a skilled
worker at Conner Steel Co.
(below), typifies new breed
of concerned black citizens.
Working with the OEO, the
NAACP, and a biracial group
of businessmen, he has helped
open up new jobs for blacks in
Birmingham. At right, Bray
relaxes with his children.

Rising fast, the South's growing black middle class owes much of its advance to industry. Civil rights laws pledged equality; now new jobs are turning promise into progress. Black factory workers today are commonplace; in 1973 blacks made up 25% of the blue-collar work force in the South. A less frequent sight is the black office worker. Blacks held only 8% of all white-collar jobs in the South in 1973, and although many firms are hiring blacks for top positions, the process has been slow. Says one southerner, "Blacks have jobs they never had before, but there is a long way to go."

In South Carolina's textile mills (below), Kentucky's bourbon distilleries (above), and countless other industries, old and new, black southerners are learning the skills they need to bring them into the nation's economic mainstream.

Two of Atlanta's leading citizens, Sen. Herman Talmadge (2nd fr. right) and business leader Herman Russell (2nd fr. left) meet at a Sunday prayer breakfast, symbolizing the city's hope for a working coalition between black and white leaders.

"Gateway to a new era, a new beginning for the cities of our land" is the way Maynard Jackson (right) described his election as the first black mayor of a major southern city—Atlanta. Georgia's capital has long been the center of the South's tiny black elite—the home of third-and-fourth generation wealthy blacks, a magnet for black professionals returning from the north. "Atlanta is . . . a new frontier city," said one man who returned after 18 years. From the Atlanta Life Insurance Co., the largest privately owned black business in the U.S., to the primarily black Atlanta University complex with its 6,000 students in four colleges, a graduate school, and seminary, Atlanta abounds with opportunities for its black residents.

Outspoken state legislator, Atlanta's Julian Bond (above) feels need for greater unity, "politically, socially, economically," in the black community.

Living the good life: at left and opposite, a party at the home of civil rights activist John Lewis.

Children of hope, these youngsters, black and white, are learning to live together in a new South. The process has been slow, fraught with tension, but integration in southern schools is now further advanced than in any other region. But an even deeper change, a change in attitude, is taking place. As one Florida schoolteacher remarked: "In 13 years I have seen mutual suspicion and fear change into mutual understanding and tolerance. Bigotry among young southerners is not merely no longer fashionable; it is socially unacceptable."

Music: sound of the south

Mountain music in its purest form still survives in the Ozark Hills. The folk songs of Stone County, Ark., many of which preserve the age-old traditions of Scottish and Elizabethan English balladry, have been handed down, virtually unchanged, from the time when the first pioneers from Kentucky and Tennessee ventured up the steep wooded passes and found winding valleys like the ones they'd left behind. Isolated from the mainstream of American life until well into the 20th century, Ozarkers endured continual hardship—crop failures, harsh winters, early deaths—yet all the while they kept on singing their timeless ballads—songs about life; about death; about love; above all, about their greatest treasure—freedom. Then in 1963, the people of Mountain View, Ark., decided to hold the first Arkansas music festival. Today that event draws 100,000 visitors every spring and has led to the construction of a $4 million Ozark Folk Cultural Center to preserve the area's songs and crafts.

James Morris (left), better known as Jimmy Driftwood, popular Grand Ole Opry performer and successful songwriter, has been greatly responsible for preserving Ozark music. In 1962, he advised against using established stars at the first folk festival, feeling that Arkansas's amateur musicians would attract just as many people. He was right. As a result the Rackensack Folklore Society, a group of Ozark musicians, was formed and the Arkansas Folk Festival (above, right, top left), an annual tradition, was born.

Folk musicians use a variety of homemade instruments, ranging from the delicately crafted dulcimer (near right), whose name means "sweet song," to the sturdy bucket, or washtub, bass (far right).

With bucket bass and banjo, mountain dulcimer and mandolin, autoharp, fiddle, guitar, and the rare mouth pickin' bow, hill country musicians can play on the emotions of enthusiastic audiences—rousing them to hand-clapping, foot-stomping frenzy with lively jig tunes, reels, and square dances, reducing many to tears with mournful ballads.

Annual events like North Carolina's Sing on Top of Grandfather Mountain (above) and the Old Fiddler's Convention (below) held for four days every August in Galax, Va., provide a stage and an audience for back porch musicians like those at left. Thousands come from all around to listen to bluegrass, country western, and folk music.

Dark and dusty, its only seating backless benches, the French Quarter's Preservation Hall (below) is the sanctuary of true New Orleans jazz. Devotees, dropping a dollar in the basket at the door, crowd in nightly to hear old-time jazzmen play.

Dixieland jazz enlivens cruises on the Delta Queen (above), the only steamboat still carrying overnight passengers on the Mississippi. Trips last from 2 to 19 days and occasionally special events are added, such as the Jazz Festival Cruise, which took place in December, 1972, and featured the lively band below.

Jazz, that syncopated "sound of surprise," with its complex, chaotic rhythms born out of a people's common past, is today acknowledged as America's only original art form. Duke Ellington defined it simply as "a music with an African foundation which came out of an American environment"; others have written whole books about it. New Orleans was its birthplace; but slavery was its creator. From the slaves' field songs, dances, and melancholy blues grew a music that captured the world.

Dancing in the streets, brass band parades, regal auto processions
pervade New Orleans at various times each year. The New Orleans Jazz Festival
(right and below), begun in 1969 to celebrate the city's musical heritage, is held every spring,
featuring not only jazz bands but also gospel singers, rock groups, Cajun bands,
and even country western performers. Every fall, the Jolly Bunch Jazz Parade
(above), sponsored by a black social and marching club, promenades
down the streets of New Orleans.

Southern soul music —blues, gospel, jazz—is meant to be felt, not merely heard. Says jazz historian William Russell: "Music is . . . for dancing and having a good time, not just for sitting there." Visitors to the New Orleans Jazz Festival would agree. Whether belting out a hallelujah chorus with gospel singer Sister Gertrude Morgan (directly below) or dancing to free-for-all jazz, they know what southern music is all about.

Creative Americans

John Gardner

Betty Friedan

Paul Ehrlich

In the Public Interest

Our innovator/leaders—these stand forth as the peculiar prophets of American civilization. And they're evident in all aspects of our national life, galvanizing and stimulating and occasionally outraging their fellow Americans from every region. First of all, in the realm of nongovernmental public service. "I'm not interested in public office.... The biggest job in this country is citizen action." So says Ralph Nader, the consumer advocate. Betty Friedan, organizer of NOW (National Organization of Women) would agree, rallying followers to women's liberation by a combination of activism and wisdom. Pounding pulpits across the land, Jesse Jackson, Martin Luther King's heir, urges blacks toward their own liberation—the recognition that they are "Somebody!" Proclaiming yet another cause, Paul Ehrlich, leader of Zero Population Growth, demands that Americans act to save their world by reducing their birthrate. Quieter but equally effective, John Gardner of Common Cause leads 300,000 Americans in a "citizens' lobby" for governmental reform.

Ralph Nader   Jesse Jackson

117

In Business and Labor

Tinkerers or technologists, American inventors have spurred industry with new ideas, benefited labor with more jobs, given our society its unfailing opportunity. Thus Edwin Land, president of Polaroid and inventor of the controversial but litter-free camera, and William Lear, head of Lear Industries and developer of a new steam automobile engine for our polluted highways, operate within the recognized pattern of American genius. Labor too has developed innovator-leaders so the worker won't be the odd man out in U.S. capitalism's cyclical growth. Both in the office, where AFL-CIO's first chairman George Meany exercises his power, and in the field, where Cesar Chavez seeks to organize agriculture's minions, labor leaders seek security for American workers.

Cesar Chavez

Edwin Land

118

William Lear

George Meany

Linus Pauling

B. F. Skinner

Buckminster Fuller

In Science and Philosophy

"Human, practical benefits flow from continued scientific work." In saying that,
James Watson (discoverer of DNA's structure) speaks for his group of American innovators.
Anthropologist Margaret Mead, though famed for foreign insights, is equally concerned
about the American family. B.F. Skinner, known for behavioral experiments, applies his
findings to the problems of U.S. industry. Dr. Jonas Salk, having produced the vaccine
against polio, now seeks to rout cancer. Buckminster Fuller, brilliant mathematician,
experiments with "synergetic" forms for our buildings and even our bathrooms. Symbolic
of this concern for man's well-being, Dr. Linus Pauling holds Nobel Prizes both for
his research on the chemical bond and his advocacy of world peace.

James Watson

Jonas Salk

Margaret Mead

121

In the Performing Arts

Leonard Bernstein, spanning both popular and classical music, epitomizes a new breed of American Wunderkinder—some are native tunesmiths (like Aaron Copland); others minstrels from abroad (like opera composer Gian-Carlo Menotti). Most inventive of all is John Cage, whose sounds spring from the music of industrial life. In dance, too, Americans have pioneered: Russian émigré George Balanchine brings athleticism together with traditional ballet; Alvin Ailey's integrated company has taken off from there. All together, they've staged a modern American revolution in the arts.

Gian-Carlo Menotti

Leonard Bernstein

George Balanchine   Alvin Ailey

John Cage   Aaron Copland

123

Edward Albee

Kurt Vonnegut, Jr.

In Art and Literature

As it goes here, innovators—first called clowns—become our grand masters. Alexander Calder, creator of bizarre "mobiles," is now hailed as titan of the plastic arts; Robert Rauschenberg, who shocked the world with his "pop art," now stands as patron to younger unknowns. (Oddly, meticulous master Andrew Wyeth seems most radical of living artists with his realistic style.) In literature Tennessee Williams and Edward Albee, whose characters blurted out unspeakable words, have achieved required reading status. Kurt Vonnegut, Jr., at first a champion only of the younger generation, now appeals to all. "Our star moon man," a literary magazine calls him. Thus does a nation honor its prophets.

Andrew Wyeth

Robert Rauschenberg

Tennessee Williams

Alexander Calder

East Coast–Modern Metropolis 3

The airport bus lurches to a stop a block uphill from Grand Central. He steps down to the sidewalk, to be engulfed immediately in a flood of New Yorkers rushing from the station. Without apology or quarter they bump him, override him, force him to the building wall, where, in a kind of eddy, he is able to fish the paper from his pocket.

The note reads: "Catch a cab (though you won't believe they're so expensive). Or walk across (east) to Second Avenue and get a bus down (south) to 19th Street. See you for breakfast."

He smiles into the face of a knowledgeable-looking onrusher and asks: "Which way's east?" The stranger glances at him with cold curiosity, pushes past, and without a word is on his way.

With the aid of common sense and a policeman he makes his way to Second Avenue and begins looking for a bus stop sign. There aren't any, but presently a bus eases up to the corner, opens its door, and he climbs aboard, pulling out a dollar bill.

"Exact fare, Mac."

"Excuse me?"

"I said exact fare. Cancha read?" Pointing to a sign.

"I spent all my change. What do I do?"

"That's your problem. Step down and let the people pass!"

In the end he walks. Through the crowds, the dirt, the traffic, above all through the noise: jackhammers; horns; sirens; shrieking brakes. The apartment house lobby, when he finally reaches it, feels like a sanctuary. But here, too, problems arise: the inner door won't open. Puzzled, he glances at the row of mail boxes and notes that each has a buzzer and a speaker grill above the name plate. Pressing his friend's button, he waits a bit, then shouts "Tom?" into the speaker. "Tom, it's me!" Ominously the door begins to buzz. What does *that* mean? He reaches for the doorknob, but the buzz stops, and the door won't budge.

He tries again: first the button, then "Tom, it's really me!" and finally lunges to catch the door while the buzzer still rasps. And it works. A few moments later, lifted to the seventh floor by an elevator, he is greeted by the opening of a door at the end of a dimly lit corridor. There stands Tom, who waves briefly before stooping to pick up his newspaper.

Tom's wife apologizes hastily for having already eaten breakfast; she has to be off to her job at the airline. A stewardess no longer, she hastens to fill executive shoes: "See you tonight!"

Tom, serving the eggs, says: "Take your time. I don't have to leave for the hospital for seven minutes. You don't mind if I clean up while we talk, do you?" In the hip-wide kitchen he runs water over the dishes. "Remind me to show you how the lock works."

The lock is extraordinary, involving a steel rod that jams diagonally into the floor so the door won't open even if the latch is jimmied. It takes several minutes to explain.

Then Tom too is gone. And the visitor sits there with a mug of coffee and a cigarette and a vague pressure in his stomach. Why do all these people have to run around quite so fast? Is it worth that much hassle? And the security at the door, and the rudeness, is that really a sensible way to live? He ponders the curious ways of the eastern urban American and then puts his head out the window to find a breath of fresh air. He doesn't succeed.

For generations it was accepted that the soul of this republic was an agrarian soul—and that the nation was the better for it. Thomas Jefferson held this view. So did Alexis de Tocqueville, that perspicacious analyst of the national character who visited here early in the nineteenth century. In those days Philadelphia had only 161,000 inhabitants; New York 202,000; but, wrote Tocqueville:

Millions of people pour into New York City each day, to work, to shop, to sightsee. Some, like the suburbanites at left, commute by train; others, 4½ million a day, ride crowded subways (right), which during rush hour often run at one-minute intervals.

The lower ranks which inhabit these cities constitute a rabble even more formidable than the populace of European towns. They consist of freed blacks, in the first place, who are condemned by the laws and by public opinion to a hereditary state of misery and degradation. They also contain a multitude of Europeans who have been driven to the shores of the New World by their misfortunes or their misconduct; and they bring to the United States all our greatest vices, without any of those interests which counteract their baleful influence. . . . I look upon the size of certain American cities, and especially on the nature of their population, as a real danger which threatens the future security of the democratic republics of the New World and I venture to predict that they will perish from this circumstance unless the government succeeds in creating an armed force which, while it remains under the control of the majority of the nation, will be independent of the town population and able to repress its processes.

What would Tocqueville think today? For far from being repressed, America's urban citizens now represent nearly 74% of the population of the nation. More than 30 million of them live along the East Coast alone, in the dense old municipalities spawned during colonial and postcolonial years. Boston, Providence, New York, Newark, Philadelphia, Wilmington, Baltimore, Washington—it was cities like these that troubled Tocqueville and that have continued to trouble people—to the point where in the 1950s and 1960s millions of citizens fled across their city lines and into the suburbs, in an epidemic of urban anxiety. Since then, however, the situation has calmed down a bit, people are having second thoughts, and statistics are beginning to change. "In the last three years," commented a Boston official in 1974 with wonder in his voice, "we've had an increasing num-

ber of young professional people between the ages of twenty-three and twenty-five moving into Boston."

More important than population statistics, a deep-rooted and effective democratic spirit is emerging in the cities in thousands of community meetings and public hearings along the 400-mile megalopolitan coastline. In Hartford, Connecticut, and Annapolis, Maryland, as well as in the giant-sized metropolises, the neighborhoods are overturning city hall and gaining more power for themselves.

When, toward the end of his final campaign for mayor of New York several years ago, John Lindsay was asked in a weary moment if he thought his city would endure, he found himself answering yes, that man would prevail, and New York, too. And so it has, for another few years. But even when a city as a whole appears beyond hope, residents will still form groups to defend their own neighborhoods, stubbornly, sometimes violently, in a spirit of indignant self-preservation.

"I've lived here all my life," says Nancy Lau, showing a visitor around Philadelphia's tiny Chinatown. "This is our gym and our auditorium. You name it, we use it, for wedding receptions, for funerals, basketball games, dances, movies, anything you can think of." She and other families in the four-block neighborhood are working together to prevent the bulldozing of their gym and adjoining church for the sake of the proposed Vine Street Expressway.

"We're such a small community," Celia Moy adds. "To fight the city, the church, and the state—how many more can you take on?"

The remarkable thing is that Mrs. Lau and Mrs. Moy appear to be winning. Many obstacles remain to be cleared; but step by step the establishment is yielding, just as it has yielded in numerous similar confrontations within other cities in recent years.

To a middle-aged schoolteacher in the Bronx, "an in-

explicable sense of camaraderie" appears to be the special secret of urban delight. John Steinbeck would have agreed. He wrote of the damp but marvelous day, when, after living through months of puzzled loneliness in New York, he suddenly felt at home under the splendid ugliness of the Third Avenue El as he looked into a rain-spattered window with the crowd going by. Walt Whitman, poet laureate of American urbanites, felt a tremendous togetherness with past and future generations of city folk when he wrote *Crossing Brooklyn Ferry*:

> Others will enter the gates of the ferry,
>   and cross from shore to shore;
> Others will watch the run of the flood-tide;
> Others will see the shipping of Manhattan
>   north and west, and the heights of
>   Brooklyn to the south and east;
> Others will see the islands large and small;
> Fifty years hence, or ever so many hundred
>   years hence, others will see them,
> Will enjoy the sunset, the pouring in of
>   the flood-tide, the falling back to
>   the sea of the ebb tide.

There is loneliness and privacy in these big cities, but you do constantly feel you're *with* people. You're with them in the sense that you're on essentially the same escalator. It's designed to take everyone up: out of small-town thinking into cosmopolitan patterns; up out of self-conscious inhibitions into a kind of anonymous freedom; above all, up out of the lower class into the middle class. And until very recently the city has served its upward function remarkably well, raising countless millions from immigrant despair to citizen pride.

What is a "typical" East Coast city? The answer: there isn't any; they're all contradictory in character. Washington stretches out languidly along the Potomac, a city of trees and marble; while New York thrusts upward, all steel and glass. New York seems to survive by holding its many ethnic minorities in some kind of balance. Boston and Washington, on the other hand, each has a once-repressed ethnic group which now holds most of the power—the Irish in Boston, the blacks in Washington. Newark has been forsaken by the aristocrats who once ruled it. But Baltimore remains in the hands of its eternal old families. Boston has profited by eradicating its notorious Scollay Square and building a mighty gov-

129

ernment center in its place. Yet Baltimore refuses to give up its traffic-blocking "arabs" (fruit peddlers with horse-drawn wagons) or its racy "strip" and seems to be getting along nicely too.

If the cities themselves defy generalization, so do the people inhabiting them. One young working couple chooses to spend its day off in Washington's Anacostia section taking part in the August People's Day celebration. "We're having a great time," they tell a newspaper reporter, holding their children's hands. "It's even better than last year—more exhibits. The vibrations are just beautiful." But then you come up against a man who lives on Baltimore's eastern fringe: "We rarely go downtown anymore. I work in the suburbs, and the whole family shops here. We find what we want at shopping centers scattered along the beltway." The chief joy of some urbanites appears to lie in getting away from their cities, off to bird watch in the Jersey

"We want to keep what we have and make it possible for our people to continue to live here," declares Little Italy resident Vincent Vitale. His words express the strong ethnic pride and love of community that is common among New York City's Italian-Americans.

A maze of exotic, sunless streets, Manhattan's Chinatown is home to more than 60,000 Chinese, many of whom are recent immigrants. More than half of Chinatown's men work in the area's popular restaurants; 75% of the women toil for low wages in neighborhood garment factories.

pine barrens, to ski in the Pennsylvania Poconos, or to sail on the Chesapeake. For others, listening to the cities' music, tramping around to the art exhibits, catching up with the latest shows is a year round occupation that makes urban life worth living. "This is the place I like to spend the summer," said a young mother with baby in stroller at New York's Museum of Modern Art. She's an urbanite—but only one of many.

So—not by looking for the typical but by falling into step first with this character then with that—that's the way to discern the American of the city. And it's probably best to begin in New York City, biggest and tallest of them all.

It's tall because of the rivers that restrict Manhattan. It's tall too because everyone wants to be there, right in the heart of town, in those magical 23 square miles. New Yorkers don't abandon an old building and move on; they tear it down and build a taller one in its place. Below the glinting pinnacles in the cramped streets, the driver leans on his horn, the pedestrian races to beat the light. When a New Yorker finds a quiet place in the sun (perhaps on one of the usually crowded benches in the park), he relaxes, but intensely. He is constantly on the watch for a break in the line, a better restaurant, a brighter idea. The sense of compressed vitality may be stronger here than anywhere in the world.

Phil Wise and Linda Orloski are a young New York couple. Their immigrant great grandparents, traveling from Central Europe several generations ago, did not pause long in this city. At the immigration station they waited in line, passively accepted radical phonetic respellings of their names by harried bureaucrats, and then headed out into the new continent's heartland to farm and raise families. Among their numerous descendants are Linda and Phil.

Phil is twenty-eight now; Linda, twenty-five. They both came to New York from the Midwest not because they picked the city but because New York picked them. Phil, about to graduate from the University of Kansas, was hired by a big New York insurance company for its corporate personnel department. Three years later, on a recruiting trip himself (with instructions to keep a particular eye out for possible female junior executives) he interviewed a self-possessed, good-looking senior at Northwestern University and induced her to accept employment with the same firm. It turned out to be an extraofficial engagement. Three months after Linda came to New York they got tired of eating out every night and she moved into his bachelor apartment in a very natural, mutually noncommital way.

Native New Yorkers are surprised and a little amused by people like Phil and Linda. In their four years in this city they've been everywhere, from Coney Island to Bedloe's, from Grossinger's in the Catskills for a socially directed weekend to the Hotel Plaza on Central Park South for Sunday brunch. They've walked the great bridge to Brooklyn, gone skiing in Corona Park, and one rainy spring morning got up at five to watch the circus enter town. They are the kind of people advertising agencies have in mind when they launch new brand-alliance campaigns, but Phil and Linda depend on their own sources. They buy their bread at Bloomingdale's, their other groceries at the outdoor stands on Ninth Avenue. Linda's fancier dresses often come from a certain high-class thrift shop on the upper East Side. For Phil's clothes they shop together at Barney's on lower Seventh Avenue, a one-time discount house which is now bigger—and, in some departments, more costly—than Brooks Brothers and has a buffet lunch bar and barbershop besides.

The couple moan when the New York Times prints a rave review of one of their special restaurants, thereby jamming it with new customers for weeks. They are so happy together in their carefree, upward-bound life that the city has the same place in their affections that a

131

Framed by a setting sun, the Empire State Building soars skyward, 1,250 feet above Fifth Avenue. No longer the tallest building in the world, it still remains one of New York City's best-known sights, attracting scores of visitors every year.

first child does in a Marin County commuter's home.

Like other, older New Yorkers they profess gloomy forebodings for the future of their welterous city, a political entity so ungraspable that its budget, for example, is bigger than that of any state government (second only to the federal budget) and its 300,000 employees only a little more cordial than the taxi drivers. But Linda and Phil see a place in the city for themselves forever. Not beyond possibility, some day, is a small co-op apartment on the upper East Side, and maybe a crude weekend shack out on one of Long Island's easternmost beaches. Meanwhile, next Tuesday, Linda and Phil are going to examine another city landmark, the Office of the City Clerk. He's going to marry them.

This is a city that people remember their first sight of, before it loses clarity to later moiling impressions— the look at the whale before he swallows you. One of the most stirring first views is from an airliner on a clear blue winter afternoon at twilight, when the pilot has time to circle the city on the approach pattern to LaGuardia Airport. Below, the millions of lighted windows readjust themselves, expectantly conveying the urgent mental quality of the place; the lights are like sparks thrown off by the abrasion of strong ideas.

Or did your first glimpse happen from behind an automobile windshield? That too has its moments. On the New Jersey Turnpike, headed north, you finally work your way past the Gehenna of foul smelling oil refineries. All at once, just past a shipping facility of some sort, you incongruously spot the Statue of Liberty, like some weird mirage; and a few moments later the whole New York skyline rears up like a stage set— before you crawl through the Holland Tunnel to become a part of it.

How is one to grasp it all? It isn't easy, particularly in the outer boroughs of Brooklyn, Queens, and the Bronx. These areas until fairly recently were really col-

An island within an island, Central Park slashes through the center of Manhattan, 840 acres of open country in the midst of one of the world's most crowded cities. Ideal for relaxing on Sundays (above) or singing in the sun (left), the park is a place for everyone.

lections of separate towns, but gradually the population grew until the grid filled in with continuous housing. You can travel for miles in such areas with very little sense of where you are. The sheer variety of this city only compounds the confusion. From a Georgian mansion on the Hudson in Riverdale, the Bronx, to a stubby new garden apartment in Flushing, Queens, seems a very long way—and it seems even farther to a cold-water tenement on 128th Street, Manhattan. New York is justly infamous for its slums. Of these, Harlem is the best known; but there are worse slums, and bigger ones, in both Brooklyn and the Bronx—Melrose, Mott Haven, East New York, endless stretches of debris-strewn desolation, where most of the buildings look as if they've been broken into and where the people look broken too. There are no signs here of any economic escalator moving upward. If anything it seems to have gone into a slow reverse. Yet every year more poor peo-

ple move in. The number of blacks and Puerto Ricans in the city has doubled in two decades. In these desperate districts live New Yorkers whose city experiences have been vastly different from those of Phil Wise and Linda Orloski.

Jesus Ramirez came here from the Dominican Republic three years ago. He's a competent carpenter, but his English is poor, he's not a union member, and he hasn't worked since a two-week job last August. His sister took him in a few months ago, but her husband recently told him to find another place to live. He has no money to rent a room, he can't afford his plane fare back home, and since he's an illegal alien he can't go on welfare. These days he's alternating between panic and paralysis.

May Jamison is a sixty-two-year-old black woman who makes a meager living, as she has since the age of fifteen, cleaning other people's apartments. At night she comes home to a two-room flat in Bedford-Stuyvesant and cooks for the four grandchildren who have been left on her hands, all of whom are in trouble of one sort or another. Her life is grim, and it's going to get grimmer.

133

Aaron Rothblatt at least has a dependable job: for twenty-two years he's been driving a bus on the Second Avenue line. But he's got an ulcer which last month sent him into the hospital, and his doctor warns him he'll be in serious trouble unless he finds a quieter line of work. He has a small, highly mortgaged home on Staten Island and two teen-aged children. What he doesn't know yet is that his wife is pregnant again; she hasn't had the heart to tell him.

On the other hand, New York City also has residents like John E. Ogburn III. Jack dropped out of Yale after a year, to find himself, and currently is working as a deckhand on a tugboat. He is one of those broad-shouldered, hairy, saintlike, equable youths with no sense of urgency to him. For Jack such complicated matters as getting a strict union job somehow open up; he does his part by handling the towlines nimbly and cheerfully.

New York City has a large shoreline, 578 miles of it,

Twin towers of the World Trade Center, gleaming glass pinnacles 110 stories high, dwarf surrounding skyscrapers along the Hudson River in lower Manhattan.

134

and the tug's duties take its crew all over that waterfront. First thing in the morning they may be dispatched to drag a barge of garbage to a fill area. That job finished, the tug may do some lighterage, unloading cargo from a freighter to barge it to one or another of the operating docks among the many rotting ones that jut shabbily out into the rivers. Before the shift is over, the tug is certain to be sent on some errand or other deep into the complex of New Jersey's containership facilities. There, from close to the Jersey shore, one gets the full panoramic sweep, the long side of Manhattan, unphotographable, from George Washington Bridge south to Wall Street and the Battery, where the tallest (so far) of all New York buildings stand in a matched pair, the World Trade Towers.

By way of contrast to this mighty sight, the tug may next be sent around the quiet, New Jersey side of Staten Island, where decrepitude prevails. On the mudflats is a junkyard of abandoned craft: tugs, old steamers, even aged remains of sailing ships. No proud towers, no glistening walls of glass.

Jack Ogburn's job is not a demanding one once the tug is under way. He can pour himself a cup of coffee from the pot in the galley and simply watch New York City as it moves by. To him the city is something to be around without getting caught in, and his present occupation is ideal for that. Maybe, he muses, he should become a docking pilot, instead of another corporation lawyer like the numbered Ogburns preceding him.

A docking pilot. When the tug strums into the Battery to pick up one of those professional personages, it is on a more elevated task than most. The pilot himself emits a certain air of elegance. Dressed most unnautically, in a business suit, leather-soled oxford shoes, and a snap-brimmed fedora, he's cordially aloof from the tug crew, a whole social cut above them. Meanwhile, down the harbor waits a tall ocean liner, helpless without his expertise. But what impresses Jack the most are those

Survival in New York City takes imagination and an anything-can-happen attitude. High above the city, an apartment dweller takes advantage of pleasant weather to vacuum the soot from his artificial grass. Below, workers dash across an empty Fifth Avenue at rush hour during one of the city's periodic paralyzing blizzards.

slippery shoes the pilot wears. For watch how he gets onto the liner from the tug: the tug speeds to the liner's side; and while both are still moving, a steel door opens in the bottom of that cliff of metal, the side of the ship, and the docking pilot jumps from the tug's rail into it, across the brink, his face expressionless.

Responding to the pilot's signals on the big horn, the tug, pounding with power, slowly pushes the enormous ship dockside; and for the next twenty minutes both Jack and the pilot are very busy. Finally the job is done. The excited passengers line up to disembark; the pilot takes the ship's captain aside to invite him out to an expense account dinner that evening and perhaps a musical comedy; but Jack Ogburn is glad to let go of the dock side and be floating once more. Just a little free of the monstrous city, but still there.

Of all the East Coast cities, Philadelphia may be the most difficult for an outsider to know, to understand. One reason is its quietude. Jokes about it have survived even vaudeville. In railroading days it was called the yawn between New York and Washington. W.C. Fields, born here, supposedly requested that his tombstone bear the words: "On the whole, I'd rather be in Philadelphia." Muckraker Lincoln Steffens spoke of the city at the turn of the century as being corrupt and contented.

And indeed, this city seems to be a large calm place. Yet not long ago it ranked third nationally in terms of violent crime. In other social matters as well, it is a complex kind of quietude that Philadelphia maintains.

The high-society image of the city is one of great privacy, with not much restaurant life nor much gaiety of any sort. This is nonsense. Well-born Philadelphians have been rich so long that they do very much as they want socially; it is just that the high-society circle knows how to close ranks and be unrevealing. Unlike their counterparts in some other cities, they really do not like to be in the newspapers. There is always New York close by if one has to blow off steam. Or if the politics of private society get boring and one wants a faster game, there is always Washington, D.C.

Philadelphia is like Boston in that the weight of the old society names is somewhat fictional anyway; families like the Cadwaladers and the Wideners, who once set the tone of Rittenhouse Square, have dissolved outward into the beautiful Pennsylvania countryside, where horses are easier to keep. Unlike Washington and New York, there is no great necessity to have an apartment in town to feel involved in Philadelphia.

Involved these people are. Back in the 1950s they startled the nation by capturing corrupt City Hall, against seemingly impossible odds, and placing one of their own, Richardson Dilworth, in the saddle. It was like a Civil War cavalry raid. The massive infantry of the minority ethnic groups finally drove off the attack and took the city back again, but the Dilworth days are recalled by many with fondness. Nor would it be very surprising if another raid were to be mounted within the next few years. One lawyer whose business pulled him away from Philadelphia in the late 1950s recalls: "What I loved about the city was City Hall. Mayor Dilworth drove out the rascals who had been binding the government in graft and favoritism for decades. For a while there the crooks were literally jumping out of the window. . . . the chief of the vice squad killed himself. The place still reeks of cigars and old wood." It is fair to mention that this lawyer's wife was less disappointed than her husband when they were transferred elsewhere. Things were too placid socially for her: "All the connections in the Main Line suburbs really go back to the schools these people attended together when they were children. Half the time I didn't know what they were talking about."

But Philadelphia's true history, like that of so many East Coast cities, is a story of wave after wave of poor immigrants who gradually worked their way up into the middle class, then got together and seized political power. There are the Irish and the Polish and the Italians—especially the Italians. And then there are the blacks. If the blacks went over to a reform candidate, the other minorities might not again elect a mayor with whom they identify as strongly as with Frank Rizzo. So far, it seems, black aspirants for the highest office in the city have only split the opposition to the other massed minorities, but there may come a day.

Philadelphia is a place that does its civic homework. Although the city does not get the national attention that New York, Washington, and Los Angeles attract, it is fair to say that many of the federal urban programs of the past twenty-five years were first invented and tried out here. The city was redesigned on paper in the late forties, and more than a few of the changes have since been moved off the drawing board and into the streets by eloquent city planners and their backers. Penn Cen-

Craftsmen gather at the old marketplace in the Society Hill district to demonstrate their skills and sell hand crafted goods.

ter was the first of the big postwar redevelopments, a complex of office buildings and apartments near City Hall, where Broad and Market Streets cross and the old statue of William Penn gazes down from on high. Penn Center is not quite so exciting physically as the redevelopments that followed it in other cities across the country. Neither is the tidying up of the area around Independence Hall, where too many of the flavorful, almost grotesque commercial buildings of the late nineteenth century were sacrificed for the sake of gentility. But Society Hill, in the run-down area east of Washington Square, is as successful an urban residential restoration as can be found. A mass of new town houses was built in a neighborhood where other town houses were being restored, and apartment towers were inserted with discretion.

Today Society Hill ranks as one of the most deliberately charming new/old residential areas created in any major American city. Cobblestone streets reflect the glow of gaslights; sporty little cars park in front of authentic hitching posts; window panes of the narrow town houses rattle with the laughter and music of the affluent liberals who have moved in. Mayor Rizzo refers to Society Hill with asperity—and some accuracy—as Philadelphia's very own Georgetown. It is not his turf. It is also in this area and its immediate environs that some swinging night spots have recently sprung up, contradicting the image of a dull Philadelphia after dark.

Urban renewal of another sort is taking place in North and South Philadelphia. Up near Temple University is a section that most white Philadelphians think of as "the jungle" and which the university hopes to eradicate by the usual combination of bulldozer and concrete mixer. The black citizenry, on the other hand, keeps hoping that it can save this neighborhood. Led in part by Episcopal priest Paul Washington, rector of the Heavenly City Church, they have set up a community development corporation. On formerly devastated Page Street stands one of their successes, a group of black-built, black-owned two-story houses of redwood and brick.

Down in South Philadelphia a similar battle is going on within the vigorous Polish community, most of whose strong-backed men work on the docks that line the Delaware River. The women watch the budgets, get the family to church, and scrub the marble front steps. In an old section called Queen Village, where many of the brick and stone houses are historically certified, developers want to build apartments that will attract young professional tenants like the smart set on Society Hill; the residents are fighting back.

"We really don't want to force (anyone) to leave. . . ." insists one developer, but then he goes on to say a little plaintively: "A lot of these people are sixty, seventy, eighty years old. A lot of them are bordering on senility. They don't understand the whole idea of moving. It stymies them. They just don't understand progress and the need for social improvement."

Maybe it's backward to want to keep Queen Village the way it is. Maybe it's old-fashioned to throw that big

"Proclaim Liberty throughout all the Land unto all the Inhabitants thereof" reads the inscription on the historic Liberty Bell. On July 8, 1776, it rang out, announcing the proclamation of the Declaration of Independence, signed four days earlier at Philadelphia's State House, now known as Independence Hall (left). The bell, displayed for centuries in the Hall (right), has been moved across the street to the mall.

party at the local tavern after the Mummer's Parade on Broad Street. And maybe it's foolish to hope your son will settle down and get a union job on the docks so he can marry and raise a family in the neighborhood. But that's what they seem to want in Queen Village.

There is a brash, gibing kind of humor peculiar to Philadelphians whatever their social or economic level in the city, and their flat, clear diction projects it well. With it, they put one another on their mettle in a seemingly merciless way but with the underlying kindness of a real feeling one for the other. Reporter Carol Byrne of *Philadelphia Magazine* caught the following conversation in Andy's Queen Village grocery store:

The Mummer's Parade, a Philadelphia institution, takes place every New Year's Day. Dressed in glittering, feathery costumes, string bands and other marchers parade up Broad Street, from South Philadelphia to City Hall, where each group is judged.

"What d'ya want, doll?" Andy leaned over the high white counter, patiently smiling at the heavy older woman scrutinizing the meat in the counter.

"Don't doll me, you shyster. I came for meat, not a lip." She pursed her lips together and glared at him. Then, ever so mischievously, she gave him a wink. It was fun, this game everyone played when they came to Andy's. Andy was a friend. If you couldn't insult your friends, they weren't friends.

"Give me two pounds chip steak. And make it nice."

"C'mon, Marie. Don't I know beauty when I see it?" Now Andy smiled broadly. "Chip steak, huh? For sandwiches, right? On a diet again, Marie?"

Marie lifted her arm as if to strike him. "I'll give you the back of my hand, you devil." But she, too, smiled broadly.

Andy finished cutting the meat. "What else, Marie?"

"Two pounds ground round, Andy. And that's it." Andy looked at her incredulously. "That's all? For the week?"

Marie's face fell and became apologetic. "Money's tight, Andy. What can I say?"

Andy just shrugged his shoulders and started grinding the meat. "Yeah. What can you say, Marie." Marie took her meat and moved to the front of the store.

In genteel Philadelphia a string trio is playing Strauss waltzes during the afternoon cocktail hour at the Bellevue-Stratford Hotel. A college couple meets, as arranged, under the eagle at Wanamakers. In a deteriorated public housing building, a tenant sets his door

chain and wonders if it will be strong enough to protect him against predatory visitors. This is a quiet city, self-respecting in essential spirit but afflicted with the hopes and ills of all the old eastern metropolises.

Washington, D.C., is a city of important—and self-important—people, of careers made and unmade in an atmosphere of relentless gossip. It is also a company town, with government as its product; the filing cabinet its most universal piece of furniture. At the same time, and underlying all the rest, it is a southern city. The vegetation is southern. The air is southern. So is the pace, curiously relaxed, even languorous, amidst all the tensions of important decisions and big events. John Kennedy once described it as a place of southern efficiency and northern charm.

As East Coast cities go, Washington got off to a late start, and a slow one. In 1790 Philadelphia was already 108 years old, Boston 160, but Washington was still mostly swamp and forest, its only mark of civilization the little river port of Georgetown. Even after George Washington picked the site for the nation's capital, not much seemed to happen. For years the city limped along as the rawest kind of New Town, slow to grow, provincial, poorly kept, L'Enfant's splendid plan almost a joke. Government was all it had, and government wasn't that important. Congressmen rented rooms in boarding houses on Pennsylvania Avenue, fleeing home as soon as the sessions ended. Even by 1850 the city numbered only 60,000 residents, and people still talked of moving the capital to some real place, like Philadelphia.

It was not until the present century that Washington

Washington, D.C., where a glimpse of the Capitol (right, background) is always just around the corner, teems with visitors every spring.

really matured. In 1970 the population of the metropolitan area hit 2.9 million, up 40 percent in just one decade. Along with the people the city has acquired homes, small businesses (though still no industry), and innumerable professional offices and organizations. It has also, rather suddenly, acquired sophistication: elegant restaurants, music, and theater to add to its long-established fine art museums. But more emphatically than anything else, starting in the 1960s it changed its character to become a black city feeling its way into self-government.

The greater Washington area sprawls over much of southern Maryland and northern Virginia. Three-quarters of its people are white. But within the District of Columbia itself, almost three-quarters of the residents are Negroes, a total of some 538,000 blacks and 219,000 whites. Because blackness is so often accompanied by poverty, Washington has deep problems and deadly slum areas. This is true even in the much vaunted Southwest section, an area of the city which has been extensively cleared and redeveloped for a mixed population of rich and poor, white and black. But despite the relative newness of the buildings, life for the poor here remains just about as bleak as in the older slums.

Nevertheless, the black community in Washington is considerably better off than in most American cities. This is no new thing. As early as the 1830s half the Negroes in the city were freemen, and by the start of the Civil War 78 percent were free. Black neighborhoods today are not all slums. Many are soundly middle-class, and a few, such as Portal Estates and Colonial Village, are very expensive, reflecting the fact that of all the big cities Washington has the highest percentage of Negroes in professional, technical, and managerial jobs. A third of the costly condominiums in the Southwest redevelopment area belong to well-to-do blacks.

The economic escalator works here—modestly but steadily, and fueled to a large extent by the civil service

140

Counselors to presidents, such as Henry Kissinger (near right), senators, and congressmen frequently lunch at the Sans Souci, one of the capital's superb French restaurants.

system. The fact that more than half of all jobholders in Washington work for government gives the place a kind of implacable economic calm, the right climate for bringing a middle class to bloom.

Sally Nesbitt might be called a representative Washingtonian. She is black and works for the federal government as a clerk in HUD. Not only that, but she is a woman—there are twice as many black women in Washington as there are black men. Mrs. Nesbitt also possesses a document peculiarly symbolic of her middle-class status: she has her name on a mortgage for a house she has occupied in the Northeast section of Washington for seventeen years. The mortgage is largely paid off. Before her husband died last year he worked at two jobs, in a laundry during the week and driving a taxi on weekends and several nights a week. With her small but steady salary added, they were able to send their son and daughter to Howard University. Both offspring are now teachers, he in Maryland and she in New Jersey. Mrs. Nesbitt has photostats of their college degrees framed on the wall of her bedroom. These slips of paper, along with that other paper in the safe deposit box, the diminished mortgage, make her small frame house on Adams Street considerably more important to her as a monument than any of the heavy neoclassical limestone government buildings so numerous in the District of Columbia.

Just past the city line, out where Massachusetts and Connecticut and Wisconsin Avenues cross into Maryland, dwells a rather special group of people, close enough to the District line to think of themselves as Washingtonians although they do not have to send their children to District schools. Their elevated incomes have turned Montgomery County into one of the richest and best educated in the country; and their parties make all in attendance feel that they too must be of importance, just like the other men and women there (whether or not they know exactly what law firm he's with or whether she's in A.I.D. or the State Department proper).

Among the impressive party givers on that Maryland-D.C. straddle line are Tom and Joan Braden who live in Chevy Chase. He's a newspaper columnist; she's an economist and Washington director of a Rockefeller-backed foundation. According to a story in *New York* magazine which quite accurately caught the who's-watching-whom feel of elite Washington society,

> . . . the powerful of the nation will assemble for them at the drop of a stiff white invitation. . . . "Women are always jealous of Joan Braden in this town," says Michael Ballentine, a public-relations man. "She has an eye for power. She works at collecting the big fish, and she doesn't mess around with small-timers, but she doesn't give a damn about the gossip. She loves being what she is." . . . Of course, elegance is always the predominant note. There are candles and vigil lights throughout the sitting rooms, fresh flowers, dandelions, daisies, or roses on every table. A fire is blazing in every hearth. The lights are low, and Joan, even if she's been at the office until seven, has bathed and changed into a long skirt. Tom always wears a coat and tie to dinner. There are mixed drinks and hors d'oeuvre. The round table in the dining room is covered with scalloped Porthault, there are fresh linen napkins, and again candlelight. Yet in the midst of it all are enormous dogs, crossbreeds for the most part, who saunter in and recline on your feet, and a variety of freckled Braden offspring who pop in to listen or to cuddle up on the couch with Joan and munch potato chips. (If Kissinger comes, the girls usually put on long dresses.)

The white population of the District of Columbia moved to the suburbs in large numbers after 1954, when it became apparent that the District was going black—

141

and in doing so, they hastened the process considerably. But interestingly, there are recent signs that the shift to near and far suburbs is now becoming as much a black as a white movement. The Washington Center for Metropolitan Studies reports that between 1960 and 1970 the suburban Negro population almost doubled, from 83,746 to 166,033. Not all of Washington's suburbs are receiving the outward bound blacks, however. Very few Negro families end up in Virginia; seven-eighths of them go to Maryland, principally Prince George's County. Virginia is still too southern.

What has been driving the middle class of all colors away, of course, is the well-known deterioration of the public school system, but other social indices are hardly more encouraging. Infant mortality is the highest in the nation. Illegitimate births run about 40 percent. Crime remains a problem, despite an improved police force. Many residents refuse to walk or even drive in some parts of D.C. after dark, and one prominent Washingtonian has been known to carry a "noise device," similar in shape to a gun, when answering his door at night.

Yet as the black middle class joins others in retreating from the perils of Washington, there is a persistent migration of whites back into the District—not large, but noticeable. The spirit of Georgetown has spread, and broken-down old row-house neighborhoods are being restored, often at immense expense. Capitol Hill is an area of old houses just behind the Capitol where real estate prices have tripled in the last few years as congressmen and other well-to-do people have moved in and made homes for themselves. Northeast of Dupont Circle a group of young, middle-income antisuburbanites have settled in a bunch of elderly town houses, and have even persuaded the government to downzone the area in order to prevent apartment construction there.

Meanwhile, a little farther out, the neighborhood of Cleveland Park has remained almost unchanged since its development near the end of the last century, when people designed their houses big and built them sturdy. The section was named for President Grover Cleveland, who owned a summer home there, and to walk down a street like Highland Place is to enter another era. Rambling old frame houses—three-storied, comfortable, portly, and full of life—stand cheek by jowl along the curved irregular roadway. Bay windows abound. So do porches—enormous ones that may run all the way around the house, sometimes two tiers of them. It is like passing a fleet of raffish old ocean liners, anxious to put out to sea again. Yet this neighborhood may be in better shape now than it has ever been. People who live in these houses today are proud of them: willing to vacuum and dust the eight bedrooms, to fuel the giant furnaces,

Historic Georgetown, a district of elegant town houses and affluent living, favorite haunt of tourists and young people, is the oldest and most picturesque of Washington's neighborhoods.

142

to repaint those endless stretches of porch every three years.

Washingtonians not only like old neighborhoods, they are relatively realistic about them, knowing you can't have your cake and eat it too. They don't replace half of Georgetown with modern apartments and expect it to remain Georgetown, as New Yorkers have tried to do with Greenwich Village. The District of Columbia has other things going for it besides the enthusiasm of residents. Legal height restrictions are one. Developers know that demolition isn't profitable unless you can replace the old building with one that is substantially larger, and this is not possible in a city where you can only go up twelve stories. So the place for a high-rise is across the line in Maryland or Virginia—which is where the big real estate operators increasingly go.

Pierre L'Enfant's plan helps too. In Washington, as in New York, it is on the avenues that most of the new buildings go up. But in New York and most other cities laid out on the grid, the avenues run parallel, just one block apart, so the streets between them feel the impact of what happens on the avenues. Washington isn't that way at all. Starting at the Capitol, the avenues move outward like slice marks in a pie and break the monotony of the street grid by angling across it oddly and grandly. Where avenue meets street you get, at intervals, the circles, focal points which by their very nature seem to generate all kinds of small parks and monuments (not to mention traffic tie-ups and lost tourists—L'Enfant did not anticipate everything).

Built low, spread out, tousled with trees, Washington is also a city of skies, a good place to study cloud formations as they roll in across the river or to watch the genesis of a thunderstorm. Washington, of course, experiences lots of the latter, and is notorious for its weather. Winters there are raw and chilly. Spring is rhapsodic, but most years lasts only a few weeks before the summer sets in. And then the heat is awful—from June through September oppressive, sodden, to many visitors almost immobilizing; the Potomac might as well be the Nile.

Long-time residents survive through a combination of stoicism and mechanical cooling. Yet screened porches remain a surprisingly big thing in this city, and on hot summer nights Sally Nesbitt finds herself out on her stoop, drinking iced tea and taking in the lambent night air. Throughout Washington the flowers, the bushes, the trees, even the grass seem to brood upon the darkness, flavoring it with a hundred mixed fragrances.

The eastern city scene, with its skyscrapers and sprawl, is truly an American social invention, a people-shaping conception, as much as the frontier was in its day. Not everyone here likes it, in whole or in part. It is crowded, tense, and dirty. It throbs day and night with the power of heating and lighting dynamos, it reverberates with the roar of engines underground and overhead, it is punctuated by sirens and klaxons. Yet Philadelphia, New York, Washington, and all the other old metropolises of the East Coast still project something grand, still give urbanites some glimmering sense that they, all together, are a part of man's enormous endeavor.

Wearing as they are, worrisome as they are, how could we do without our cities? Try getting up at dawn some Sunday morning, go out and walk around—in New York, in Boston, in Washington, Philadelphia, or Baltimore—and the full wonder of it all will strike you. Each is an enormous and solemn artifact, a monument to human vitality. People made this thing. And bit by bit they are still making it, and tomorrow and next month and next century they will continue to make it. Meanwhile they go about their daily lives, innocent of what they have wrought.

—WALTER MC QUADE AND ANN AIKMAN

143

New York Streets: sights and sounds

The most exciting city in the world is home to 8 million Americans of every race, creed, and color. To outsiders who know nothing of its varied and cohesive neighborhoods, it is a faceless and frenetic urban nightmare. To experts addicted to computer forecasts, the city is on its deathbed—too big, too complex, too troubled to survive. To the New Yorkers at left, however, the apostles of doom deserve nothing more than a resounding Bronx cheer. If the city is dying, what's going on there today must be the liveliest wake in history.

Shopping in the streets of New York is an adventure, whether in a West Side flea market (above) or on the lower East Side (below).

Lunchtime in Manhattan brings thousands into the streets. The young executives in the financial district (below) line the sidewalks on sunny days to do a bit of girl watching. Would-be orators use microphones instead of soap boxes (facing page), but most of the crowd prefers to watch the inevitable street-repair crew at work. Uptown on Park Avenue (at right) young couples do their thing, and nobody gets hassled when retaining walls are used as benches. At Rockefeller Center (far right, below), the management welcomes the public with seat-high walls, masses of flowers, and special events free to all. Afraid of attracting "undesirables," the owners of some skyscrapers built forbidding plazas with no place to sit. But more enlightened managements are rejuvenating such areas, having discovered that the problem of undesirables vanishes when plazas are made attractive to all kinds of people.

A good time in New York doesn't have to cost money. There are fashion and puppet shows, pool exhibitions, street theater groups, and a hundred other programs that bring life and color to summer streets. Community groups in once-deteriorating neighborhoods of Brooklyn's Bedford-Stuyvesant have opened a cultural center, and local talent gets together for day-long events like "Soul Sunday," which includes a show put on by the Total Fashion Theater (at left, below). In Harlem, the more sedate residents get together for a game of checkers while younger and more adventurous spirits gather round an outdoor pool table. The "Pool in the Streets" program (below) gives the local pool sharks a chance to pit their skills against traveling experts who show off a dazzling assortment of trick shots. In midtown Manhattan, itinerant entertainers like the cycling circus pro from Paris (facing page) always attract a good crowd. They say the police are more tolerant and the people are more generous in New York than elsewhere.

Puerto Rican theater group (above) entertains a lunchtime crowd
at City Hall Park with an extravagant island folk tale.

Wall art enhances many of the dreariest areas of New York, bringing a touch of gaiety and color to drab, nondescript buildings and streets. Some of it, like the dramatic creation at right, is painted by professionals, endorsed by the city, and financially supported by philanthropists and corporations. Down at street level, however, wall art is the work of amateurs who express themselves by decorating the impersonal walls that enclose their world. The backdrop for the youngsters skipping rope below is a school. What may have started out as graffiti eventually developed into a bright and lively abstract design that introduces a note of cheer to an otherwise depressing block. The painting in Chinatown at left was done by artists who didn't know much about scale but had a natural feeling for perspective. The touching painting (bottom right) brightens a tenement which might have inspired expressions of rage and frustration instead of a graceful flower, "love," and "amor."

151

Block parties, street fairs, plant sales, carnivals, cleanup parties, and countless other events are sponsored by New York's 4,500 block associations to help neighbors get to know each other and to raise money for improvements. These groups, spontaneously organized in slums as well as more affluent areas, are helping to turn large sections of a huge, impersonal city into a collection of friendly neighborhoods. The crime rate has plummeted on such blocks because people watch out for each other. Some associations equip residents with police whistles—when one is sounded, everybody runs to the window and blows like mad, alerting the police and scaring would-be muggers half to death. The associations also give members more clout at City Hall. Money raised at block parties like the community festival in Brooklyn (at right) or the Grove Street Country Fair (below) may be used to plant shade trees and flowers, light back yards, or install a bench or two in a cleaned-up vacant lot.

The West 74th Street Block Association's annual fair (above) features a sale of clothing donated by residents, homemade delicacies, and a puppet show. The mod gentleman (below) is involved in a similar affair in the Bronx.

Street musicians come out in force at winter's end, reminding older New Yorkers of the hurdy-gurdies and costumed monkeys that played pied piper to their youth. A visitor strolling along Fifth Avenue some time ago found a trio playing Bach at 49th Street, a Hari Krishna group at 53rd, two girls singing folk songs at 54th, a flutist at 59th, and a steel drummer at 60th. The folk singer playing his guitar at Washington Square Park at right always draws a good crowd. The young violinist below is a talented music student at the prestigious Juilliard School of Music who helps pay his expenses by giving violin recitals on Manhattan street corners. A discreet sign propped against his open violin case reads: "Music student, please help." Many people do—including some who do not look like lovers of classical music. The clarinetist at left, also a music student, keeps a tin can handy for contributions. The police, who value their image, try to ignore such musicians because they are so popular with passers-by.

The Hari Krishna group on Fifth Avenue (above) chants and beats
drums for an appreciative crowd at Rockefeller Center.

Turning vacant lots into gardens on the upper East Side of Manhattan was the brainstorm of a young designer living in the area. He enlisted two friends, and the trio soon won the enthusiastic support of neighbors and block associations. These, in turn, helped to obtain the cooperation of city agencies and then pitched in to clear the rat-infested lots of trash and rubble. The Vincent Astor Foundation donated $15,000 worth of topsoil—2,000 cubic yards of it—and the city sent four truckloads of sludge which was used as fertilizer. But disaster struck soon after the first gardens had been planted, when the amateur gardeners were evicted to make way for a housing development. New Yorkers are a determined breed, however, and this particular group soon found and cleared another site, then conned city agencies and a friendly contractor into helping them move the topsoil and everything else three blocks north. A simple playground, using telephone-wire reels and other inexpensive materials, is being put together (at right in the picture below), and anyone who wants a garden is assigned his own 10-by-20-foot plot. The determined young woman wielding a pick (facing page) wound up with blisters and aching muscles, but like everyone else she finds gardening a welcome respite from the confinement of an office. The lady at left specializes in Chinese vegetables, which she weeds and waters with loving care. Children may have their own gardens—one little tyke was amazed and delighted when his sunflowers grew to twice his height. Some people plant flowers while others are partial to vegetables, but everyone enjoys working the earth and making new friends they would never have met otherwise.

Life styles in stable neighborhoods—and there are many such areas—
do not differ markedly from life styles anywhere. Single-family houses—2.3 million
of them—outnumber the city's 2 million apartments. In Brooklyn (at right) and
elsewhere, working-class families pass the time of day by their front stoops. The well-
dressed barbecue expert (below) differs from his suburban counterparts only because
there's no grass underfoot. On the sidewalks of New York there is always somebody to
talk to—it's a dynamic place where all kinds of people come together, face-to-face.
Millions are spent in other cities to coax people out of bland and homogenized suburban
shopping centers and back into downtown areas. But in New York the people are
already there. When they meet on street corners, they delight in telling each other
how bad things are in the city these days. But to an eavesdropping outlander,
it almost sounds as though they're bragging! They're New Yorkers—these brash,
energetic, sophisticated people. They like it here; they're comfortable here.

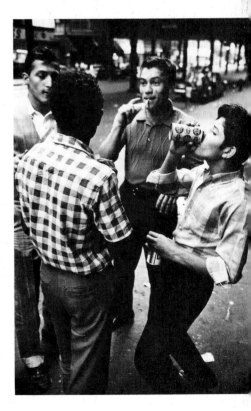

New York children grow up in
neighborhoods that contain a cosmopolitan mixture
of cultures, races, languages, and ethnic groups.
To the visiting outlander, they may appear to be
deprived because they live in a vast, crowded, complex
city. But they also live in one of the most culturally
vibrant environments in the world. There are great
museums, superb parks and zoos, and an endless
variety of free programs designed to enrich the lives of
city children. In summer, play streets are closed off
to traffic; playgrounds and neighborhood mini-parks
are staffed and ready. The city does not inhibit
young imaginations—it is more likely to stimulate
them. The children below live momentarily in
another world—where a broomstick becomes a
flashing rapier; a hat turns into a plumed helmet.
And when a young New Yorker wants to get off
somewhere by himself, he can always scale his own
private mountain. It's a good place for getting a fresh
perspective on the known world far below, a
good place for dreaming of worlds still unknown.

Suburbia: in search of a better life

The cheery ladies enjoying themselves at left while their husbands work in the city may not be typical suburbanites, but they fit well into the Census Bureau's 1970 population profile. They are both more affluent and younger than city dwellers—53% of suburbanites have incomes above $25,000 and 60% have children under 18. Suburbanites are now the largest group in the population—37% of Americans live in the suburbs, 32% in the cities, and only about 31% are left in rural areas. By 1985, only a quarter of the population will be rural, another quarter will be city dwellers, and half the people will be suburbanites.

Only 5% of suburbanites and 19% of city dwellers go to work by train, bus, or subway, while 84% and 69% respectively travel by car.

163

Life in the suburbs of Philadelphia gives Tony Regensburg, the avid golfer at right, a chance to practice his iron in the front yard. The family has a nine-room house, a pool, and three cars. Tony's wife and son both attend nearby colleges; his daughter is away at Stanford University. Suburbanites have had more years of education on the average than city dwellers, and many move to the suburbs in search of better, safer schools.

Milton Abowitz plays football with one of his two children in front of his home (above) in Wyncote, Pa. He and his wife both work full time —he as a tax lawyer, she as a junior executive with Sun Oil. On weekends they find time to invite friends over (below) for an informal meal.

Natalie Bogash (above) lives with her husband in a Merion, Pa., suburban high-rise. One corner of her sunny kitchen serves as a studio where she paints abstract oils.

164

Sailboats skim the waters of man-made, 30-acre Lake Anne—rimmed by town houses and Reston's first village center.

The new town concept —hailed in the booming 1960s as the answer to suburban sprawl—has run aground on the shoals of inflation and skyrocketing interest rates in the 1970s. Forward-looking developers expected start-up costs to be enormous and knew the eventual payoff would be years in the future. But they now find that new units cannot be sold fast enough to keep creditors at bay. Even a comparatively successful new town like Reston, Va. (below) —which has a population of 26,000 and has attracted 200 business firms that employ 4,600 people—has its problems. But from the fortunate few who live—and often work—in the best of these new towns there are few complaints.

Apartments, town houses, and private homes (above) house 36,000 at Columbia, Md., which has four village centers and a stunning central Mall (at right).

The young family strolling through Reston (above) is within walking distance of playgrounds, swimming pools, golf courses, and many other recreational amenities.

Washington, D.C.: the people's city

Teen-agers—thousands of busloads of them—pour into Washington during their spring vacation. It has long been a tradition for senior classes from all over the country to visit this storied city just before they graduate. They raise money all year for the trip, stay in local motels with adults who would once have been described as "chaperones," and everyone has a memorable time. They tour Washington's home at Mt. Vernon (facing page), and—like the 4-H group above—get special tours of the White House. They are bursting with energy, these young Americans, as they race down the steps of the Lincoln Memorial (below)—second only to the Capitol as a mecca for tourists. Years later, they will smile when they look at the inevitable group portrait—often taken, like the one at right, with the gleaming white dome of the Capitol as a backdrop.

A cathedral of democracy, the great hall of
the National Archives (at left) houses the original
Declaration of Independence, Constitution, and Bill of
Rights. A hush falls over even the most ebullient
visitor as he enters this serene place and reads the
stunning words—faded but no less meaningful after
200 years: "We hold these truths to be self-evident. . . ."
The Americans who now celebrate their Bicentennial
differ in many ways from those who first enunciated the
great concepts contained in these documents. But they
remain deeply committed to these principles—
sometimes losing faith in men and institutions charged
with implementing them, but never in the visionary
ideal of self-government that still inspires and animates
the nation and much of the world.

Every tourist visits the Capitol—"the most important
part of America," as one Kansan put it. Very few
could be present when Gerald Ford was sworn in as
Vice President (above), but millions crowd each year
into the Rotunda under the great dome (below).

172

There's something for everybody in Washington, a city of less than 1 million residents overwhelmingly outnumbered by the annual influx of almost 20 million tourists. A few of the 1.5 million foreign visitors attend official functions at the State Department (left), where they have a superb view of the city's monuments. The others, along with visitors from all 50 states, may enjoy the rich cultural life of a renascent capital at the Kennedy Center's Eisenhower Theater, Opera House (above), and Concert Hall, or at any number of other establishments devoted to the visual and performing arts. But for the visitor whose budget is limited, there is more to see and do—for nothing—in Washington than anyplace else in the world. What is most worth seeing belongs to the people, and the government sponsors an endless variety of free exhibits and activities designed to interest people of all types and ages.

The Smithsonian's complex of 11 galleries and museums offers lively exhibits on every conceivable subject. The antique popcorn wagon (far left) adorns the Mall in summer, and the Wright brothers' plane (near left) vies for attention with a model of the Apollo spacecraft that landed on the moon. The National Gallery (at right) houses over 30,000 works of art.

Outdoor programs are lively and informal, with residents and visitors sharing the summer fun. The annual Festival of American Folklife attracts hundreds of thousands to the Mall for a varied and fascinating program of regional, ethnic, children's, and other activities. The Smithsonian sets up a merry-go-round (at left), and there are plenty of trees to shade a family picnic (below). During the Bicentennial in 1976, the Festival—usually a ten-day happening around July 4th —will be a summer-long event. The Summer in the Parks program offers rock, soul, symphony, and folk concerts for office workers and visitors alike in some of the city's hundreds of mini-parks. There are free band concerts at the Watergate and free Shakespeare in the Sylvan Theater. There are puppet shows (facing page), arts and crafts, sports and games, pony rides, bicycle rodeos, and a great deal more. It's a family reunion for the nation—all summer and every summer.

The earnest little Indian above is all set to do an Indian dance. Her enthusiasm, if not her skill, matches the verve of the real Indians who demonstrate their culture at the Folklife Festival.

Spring comes to Washington in a blaze of color, bringing with it a flood of visitors. In Rock Creek Park, running for more than four miles through the city, the daffodils cascade down hillsides in March. Soon afterwards, the fragrance of blooming magnolias fills the air in downtown mini-parks—a sign that it's time to keep an eye on the cherry trees. For a week to ten days in early April, 3,000 of them blossom out around the Tidal Basin and the Jefferson Memorial (below). Hundreds of thousands of people stroll under their overhanging branches—sun-dappled during the day and highlighted by searchlights at night. Then great beds of tulips, like those marching toward the White House at right, bring color to every circle, square, and public lawn area. Finally, in May, the azalea and dogwood so favored by Washington residents burst into flower in front yards and public parks throughout the capital.

The annual Easter egg-rolling contest (below) attracts thousands of children 8 years of age and younger to the south lawn of the White House. They win prizes and cheer the antics of Disney characters. Some of them even get a glimpse of the President and members of his family. The custom—abandoned in World War I—was revived by a doting grandfather, President Dwight D. Eisenhower.

Heartland – Hub of the Nation   4

Midwest, Heartland, Mid-Country, Mid-America — whatever the term, it is stretched and strained to encompass an area three and a half times as big as France. It means both unity and diversity. It contains endless fields of flowing grain, silent wilderness, teeming cities. It is veined by three of the world's great rivers and bordered by four of the greatest lakes. Beneath its farms and forests lies a wealth of coal, salt, limestone, lead, and iron ore. It has been called the world's most favored region.

A glance at the map shows unity. This is the land between the mountains, the 1,500-mile-broad basin of the Mississippi waterways. An immensely productive region, it yet appears monotonous—no heights and depths, no barriers, nothing hidden, little contrast, few difficult or dangerous places. All its horizons seem alike. Its most insistent feeling is spaciousness.

A closer look reveals diversity; the hilly sheep pastures of Ohio, the vast cornfields of Illinois and Iowa, the lake and forest counties of Michigan and Minnesota, horizons of ripening grain beyond the Missouri River. Straight country roads lead to a county seat with its tree-shaded courthouse square, and four-lane highways circle the spreading cities. Mile-long trains of corn, wheat, and soybeans whistle past towboats pushing 1,000-foot barge loads on the rivers. Midland means tractors and gangplows striping the level land, government grain bins glinting in the sun, livestock milling in the loading pens. It also means the smoke and glitter of steel mills, mile-long motor factories, and cities of soaring beauty and sullen ugliness beside the lake shores and the river landings.

A hundred thousand Indians froze and starved in this region that now supports 50 million people. The Indians lived in it like deer and foxes, leaving the land unchanged. Theirs was a timeless country, with all its memories yet to come. Blackbirds swayed on the reeds of the Chicago ("wild onion") River. Wolves roamed the prairies where Abe Lincoln, with law books in his saddlebag, would ride the court circuit. Beard grass waved where John Deere would hammer a steel plowshare from an old saw blade and Joseph Glidden would twist the first filed barb around a strand of fence wire. Indian signs on a beech trunk were the only writing in a realm where Spencer would teach penmanship, McGuffey would compile his *Readers*, and Ray his *Arithmetic*. Black night hung over the Lake Erie river mouth where young Edison would watch the whale oil lights of wheat schooners, and passenger pigeons streamed over the Miami valley where the Wright brothers would experiment with flight. Indian women gathered ears of maize where agronomists would develop the miracle hybrids. Buffalo roamed the plain where covered wagons would toil toward Oregon and California.

History came with a rush to the wild land. When Queen Victoria was crowned in 1837, Chicago was incorporated as a city with 4,117 persons—a place of mud streets, bare board buildings, and an empty army fort. When Victoria died in 1901, Chicago, with 2 million people, was the hub of an area more productive than all of England. No other great region, anywhere, has been so transformed in a single life span.

Land, freehold land, was the lure to the mid-continent. The Northwest Territory Land Ordinance of 1785 projected its settlement and organization into new states of the Union. But the Indians were still there, and legal possession waited on cession by the tribes. Congress ordered a survey of the public domain into townships six miles square. This rectangular system, so much more orderly than the colonial surveys that used rivers and ridges for lines of demarcation, would eventually measure all the land from the Alleghenies to the Pacific Coast.

The migration to this midland country came in

waves: first, settlers from the eastern seaboard; then, in the mid-1800s, peoples from northern Europe. In the late 1800s southern and eastern Europeans thronged to the cities, and in the mid-twentieth century migrants from the states of the Deep South came north. Yet it was a mixed populace from the start. As early as 1802 the French naturalist François André Michaux journeyed down the Ohio filling his notebook with observations of the new country. Everywhere he stopped he heard the repeated greeting: "'What part of the world do you come from?'—as if those immense and fertile regions were to be the asylum common to all the inhabitants of the globe." The movement was one of the most momentous in history, with a drama too vast and too familiar for Americans to understand. New citizens came in many garbs and costumes, with different memories and traditions behind them. But the land was large enough, the tasks were big enough, and the Midwest made them all its people.

A high tide came in the 1850s—Germans, Irish, English, Scandinavians streaming into the upper Mississippi valley. The rich land spawned villages like mushrooms. "Little towns peep up on the prairie," wrote Sandburg, "where there used to be only gophers and jackrabbits. Cities swell from little towns."

Throughout the midland country there were no unemployed and virtually no servants. In frontier Michigan in the mid-1830s Alexis de Tocqueville was told by a Yankee settler:

> It is not here as in France. With you labor is
> cheap and land is dear. Here the cost of land is
> nothing, but the labor of man is beyond price.
> . . . In Michigan the acre never costs more than
> ten shillings. That's about the price of a day's
> work. A worker can therefore earn enough in one
> day to buy an acre of land. But the purchase
> made, the difficulties begin. . . . Later come ease,
> and then wealth.

Neighbors were important to frontier settlers, even the *idea* of neighbors who lived miles away and only met occasionally. In communities along the Wabash River, the Englishman Morris Birkbeck found "a genuine warmth of friendly feeling, a disposition to promote the happiness of each other." Continuing, he wrote: "Their importance to each other creates kind sentiments. They have fellow feelings in hope and fear, in difficulty and success, and they make tenfold more of each other than the crowded inhabitants of popular countries." It was not Farmer Rosicky but "Neighbor Rosicky" who in Willa Cather's story is best described by his "warm brown human hand, with some cleverness in it and a great deal of generosity."

The midland settlers helped each other with house-

Grain elevators are to the Heartland what steepled churches are to New England. This one in Kansas, owned by the largest cooperative in the world, holds 18 million bushels of grain.

180

raisings and barn-raisings. Neighbors gathered for husking bees and quilting bees. For many years local farmers formed threshing rings, the men going from one farm to another to harvest the ripened grain.

Now a tractor-driven combine does the threshing and mechanical corn-pickers do the husking, but the sense of community remains. When a farmer is ill or injured, his neighbors move in with a parade of machines and his fields are harvested by sundown. A man on a back road, with term nearing for his pregnant wife, need not worry about the January weather forecast. A voice on the telephone assures him: "Just let us know, any time of day or night. We'll plow you out." Once it was a horse-plow; now it is a tractor. Technology has changed farming but not these farmers.

Traditional neighborliness has also been at work in the cooperative movement that has spread throughout the midland states. Farmers' mutual elevators and farmers' mutual insurance companies have given the land worker an increasing share in the regional economy. After a century of development, local marketing cooperatives are merging into regional associations. Though the number of farms and farmers is declining, membership and volume of business in the co-ops continues to grow. In Minnesota, where huge tapered elevators dominate the towns, the Farmers' Union Grain Terminal Association has been called the nation's largest cooperative marketing firm. In Kansas the Cooperative Grain Dealers' Association gives thousands of individual farmers collective support and bargaining power. So far in the 1970s more than 80 percent of Wisconsin's farmers have bought supplies, equipment, and services through cooperatives.

The co-op movement has been strongest in areas of dairy farming. Many farmers have gained an ownership interest in cooperative creameries, taking their milk to factories where they share in its processing and marketing. Dairy co-ops have spread throughout Michigan, Wisconsin, Minnesota, and Iowa.

Cooperative associations have also reached into other areas: telephone systems, farm supplies, and credit unions, even electric power plants. Since World War II, communities in the prairie and plains states have joined efforts to create nonprofit, consumer-owned electric systems. In South Dakota more than thirty cooperative associations serve nine-tenths of the electrified farms in the state. Where once a lone windmill broke the skyline, now high voltage towers march over the horizon. They go where people are few and far between; in some places five or six miles of line are strung to reach one consumer.

A line drawn westward through Saginaw Bay on Lake Huron passes through Green Bay on Lake Michigan and crosses the Mississippi close to Minneapolis and St. Paul. At that line the Heartland's north country begins.

Hibbing, Minn., has a statue of the legendary logger, Paul Bunyan, and Babe his Mighty Blue Ox. Paul was so strong that—at the age of three weeks—he strangled a full-grown grizzly with his bare hands and so big he used a pine tree to comb his curly beard.

Prevailing winds in the lower midlands blow from the southwest; here the weather comes from Canada.

From the sandy and rocky soil of these upper midlands sprang the great coniferous forest—spruce and tamarack in the lowlands and in higher ground stately stands of pine with dark trunks rising to a crown of green. A century ago reports of government surveyors described "one immense pine forest" 400 miles square. Into that empire came the timber cruiser and the lumberjack, the seesaw clang of the crosscut, and the snarl of the sawmill. After the Civil War, log rafts as big as a cornfield went down the Mississippi, and lake schooners took northern pine to the lumber yards of Detroit, Milwaukee, and Chicago. Millions of people needed houses, barns, and shops. Hundreds of towns needed churches, schools, depots, courthouses. Cities needed wharves, bridges, streets, and sidewalks. Here was timber to house, pave, and furnish a new country.

By 1910, however, the north woods were laid waste, and the lumber industry moved on to the Pacific Northwest. Scattered over the upper midlands are

Fog-shrouded freighter traverses Lake Superior at reduced speed. Such ships can carry enough grain to fill 200 freight cars.

River barges on the Ohio (above) carry huge loads at low cost.
At right, a freighter officer charts a course through the Great Lakes.

memorials of a hearty age—museums of logging tools and implements, collections of posters, photographs and drawings, annual lumberjack festivals in the old woods towns. On the shore of Bemidji Lake, Minnesota, carved figures of Paul Bunyan and his blue ox, Babe, rear up from the old rollway where sawlogs rumbled into the water. Now the logging camps have been replaced by resorts where people from Detroit and Chicago escape the summer heat.

Geologically the northern midwest is the oldest land in North America, so old its rocks contain no fossils; instead they held riches of copper and iron. Now the fabulous copper mines are marked by empty mill sheds with fireweed blazing around them, but iron ore trains still clank through the woods to Escanaba and Marquette. Coal from the Ohio valley, limestone from lower Michigan, iron ore from Lake Superior—the endowed midlands held not only the resources of a steel age but a chain of spacious waterways to bring them together. To the region's economy Great Lakes transportation brings vast enterprise and wealth.

For a thousand miles the midland states are bordered by blue water. Millions of inland people have a horizon of sea and sky. They watch a commerce greater than Panama's, the long ships passing through the connecting rivers and over up-and-down-bound lanes on the open lakes. The efficiency and safety of Great Lakes transportation is so well known abroad that the Lake Carriers' Association was asked to help establish new shipping lanes in the congested English Channel. Lessons learned on Lake Michigan and Lake Huron went into a system adopted in 1971 by the institutes of navigation of Great Britain, France, and Germany.

In spite of its hectic history the northland is still haunted by Ojibway legends of the gods of thunder and lightning who lived in caverns on the shore. Passing the Pictured Rocks of Lake Superior, French voyageurs crossed themselves and tossed twists of tobacco to the manitous. Now the Indians are mostly gone, but ghostly northern lights still stream across the midnight sky. Here the youthful Hiawatha lived with old Nokomis, learning the lore of the earth and the heavens. More than any other part of the mid-continent this area has color and character, a wild stern beauty and tradition.

Upper Michigan, for example, is as distant from Detroit as Detroit is from Washington, and even farther removed in feeling. This is the country of Hemingway's Two-Hearted River. As a young writer learning his craft, he reached for its loneliness and strove to find words for its forbidding beauty, its hard seasons, and its tough-fibered people who would not trade it for any country less severe.

The Minnesota arrowhead, on the north shore of Lake Superior, is equally far removed in spirit from St. Paul and Minneapolis. It is an elemental land, where people are closer to things than to ideas. Its remembered men are explorers, prospectors, surveyors. At Frank Hibbing's lumber camp in the old hills the Indians called Me-sa-be, men found iron ore while digging a well for drinking water. After years of hardship and frustration the seven stubborn Merritt brothers developed the iron formation in the 1890s. "Mesabi" means "Giant." In its first four years of production the Mesabi rivaled the older ranges. In ten years it outdid all the rest combined. Hibbing's camp became the city of Hibbing with its great Mahoning Mine yawning at the edge of town. Hibbing has broad streets, churches using a dozen languages, and some of the finest schools in the nation. With iron ore royalties all the range towns prospered, while producing fortunes for industrialists in Ohio and Pennsylvania. In eighty years the Mahoning Mine yielded 130 million tons of rich red iron ore.

In November, 1973, came the end of a legend on the Mesabi. The Mahoning Mine was finished. The last truckloads came out of the pit and the traditional "clean sweep" broom rode down to Duluth on the last

183

trainload of Mahoning ore. But Hibbing was not
finished. While the vast pit filled with silence, a roar
and rumble began just beyond the Mahoning's northern rim. In the tangled woods bulldozers were clearing
a 150-acre site for the Hibbing Taconite Company
plant. With full production in 1976 the plant will sur-
pass the fabulous Mahoning, producing an annual 5½
million tons of iron ore pellets for many decades to
come.

There is nothing severe about St. Paul-Minneapolis,
with its famous universities, orchestras, museums, art
galleries, the internationally known Tyrone Guthrie
Theatre, and 170 technical and electronic industries.
Yet people of the Twin Cities share with other Minnesotans a zest for outdoor life and a feeling for the land.
Their license plates read "Land of 10,000 Lakes"; the
actual number is closer to 30,000. There are thirty
sparkling lakes within the Twin Cities alone, and hundreds within an hour's drive. Most Minnesotans vacation close to home. They relish their rugged, bracing
winter; both Bemidji and International Falls claim to
be the "coldest spot in the nation." Throughout the
state there is a gusto for hockey, sledding, skating, snow-
mobiling, cross-country skiing, ice-boating.

For these people winter is a bond, a challenge they
meet together. In the early years of settlement winter
closed them in, heightening their sense of community.
Now roads are kept open and zero weather is no reason
to stay home. But the community sense remains—a
larger community now, extending from the neighborhood through the entire state. Said a young man who
worked his way through St. Thomas College in St. Paul,
became a Minneapolis alderman at twenty-six, and
three years later chairman of the metropolitan council:
"I would like to make politics my life. There is a purpose here."

The loggers came to the north country and went on.

The farmers came to stay. They were a rich mix of people: Yankees, Irish, Germans, Bohemians, Norwegians, Swedes, Danes, Poles, Slavs, Finns—alike in their willingness to pay with toil and privation for independence and possession of their own land. No ethnic strain has kept its culture apart from the others, but each has added something to the community. The Danes brought the cooperative movement in marketing and distribution. Finns brought the sauna; Swedes the smorgasbord. The Germans brought a love of choral singing; the Czechs brought Sokol, their national gymnastic society. Every year the Norwegians have a festival in Minneapolis; gathered around the statue of Ole Bull playing his violin, they sing *Ja, vi elsker dette landet*. On a December night in a Minnesota town, one can follow the rich aroma to a *lutfisk* supper in the Swedish church.

One worry is common to the mixed people in the farming counties: they are concerned about the prospects of their children. Five years ago high school seniors in southwestern Minnesota were asked to rate their father's occupation on a scale ranging from very satisfied to unsatisfactory. Twice as many farm youths as city youths marked "very satisfied." Just over Minnesota's stateline in Iowa, a farmer said, "I'm just fifty paces from my work. I love the land and it's a family way of life. When we go to town we don't even have to lock the door."

Yet on the modern mechanized farms continually fewer farmers produce continually greater harvests. Many of the boys enrolled in Future Farmers of America will not be able to find a future on the farm. Today increasing numbers of factory workers live in the countryside, and the 4-H Clubs are enrolling town as well as farm youths. Thus in many ways town and country cultures are intermingling.

Illinois was the first great grassland the frontiersmen found. It was unlike any part of England, and no English word would fit it. The French word *prairie* originally meant meadow, but it expanded to include spaciousness and wildness when used to designate the grasslands that began beyond the Wabash. And where

Ice fishing in zero weather requires patience and fortitude. The Wisconsin man peering hopefully into his hole and the huddled Illinois couple at right have their share of both qualities.

The annual speed skating races in Madison, Wis. (above), have special events for all ages and both sexes.

185

did the prairie end? In 1834 a New York journalist, Charles Fenno Hoffman, came suddenly to Door Prairie in northern Indiana. "It forms a door," he wrote, "opening upon an arm of the Grand Prairie, which extends if I mistake not to the base of the Rocky Mountains." He was not mistaken. Illinois was but the beginning of the wind-rippled prairie and the marching plain.

As a sailor is aware of the sea, prairie people have always been conscious of the land. Whether rural or urban their lives and fortunes are interwoven with the earth. The first State House of Nebraska, built in 1869, crouched under the wind on the Salt Creek flats of Lancaster County. It was built of local stone, as the settlers' huts were made of local sod. In 1923 a more prosperous and assured people built the monumental Nebraska capitol, but they did not forget the land. The 400-foot limestone shaft is crowned by a glazed dome that supports a 27-foot bronze Sower—a striding figure broadcasting (how far that earthy term has traveled) with a seed pouch and a circling arm. The lofty Sower comes into view over many miles of prairie.

One of the contradictions in mid-America is the isolationism of a region made up of many strains of Old World people. Isolationism—America First—Americans for America—has been voiced by many midwestern editors and politicians, while hundreds of communities continued to honor ethnic customs and traditions. Where it persists, the isolationism of mid-America is a half-conscious memory of people who left the Old World in protest. They were drawn as much by what America did not have—"No king there"—as by its promises. Even in the twentieth century these people have been reluctant to join in wars abroad. A Kansas farmer bringing his son home from an army cemetery in France said that when rain fell on the young man's grave it should be Kansas rain. In American Legion parades a familiar float shows red poppies on a field of green under the words "We Must Not Forget." These people care less about Old World rivalries than about their own hard-won aspirations. Another familiar float extols "Christian Homes, Honesty and Truth."

From these windy plains came politicians who rarely looked beyond the middle border. Out of Nebraska strode the silver-voiced William Jennings Bryan, shouting the faith of the populists, converting economic issue into sectional contest: gold was the greed of Wall Street; silver was the hope of the prairies. In spite of his Biblical fervor and west-wind charm, Bryan lost by the largest plurality then recorded.

Rooted in locality yet never provincial, William Allen White of Emporia, Kansas, became an internationally known editor and writer. Genial and neighborly, outspoken and incisive, both practical and idealistic, he was the harshest critic and the best supporter of the Republican party. His *Emporia Gazette* spoke for the small-town conscience in language heard and respected across the nation. In half a century of editorship he never forgot the words of a teacher at the state university: "It's vastly more important than many pious prayers and high-falutin' aspirations to get a street in a country town made wide enough so that two loads of hay going in opposite directions will still leave it possible for a woman to drive a horse between them without getting hay wisps on her buggy top." Knowing Emporia, many people observed, he knew a lot about America.

In the summer of 1959 a group of high school girls in Hutchinson, Kansas, corresponded with a self-styled beatnik group in Venice, California. Taking the offensive, the Californians told of their beach and boat parties, their convertibles and freeways, their uninhibited life style. After the Kansas girls had described their swimming pool, roller skating rink, movies, and Scout camp, the California girls still asked "What do you *do* in Kansas?" The answer had a certain finality. "We *live* here." In Kansas the young are not yet world-weary.

*Thomas Hart Benton's painting,
Frankie and Johnnie, celebrates a
Missouri legend. It is part of a
series of Benton murals that hangs
in the Missouri capitol (at left).
Frankie shot her lover when "he
done her wrong" with Nellie Bly.*

Though other Kansas towns had the amenities of Hutchinson, the girls added, their town was the best.

This is a familiar claim in the midland country. The village of Gordon, Nebraska, announces itself on the highway as "The Little Town With the Big Smile." Emporia claims an open door like its name, and the capital of Kansas declares that "Integrity, courtesy and initiative are words of real substance in Topeka." In 1972 the 625 citizens of Verdigre, Nebraska, built a new elementary school, a fifty-five-bed nursing home, a thirty-acre park, and a medical clinic. The next year it was named an All-America city.

Self-satisfaction in the area is tempered by a strain of realism and skepticism. Missouri people early adopted the mule as a token and took a possessive pride in that headstrong, perverse, unlovely creature. "I'm from Missouri," they repeat, "show me."

That earthy realism reached into Missouri's handsome capitol at Jefferson City when Thomas Hart Benton, a grandnephew of the old western war-horse, adorned the building with sardonic murals. With unanimous satisfaction the legislators in 1935 commissioned Benton to depict a history of Missouri on 45,000 square feet of wall space in the State House lounge. Unveiled in January, 1937, the mural made national headlines. What the legislators had expected was an epic procession of steamboats and covered wagons. What they got was a slave auction and a lynching, a baptism of Holy Rollers in a muddy stream, a team of mules and a mired wagon, a judge dozing on a courtroom bench above a stained spittoon. Bigger than life were Jesse James robbing a bank and holding up a train and Frankie and Johnnie in a barroom shoot-out.

Asked why he didn't include General Pershing, Benton replied: "Pershing is of less importance in the history of Missouri than a bucksaw." In his gravelly drawl Benton said he had aimed at realism and couldn't be encumbered with what ought to be. The most famous characters spawned by Missouri, he said, are the disreputable and half mythical ones—like the James brothers and Huck Finn.

Complaining that Benton had pictured a "houn' dog state," some citizens wanted the murals obliterated. But Benton had been paid $16,000, and the legislators

*The annual Fence Painting Contest in Hannibal, Mo.,
commemorates Tom Sawyer, who conned his friends into
trading tadpoles, marbles, and other treasures for a chance to
whitewash Aunt Polly's fence.*

187

decided their bad bargain should remain. When people looked at the walls more calmly, they saw grassroots reality and vigor. There were slumped figures in city slums and hearty church women preparing a church supper, men at work with beef carcasses and a serene view of the Nelson Art Gallery in Kansas City, a team of long-eared mules under a silo and giant elevator, a smoking threshing machine, billowing wheat fields, and a windy sky above spring plowing.

Today Benton's murals attract visitors from distant places. School children from all over Missouri are brought to see the paintings. They are told that Thomas

Hart Benton is only one of several artists who developed an American viewpoint and concentrated on the local scene: men like John Steuart Curry of Kansas and Grant Wood of Iowa shared with Benton a mid-American background and went not to art but to life for their models.

Isolationist or not, midwesterners have a well-de-

Dust fills the air at sunset as combines harvest a tinder-dry field. Custom cutters use headlights to work late into the night in such weather—each day increases the risk of prairie fires, but a heavy rain would reduce the yield and bog down the combines.

Custom cutters like those lunching in the shade at right follow the harvest from Texas to Canada. When bridge clearances are too low for combine-laden trucks (at left), they sometimes inch their way through by letting some air out of the tires.

served reputation for hospitality toward strangers. When an agricultural mission from the Soviet Union toured American farmlands, their warmest welcome came in Green County, Iowa. They saw miles of hybrid corn tasseled out in late summer and were shown the plows, planters, cultivators, and harvesters that work the endless fields. In the county seat of Jefferson they watched a 4-H Club demonstration—sunburned boys killing corn borers and aproned girls baking frosted rolls. They soon learned to raise an arm at the right line of the hearty song: "Iowa! Iowa! That's where the tall corn grows."

A few seasons later Premier Khrushchev came to see for himself. In Carroll County, Iowa, he visited a prize farm at Coon Rapids. After inspecting white-faced feeder cattle and wading through a mound of silage, he was given samples of new strains of hybrid corn. Following his visit, a women's political study and discussion group in Des Moines was besieged by women who wanted to learn about public affairs and foreign relations.

Some 200 miles apart, running due west like parallels of latitude, the national highways cross the plains—Interstate 40 in Kansas, 80 in Nebraska, 90 in South Dakota, 104 in North Dakota. Erased by time are the old historic roads: the Santa Fe Trail to Colorado and the Southwest, the Morman Trail to Utah, and the Overland Trail to Oregon and California. When the first wagon trains crept westward, the Great Plains were buffalo and Indian country. After the Civil War, settlers pushed into the treeless land that explorers had called Great American Desert. Half a century later it was the nation's breadbasket.

The buffalo range has been plowed, planted, and brought to bounteous harvest. Yet there remains the elemental land, scratched by man and his machines, dotted here and there with his farm buildings, but roll-ing on, limitless, under the arching sky. From miles away you see a windmill, that tall-stemmed flower of the prairie with its head always seeking the wind. Even farther away you can see the water tower and grain elevator, signs of a town in this flat land. From the great Bismarck plain rises the North Dakota capitol, the only skyscraper within 500 miles. Before there is any sign of habitation that twenty-story tower breaks the skyline, as though people in this horizontal land wanted to accentuate their presence.

Nowhere are people more conscious of the weather. The fierce winds of winter, the fitful capricious spring, the hot dry summer, and the grateful golden autumn—they live close to them all. Seasons determine the harvest: winter wheat in Kansas and Nebraska, spring wheat in the Dakotas. The hard winter wheat provides both bread and beefsteak; cattle feed on its green winter growth and are herded out of the fields in early spring so kernels can develop for the flour mills. Dry seasons are still a problem, but deep cultivation brings up moist earth to hold the topsoil down. New equipment and new farming methods have evolved since the Dust Bowl years.

Sixty years ago thousands of field hands moved north with the harvest, men dropping off freight trains at the huge elevators. They worked one farm after another, sleeping in the barn or on the haystacks. Now the fields are bigger, the new seed strains produce more harvest, and the many migrant field workers have been replaced by a few men with machines.

In June on the north-south roads, lines of trucks drone northward, flatbed trucks carrying big red combines that are on their way to the spring wheat country of the Dakotas. "Custom cutters" make contracts ahead of time with farmers whose wheat runs to the horizon. Over the fields move four, five, or six combines, one behind another, each mowing a twenty-foot swath, spitting yellow straw and pouring a stream of grain into the

trucks (now framed with sideboards) that will haul it to elevators or storage bins. Short-wave radios coordinate the operation. All summer the cutters march on, northward and westward, till the wheat gives way to range land where cattlemen hope for a mild winter and enough spring moisture to keep the bunch grass green.

The migrant harvesters of the past were men only, but custom cutting is a family business. A typical family —call them Durum for the high-protein, disease-resistant wheat developed by years of crossbreeding in the Experiment Stations—has a home in Kansas but lives in a house trailer half the year. Roy Durum has been cutting since he and Debra married; their wedding trip was a cutting season from Oklahoma to Canada. Now young Roy, between terms at the A and M college, drives a combine. His twin sister, Barby, always in shirt and levis, helps with cooking for the crew—three big meals a day for a dozen men. She hauls the food out to the fields in a station wagon, and the men eat in a combine's shade. After the noon meal Barb maneuvers a ten-geared truck, filling in for her father who has gone ahead to schedule next week's work.

Most of the Durum crew are farm boys in their early twenties. In 1971 one was a Vietnam veteran. After months in an army hospital, he was glad to be driving a grain truck, circling the huge field beside a noisy combine. "I like it here," he said. "It's never too busy for me." A poor crop in a dry year is a "lazy harvest"; the Durums prefer the bumper crops that keep them in the field, headlights blazing, long after sundown. Says Debra Durum of her husband: "He likes the pressure. Says it gives him energy." That goes for all of them.

In past years the Missouri was a seasonal river, surging into a mile-wide flood when snow melted in the Rockies and baring its humped sandbars in midsummer. Nobody knows who first called it the "wide Missouri," but many saw it as a divide. A man with a piece of land on the east was a farmer; on the west a rancher. A cow on one side is milked; on the other punched. Said a veteran railroad conductor: "A great difference between the east and the west is in regard to talking with strangers. The Missouri River is the dividing line. The minute passengers get east of Omaha and Council Bluffs they freeze each other."

The Missouri is wider than ever now, though less of a cultural boundary. Below Sioux City, Iowa, it is a reliable river of commerce, carrying long barge tows of corn, wheat, soybeans, phosphate, salt, molasses. Above Sioux City, where the channel swings westward, a series of dams have created Lewis and Clark Lake, the Fort Randall Reservoir, the 200-mile Oahe Reservoir—all in South Dakota; and the huge, twisting, many-armed Lake Sakakawea in North Dakota. These reservoirs provide electric power, irrigation, and flood control.

Some Dakota farmers have never seen the Missouri River, but all are affected by it. Since 1945 the Missouri Basin Project has given them a more stable and balanced economy, guarded against flood, and brought low-cost electric power to farms, towns, and industries. It has benefited fish and wildlife and provided recreation in a one-time desert. The "great lakes" of the Dakotas attract 4 million vacationers every year.

Main Street in Sauk Centre, Minn. (at right), doesn't change much over the years, but downtown Minneapolis has a handsome new plaza (at left) with three floors of shops and business offices above.

When the sociologists Robert and Helen Lynd sought a representative American community for intensive study, they refused to select a New England town, a southern town, or a town in the Rocky Mountains. It had to be, they felt, in "that common denominator of America, the Middle West," near the national center of population that was then in west central Indiana. They chose the city of Muncie, which they called "Middletown."

In 1885, Muncie, Indiana, was an agricultural market town of 6,000 people. Little change came with the first stirrings of industry: a bagging plant using local flax, a tile-yard using local clay, a roller skate company (wooden rollers, cowhide straps) in an old barn, a feather duster shop, a planing mill, and two flour mills grinding local wheat. There were also a barrel shop and a wooden pump works. Such a mix of small enterprise was common in county seat towns.

Omaha (below) is a major insurance center and global headquarters for the Strategic Air Command. Kansas City's $250 million Crown Center business and apartment complex (at right) covers 25 square blocks.

Then, just north of Muncie, a work crew boring for coal struck gas. As the flame burned night and day, builders, bankers, businessmen, and reporters poured into town. The population doubled in three years. Industries were offered free fuel and free building sites. With glassworks, foundries, a pulp mill, and shoe factories, sleepy "Middletown" became a restless manufacturing city. Yet at the turn of the century crop reports still appeared on page one of the paper, and hardware stores sold harness and hayrakes along with lathes, drills, and piping.

This commingling of agricultural and industrial production was repeated in scores of towns like Muncie and multiplied in cities like Cleveland, Indianapolis, Detroit, Minneapolis, St. Louis, and Omaha. The Ohio River, having brought home-seekers to the empty country, now became a corridor of commerce. Along the Great Lakes stretched another band of industry: steel at Cleveland, Youngstown, Gary, South Chicago; rubber factories at Akron; glass at Toledo; automobiles at Detroit and South Bend. Railroads on the "water level route" brought the materials of heavy industry and hauled away tanks, pipes, girders, rails, machine tools,

191

generators. Scores of small cities like Muncie became known for their special products: tractors, trucks, electrical equipment, corn and soybean products, plumbing fixtures, and kitchen appliances. From midwestern factories came the machines that plow, plant, and harvest midwestern farms.

In the big industrial cities people formed ethnic neighborhoods—Italian, Greek, Polish, Slovenian, Croatian, Puerto Rican, Black American. But the "Middletown" worker is likely to be Hoosier born and bred. From an Indiana farm he brought to town the independence and individualism of the country. He is slow to join in political and trade union movements. Though a factory worker, he has kept contact with the land. Generally he lives in a single-family house, tree-shaded, with a back garden. He has a recent-year automobile and is thinking of getting a used car for his wife, who may take a factory job herself. He wants his children to go through high school and perhaps to college; he expects them to have a better life than his—perhaps away from Muncie, though he likes it here. In spite of what newscasters tell him about crime, corruption, pollution, and congestion, he looks forward. He knows the present is better than the past, and he refuses to see a dead end now.

Big cities, having the most people, have always had the most problems. "Hell is a city much like London," Shelley wrote 150 years ago, "a populous and smoky city." Though the problems seem endless, the midland cities are better governed, more aware of people's needs and hopes, and more pleasant to live in than ever before.

Forty years ago the writer Christopher Morley wrote a fond letter to Chicago, including even "the wide barren plazas of Grant Park . . . the dense and gloomy regions of the Loop." Since then Chicago has pushed the water back to make park space; now the Grant Park plazas are shaded and gardened, lively with playgrounds

and bubbling with fountains. The gloomy regions of the Loop have been replaced by open areas in which garden pools reflect fifty-story facades. The Civic Center has green trees, sparkling water, and enough space to put its four-story Picasso steel sculpture in perspective. Walking south from the Civic Center one passes, within four blocks, the huge Calder metal design and Chagall's freestanding mosaic, "The Seasons," each in its own airy plaza. On the western edge of the Loop soars the sleek Sears Tower, at 1,450 feet, the tallest building in the world.

Chicago also has one of the world's most beautiful and expansive lakefronts: the whole city is open on one side, with parks and gardens, museums and galleries, office and apartment buildings facing the sea and sky.

Overwhelming as it is, Chicago prompts a kind of possessiveness in its people. Frank Lloyd Wright, age eighteen, arrived from Wisconsin on a drizzly spring evening in 1887. From the railroad station he moved with the crowd to the Wells Street Bridge, where masts

Chicago, the nation's second largest city, has lined its beautiful lakefront with elegant apartment buildings (below) and carefully manicures the planting along North Michigan Avenue (right). A much-acclaimed statue by Picasso (at left) dominates its Civic Center.

and funnels loomed through the rain. Suddenly a bell clanged and the crowd rushed past, leaving him on the bridge as it swung out over the channel to let a fuming tugboat towing a huge iron freighter pass through. Wright stood there, dazed and wondering, till the bridge swung back again. "Later," he wrote, "I never crossed the river without being charmed by somber beauty." Carl Sandburg, age eighteen, arrived from Galesburg, Illinois, on a spring morning in 1896 with $3.50 knotted in his pocket. Walking was free, and the teeming streets were a kaleidoscope. He walked miles past foundries and factories, markets and tenements, and along the shore where strident streets ended in the gleam of lake and sky. Years later, when Chicago was "my city" and he had traveled far enough to make comparisons, he wrote: "Show me another city with lifted head singing so proud to be alive and coarse and strong and cunning."

Chicago is like that—"my town"—to all kinds of people. Within its immensity are scores of communities; "Chicagoland" the *Tribune* calls it. A community sense pervades the Near North Side, as it does the

Carl Sandburg's "City of the Big
Shoulders" vibrates with energy.
The metropolis produces more steel
and machinery than any other
area in the world. Along its lakefront are crowded beaches (below),
the world's largest water filtration
system, a great aquarium, and an
outstanding planetarium.

From the scalloped balconies of Marina City (background, at right), apartment dwellers get a bird's-eye view of downtown Chicago or can see all the way to Indiana. Boating enthusiasts reach Lake Michigan directly from the basement marina fronting on the Chicago River.

scattered ethnic neighborhoods and the spacious, tree-shaded northern and western suburbs. Oak Park with 61,000 people calls itself the "biggest village in the world." Evanston, grown up around Northwestern University, enjoys a touch of aloofness, seasoned with humor. Its own jest is that a stone tossed in the city center would probably hit an intellectual, which would probably be a good idea.

The newly emerged communities of Old Town and New Town border Lincoln Park. Old Town is a Bohemian quarter, a place of verve and variety, mostly young people and much innovation. Here Sachio Yamashita has covered a grubby three-story building with a Mt. Fuji mural. On Wells Street artists, writers, and actors jostle with visitors on their way to candlelit restaurants, arts and craft shows, and a wax museum.

New Town, where people say "Hi" even if they've never seen you before, rescued a rotting neighborhood west of Lincoln Park. Among expresso bars, health food stores, studios, and craft shops are storefront theaters that offer stage shows for half the price of a movie. Music pours from bars, cafes, and record shops. The first jazz came north from New Orleans and Memphis; now Chicago writes its own folk music.

Hull House, where Jane Addams helped poor, bewildered people to help themselves, has become a museum in a district transformed by the surging Chicago Circle Campus of the University of Illinois. Today a new Jane Addams Center on North Broadway serves Mexicans, Puerto Ricans, Appalachians, Indians, and some Eskimo families. The present Hull House Association, with seven scattered centers, seeks "to establish a true sense of community with our neighbors."

With room to spread out, Chicago is a city in which huge apartment clusters have failed to outmode separate homes. Middle-class streets extend mile after mile with close-ranked houses and dooryards of green grass. Said a British official who had lived there ten years:

"It is a city of home-proud, city-proud citizens whose fathers and grandfathers came there to make a home—and made both a home and a city." In the 1960s "Chicagoland" added more family-owned homes than any other metropolitan area in the United States.

A million foreign-speaking people poured into Chicago between 1900 and 1920. Later came multitudes of black immigrants from the Deep South. Now a black publishing industry is centered on South Michigan Avenue. Operated by blacks for blacks, the Johnson Publishing Company issues *Ebony, Jet,* and *Black World*—some 2 million combined circulation. A few blocks south is the million-dollar plant of the *Chicago Daily Defender.* Black editors, writers, and reporters look out past the Field Museum and the Shedd Aquarium to Lake Michigan, heaving and tossing in winter, sparkling under the summer sun—the matchless front horizon of their town.

On the South Side the Hyde Park-Kenwood district, recently festering with poverty and violence, has been transformed by the University of Chicago. Acres of blighted buildings were torn down and replaced by bright new shopping centers, town houses, and apartment blocks. The result is a community part town and part gown, half black and half white, a neighborhood of endless variety and vitality. To break up remaining ghetto areas, the city housing authority is at last scattering new projects throughout various districts. Staggering as its problems are, Chicago seems to have the will and the energy to surmount them.

River and lake fronts have also been handsomely reclaimed in Cincinnati, St. Louis, Cleveland, Milwaukee, and Detroit. In Kansas City a decayed district beyond the Union Station is being transformed by the dramatic Crown Center Project—hotel, shops, restau-

The ladies of Quinter, Kans. (at left), lead a very active social life. The town—with a population below 1,000—has 7 nationally affiliated women's clubs and 20 women's social clubs, including P.A.L. (Peppy Aproned Ladies). All P.A.L. members, except one, are grandmothers.

The graceful Gateway Arch (at left) dominates the skyline in St. Louis, Mo. A new Performing Arts Center (at right) adorns the waterfront in Milwaukee, Wis. The city is the nation's largest producer of diesel and gasoline engines, motorcycles, tractors—and beer.

rants, theater, recreation centers, office and apartments built into the abrupt limestone hillside. A working and living community of 50,000 people covers eighty-five acres of an old shantytown.

In St. Louis the historic riverfront was left to decay when business moved northward. Reclamation began in the 1960s with construction of the 640-foot Gateway Arch and development of Gateway Park that replaced forty blocks of sooty streets and railroad tracks. Beyond Busch Stadium and the freeway a tract of 44 acres has been cleared of blighted buildings. This is the site of the first phase of LaSalle Park that will become a 140-acre community. At the edge of the razed ground rise the research and administration buildings of the Ralston Purina food company. LaSalle Park is a Ralston Purina project of housing, shopping, recreation, business, and light industry. It echoes the past—Robert Cavelier Sieur de La Salle was the first man to descend the Mississippi River to its mouth. There he claimed the entire valley for his king, whose name was given to St. Louis. The LaSalle Park emblem shows a green tree against the St. Louis skyline and a winged griffin from the coat-of-arms of the governor of New France. It looks toward the future of a revitalized city.

With the Midwest's urgent development there has been little inclination to look backward. In the region's cities the newest building is more important than the oldest; modern features replace outworn ones; change obscures continuity. Until a decade ago one could simply say the future has more pull than the past. But now, amid hurrying change, the region is reclaiming its memories. Throughout America, National Historic Landmarks are being identified and preserved. In the midland states that designation has gone to such diverse places as the "Beginning Point of the Public Land Survey"; the Mahoning Open Pit Mine; the showboat *Goldenrod*; the homes of John Deere, William H. Mc-

Guffey, Eugene Debs, and Ernest Hemingway; the site of the first atomic pile. Ohio at present has more than 200 registered memorials, ranging from the Great Serpent Mound to Louis Bromfield's Malabar Farm. In every state there are restorations of old market squares, railroad depots, one-room schools, blacksmith shops, and covered bridges. This is more than nostalgia in a time of rampant technology. It is perhaps an unconscious wish to draw upon the purposeful generations that turned a wilderness into a commonwealth.

Past and future are parts of the same river. Always and everywhere they intermingle, perhaps nowhere more strikingly than in two neighboring counties in western Ohio. The Piqua Historical Area includes a restored "Pioneer Farm" on the Great Miami River and a restored segment of the Miami and Erie Canal where a barge carries visitors at mule-pace, four miles an hour, under the white-limbed sycamores. Thirty miles north, beside Interstate 75, a proud little country town quietly identifies itself: WAPAKONETA, Principal Village and Council House of the Shawnee Nation. Wapakoneta is also the home of astronaut Neil Armstrong, and there, just off the highway, bordered on two sides by cornfields, is the Neil Armstrong Air and Space Museum—a windowless building of geometric lines surmounted by a great dome. Inside the many-angled building, visitors find the Gemini VIII spacecraft and Armstrong's Apollo XI space suit. An infinity cube takes them on a simulated launch into space, and in the darkened astro-theater they hurtle toward the moon. When they come out of the museum a west wind rustles the cornstalks as it did when Shawnee women tended their Wapakoneta field.

Technology has changed the Heartland in many ways and altered the lives of its people. But the oldest realities remain. Beneath all else lies the perennial and unceasing growth of the soil.

—WALTER HAVIGHURST

Midwest Industry: a dazzling diversity

The skillful, hard-working people who live at the industrial hub of the nation are among the most productive in the world. They produce 37% of our exported manufactured goods, 35% of the value added in our manufactures, 24% of our coal, 50% of our steel, and 65% of our cars and trucks. Thanks to them, and to their fellow workers in other states, America—with only 6% of the world's population and 7% of its land area—is able to produce approximately half the world's industrial output. The industrial revolution that began in 1913 when Henry Ford put together the first primitive assembly line to speed the manufacture of the Model T has had repercussions all over the world. Today, in less than 55 minutes, skilled auto workers can assemble some 13,000 parts into a finished automobile that's ready to be driven away.

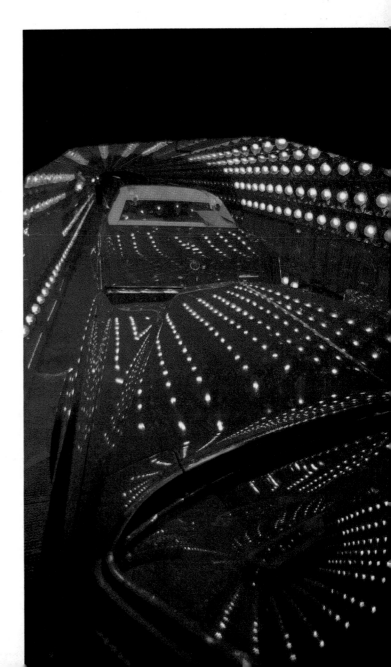

Workers on the GM line in Detroit (at left) assemble the Cadillacs shown going through the paint dryer at right. Increasing numbers of women have been hired by auto manufacturers in recent years. Those pictured above are installing headlights.

Shouting to make himself heard over the din, the Polish-American steelworker at right directs a crane operator at the Jones and Laughlin steel plant in Cleveland. Average weekly earnings in the industry are $204 for 43 hours of hot and exhausting work. At left, workmen pour accumulated slag from a giant mold. The technicians wearing heat and fire resistant outfits (below) are injecting pure oxygen into a miniature Basic Oxygen Furnace at the Graham Laboratories of Jones and Laughlin in Pittsburgh. The oxygen intensifies the heat and burns out impurities in the "pot" of scrap metal and molten iron. The U.S. produces 25% of the world's steel, half of it in Ohio, Indiana, Illinois, and Michigan. The mines of Minnesota provide 63% of the nation's iron ore.

Only one man is needed to monitor the computer controlling this 900-yard-long finishing train at a National Steel plant. Insulating glass protects operating pulpit from the "stands" of white-hot metal.

Heartland coal is moved
by rail (above) or by
barge (top) on a vast
network of waterways.

An abundance of coal is mined in the Heartland—
most of it used to power the region's cities and its concentration of heavy
industry. The U.S. produces more coal than any other nation—its miners
provide a quarter of the world's total. Ten percent of U.S. production comes
from Illinois, most of it from the southern part of the state. The Illinois
miner below is working 800 feet underground in one of the deepest
shafts in the country. Before introduction of monster machines like this
one, a miner could produce only about 6¼ tons of coal a day. But in a
mechanized mine, production can reach 37-38 tons per man per day.

To salt a batch of pretzels in a garage-size plant at Tell City, Ind., the lady simply whacks a sieve-bottomed wooden box with a hammer.

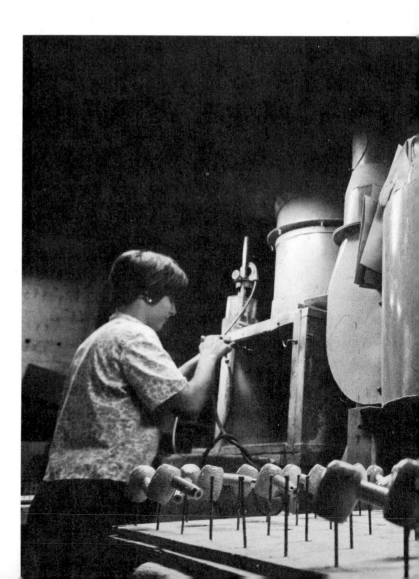

Thousands of diverse products are turned out in almost every city and town in the Heartland. Heavy industry—which employs hundreds of thousands of workers—contributes in a major way to the prosperity of the region. But light industry—including 53,600 plants that employ fewer than 20 people—helps to give it one of the best-balanced economies in the world. Precision craftsmanship and assembly-line techniques are combined in the larger plants, like the C.G. Conn band instrument factory (at left) in Elkhart, Ind. Assembly lines and streamlined equipment are less important in Washington, Mo., where all the nation's corncob pipes are manufactured. The Missouri Meerschaum Company (below and at right) provides special seeds to local farmers, buys the harvested cobs, and ages them for up to seven years before crafting them in the plant. General MacArthur, whose portrait hangs in the office of the company president (at right), continued to order yearly shipments of pipes until his death. He made the corncob famous during World War II and helped give respectability to a product once identified only with hillbillies.

Completed pipes are sprayed with shellac (at left). At day's end (above), some of the plant's three dozen workers head for home.

205

The largest inland waterway system in the
world—including the Great Lakes, the St. Lawrence Seaway,
and the Mississippi, Missouri, Ohio, and Illinois rivers—
connects the Heartland with both the Atlantic Ocean and the
Gulf of Mexico. It provides inexpensive transportation for
the ore, coal, grain, and manufactured goods produced in the
area. A laker crew can pick up iron ore at Duluth, Minn.,
carry it through the Soo locks (at left) into Lake Huron or Lake
Michigan for delivery to the steel mills of Michigan, Ohio,
Indiana, or Illinois. The crew can then load grain at the huge
elevators in Chicago's Calumet Harbor (below) and carry it
through the Seaway to a port on the Gulf of St. Lawrence
for shipment overseas. On the return trip, there may be a
load of iron ore from Canada. Nearly 250 million tons
of shipping are moved each year by the lakers—about
94% destined for lake ports and the remainder for export.

Navy Pier at Chicago, the world's greatest
inland port. Here freight is shipped between
the Great Lakes-Seaway system and the
Mississippi River-Illinois Waterway system.

Mascoutah, Illinois: "it's a nice little town"

"The people are all so friendly. . . . Everyone knows each other. . . .
Everybody has a good morning for you and things like that. . . . We've got
good schools, nice churches, and the swimming pool and all. . . . It's a
real good community to live in!" These were typical descriptions given
by Mascoutans to photographer Ken Heyman, who visited the town three
times to do a sociological study of the 1970 population center of the U.S.
The complex process used by the Census Bureau to locate this center
can best be understood by visualizing the nation as a flat, rigid surface.
If every American weighed the same as every other, the population center
would be the point at which the flat surface would be in balance if
everyone stood where he lived. The town (actually about five miles
from the demographic center) has a stable population of about 5,000—
mostly of German extraction—and had a median family income of $9,750
in 1970. It is surrounded by rich farmlands where the major crops are
corn, soybeans, and wheat—in that order. Mascoutah has the usual
fraternal and social clubs (above), plus many local groups that provide an
active social life for the townspeople. Everybody turns out to fill the
new bleachers (at left) during high school football games, but the biggest
event of the year is the Homecoming und August Fest—which in recent
years has featured the float shown below.

Mascoutah is a great town for parades. They have two on successive days for the Homecoming und August Fest, and there's a High School Homecoming Parade, a Halloween Parade, and a Santa Claus Parade—to say nothing of parades celebrating special events. The line of march includes Shriners, Scouts of both sexes and all sizes, the High School Marching Band, innumerable floats, and the irrepressible members of the Senior Citizens Kitchen Band (middle left)— who ride a wagon and play a variety of homemade instruments. During a 1971 August Fest parade, Lawrence Friederich— who farms the land where census officials placed the original population center survey marker—rode with his wife and father (below) in a specially assigned convertible. After a special parade in May of that year, he took part with Illinois Governor Richard Ogilvie and Secretary of Commerce Maurice Stans in ceremonies in front of City Hall dedicating the permanent standard that now marks the population center.

The August Fest carnival lasts for two days and attracts people from all over the county. Hot German dinners are sold, beer is bought by the bucket (below) with refills costing less than the original purchase. Equipment is rented from carnival suppliers, rides are sold by volunteers, local clubs prepare and sell food, and the Boy Scouts clean up the trash. The Mascoutah Improvement Association nets about $40,000 from homecoming fest activities. Sometimes volunteers have to be pressed into service—athletic coaches and teachers are the favorite targets for "Dunk the Punk" marksmen (at right). Mascoutah has no movie house and its Main Street is less than a mile long; but there are turkey shoots, picnics, wurstmarkts pancake and sausage breakfasts, chicken fries, occasional Saturday night dances, slow-pitch softball tourneys, and a host of other social activities.

Farmers around Mascoutah are a thrifty and conservative lot who have invested their money for generations either in adjoining land or in savings banks. The average farm is probably a little over 300 acres, but 1,000 or more acres are not uncommon. With farm land valued at $1,000-$2,000 an acre and farm equipment worth $40,000-$100,000, some of these farmers —perhaps 25 of them—are millionaires in land. "But their wealth is never displayed—they drive beat-up trucks, wear overalls, and look like everyone else. People in Mascoutah believe in working, and they think anybody who doesn't work is shirking his duty, regardless of what kind of money he's got or anything else." Both farmers and the long-established business people of the town are resistant to change—which is somewhat frustrating to the younger men. "We run into the problem of people who are very, very comfortable here. They're not interested in growth, in industry. They don't want the hustle-bustle some of us are looking for."

Roger Roehrig (above) produces some 800 pigs yearly; selling some as breeding stock, exporting some, marketing some. Roy Knipp (below) fills his bins with a bumper corn crop, while Raymond Haas (facing page) has more help than he needs at harvest time.

Weekly bingo games draw a good crowd on Monday nights. Pots are kept low, the state gets a cut, and profits are put to good use by town groups who sponsor the games. Farmers and townspeople drop into a local tavern for a beer, and there is usually an informal card game going on somewhere—euchre seems to be more popular than poker. Townspeople tend to be somewhat clannish about inviting outsiders into their homes: "newcomers" and people from Scott Air Force Base who live in the town, even those who retire there, are usually included only at school-related parties. "You're accepted up to a point and people are always friendly and polite. But if anyone has an accident or needs help they give it to him in unlimited quantities—often anonymously. They'll raise money for you with a raffle, take your car down to get it washed, bring you food. They show that they care."

Someone always holds an after-the-game party during football season. High school principal William Bach (above) and the air force parents of some of the players are included in this one at the home of the owner of a local trucking firm.

216

217

Townspeople get together to watch as Mayor Hassebrock cuts the ribbon (below) to open the new library. It was financed without extra taxation by using a surplus in the general fund, and citizen-sponsors raised the money needed to furnish it. Mascoutans belong to a variety of organizations—Rotary, Lions, Moose, Masons, Grange, American Legion, VFW, Jaycees, Sportsmen's Club, Knights of Columbus, and others. There are several active women's clubs—they, the church groups, the Scouts, and the 4-H often hold bazaars and bake sales (facing page) to raise money. The wedding of Patricia Klingel and Alan Riddle (at right) is being held in one of the town's six churches—roughly half the townspeople are Protestants and half are Catholics.

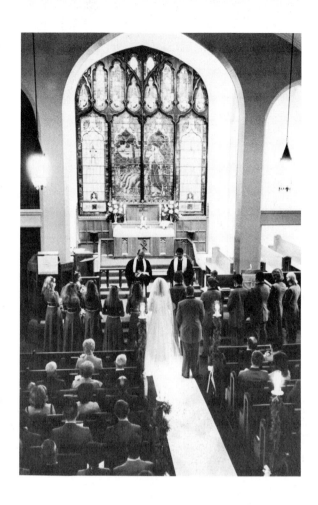

The Mascoutah Rotary Club sings during
the opening of the weekly meeting (top)
held in the Moose Home. Farm families,
including the ladies below, belong to
one of three nearby Granges.

The high school football team is cheered by excited team members and fans during the big homecoming game with an archrival. The band and a precision drill-dance group of 20 pompon girls (at left) perform at half time. Until six or seven years ago, the financially conservative farm community which controls the school board opposed football; but once the initial investment was made, the game became as popular as basketball. Little League softball teams compete in season, and there is also a girl's softball league. The most popular game for young adults in summer is slow-pitch softball. Ten or more teams compete three nights a week at the VFW park.

The Homecoming dance in the high school gym follows
the big football game. Mascoutah has no problem with hard drugs, though a
few students use marijuana. There are no real disciplinary problems and 70%
of the students go on to college at least for a year or two. Although school taxes are
very low, the system is exceptionally well funded because the federal government
contributes generously for the 65% of students who are military dependents
from the nearby air force base. The school system could not survive at present
levels for three months if the base were to close, so the thrifty—and 100%
nonmilitary—school board maintains a cash reserve of nearly $2 million.

Farming:
wealth from fertile fields

The Heartland farmer, a legend in his own time, produces 37% more food than in 1950 on 7% fewer acres using 41% fewer man-hours of labor. To achieve this miracle of productivity, he uses equipment like the tractor at left, with attachments that make it possible for him to open irrigation furrows and plant eight rows of Kansas corn simultaneously. The Nebraska farmer below uses equipment that plants corn or soybeans and at the same time applies fertilizer, herbicide, and insecticide. In 1974, farmers in Kansas produced almost 20% of the huge U.S. wheat crop; in Iowa they harvested more than 20% of our corn; in Illinois and Iowa they brought in about a third of our soybeans. American farmers today receive about 42¢ out of each market-basket dollar. The remaining 58¢ covers marketing costs and profits.

Life on the farm, in the 1970s, has many compensations. Electrification, mechanization, and a superb network of rural roads have brought once-isolated farm families into the mainstream of American life. Hard work and long hours, however, are still a necessity, and the farm population continues to decline as farm children move to the cities. The family farmer is not likely to get rich, since 46% of cash receipts from farming go to the 4% of large U.S. farms with sales of over $100,000 a year. But for people like Jay and Zada Hoeh (below) who can make a go of it, farming provides a very good life indeed. With the help of their son, Roger, Jay works his 160-acre farm near Salina, Kans., and 740 rented acres of adjoining land. When the Hoehs need help, Zada's brother comes over from his own farm nearby. Two-thirds of Jay's income comes from 110 head of cattle, the remaining third from the surplus grain he harvests each year.

The cheerful Wisconsin pair above are selling their farm produce at a roadside stand. Amenities accessible to modern farm families include the community pool in Iowa (at right) and the rural golf course in Nebraska (below).

Combines, family, and crew may work 16-18 hours a day without a day off. They eat in the fields, take a break only in wet weather.

Custom cutters, using combines that reap and thresh a 20-foot swath of grain at an average speed of three miles per hour, harvest most of the country's 1.8-billion-bushel wheat crop. Few growers can afford the costly equipment needed, since it would stand idle for 11 months out of 12. Max Louder, a Kansas harvester, has invested $130,000 in four combines and hauling trucks, two travel trailers and pickups, spare parts, two-way radios, and other equipment. He travels with his family and a seven-man crew from early May to mid-September, harvesting over half-a-million bushels during a 1,750-mile odyssey that begins in Texas and ends near the Canadian border—enough to put bread on the tables of 125,000 American families for a year. The entire trip is an exhausting race against time and the weather. The combines must reach each field when the grain is ripe and harvest it before rain, hail, or prairie fires can ruin the crop.

Harvester (at left) struggles to free a straw-clogged combine. In dry, windy weather loose straw may be ignited by an overheated muffler or a spark, burning acres of grain, encircling and endangering the lives of combine operators before fire can be contained.

When weather conditions slow the harvest, family and crew relax in the trailers and watch television (below), and Max Louder has time to teach his young son to box (above). At left, an awe-struck youngster watches as her father operates a roaring combine.

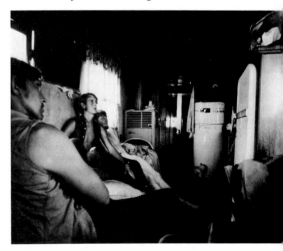

Food processing and marketing
are big business in the Heartland, where a
third of all U.S. food manufacturing plants are
located. The value of its processed food shipments is almost $41 billion—17% of the value
of all manufactures in the region. Meat
products, prepared in packing plants like the
one in Du Quoin, Ill. (below), account for
nearly $13 billion of this total. Baked goods like
those on the conveyor belt at Chicago's Sara
Lee Bakery (at left) swell the area's economy
by more than $2 billion. There is continual and
frenetic activity at the Chicago Board of Trade's
Mercantile Exchange (at right), where foodstuffs, silver, lumber, and plywood are traded.
In 1974 the nation's largest commodity
market handled more than 14.5 million
contracts valued at $325 billion.

Young Americans

The accents are regional but the young voices all speak American. With youth's special tones and rhythms, they speak to each other across the borders: the new enthusiasms and the old worries; the best and worst opinions of the nation that will one day be theirs to run.

Hear them:

"Everyone now is exposed to so much, it's like being made to grow up too fast."

"My mother is scrubbing floors so I can become a doctor. Now my school is running out of money."

"I'm concerned that the world will eat itself up."

"Black is beautiful, but what good is it going to do me?"

"Missionaries aren't very popular these days, but I'd still like to be a medical missionary."

"I want to be happy. And I want comfort—nice clothes, a nice house, good music and good food...."

"We need to put a little brake on our selfishness."

"I think a woman can do as good a job as a man. It all depends on the person."

What are they really saying? There seem to be two major themes here—one of cynical egoism and one of

The exuberance and sheer joy reflected in these young faces remind us that youth, after all, does not change so very much from generation to generation. Appearances and status are no longer so important—the young mother below thinks nothing of going to market in her bare feet, and the young father (below/right) does not consider it unmanly to serenade his enraptured infant with a guitar. Life styles are easier, less formal, less inhibited. But the basic warmth and companionship of family relationships remain the same.

idealistic involvement. Is that how it goes today? Perhaps. But whatever the meaning, the words are important to the rest of America. Cutting across all sections of the country, American youth is charting a new course, a course that ultimately will help determine this nation's destiny.

Being young in the USA is a unity of experience shared variously by some 45 million people between the ages of fourteen and twenty-four. And though American youth has always shared a certain generational closeness, this present generation is particularly aware of its interrelationship.

They are different from older Americans in many ways: their dress, their language, their music. But, most important, they have different things going on in their heads. The words "passive" and "self-centered" have been used to describe the youth of the seventies, in dramatic contrast to their more violent, more committed older cousins of the sixties. "Why don't they do something?" sputters one exasperated former rebel of the sixties. "Swallow goldfish . . . anything."

Yet perhaps tolerant, open-minded, questioning are better descriptions of today's youth than self-centered. As one observer of today's young put it: "Freedom to choose—whether you call it lack of discipline or tolerance, amorality or open-mindedness—is the ethic that makes the [high school] class of 1974 different from its generational predecessors. 1954 didn't bother. 1969 had to fight for it."

Daniel Yankelovich's 1974 poll of college students further confirmed the open-mindedness of today's youth: "Young Americans now in college are tending to be less radical and more conciliatory toward society and its system of values."

Along with the new tolerance, however, has come a new cynicism—a feeling among many young people that idealism by itself doesn't get one very far.

234

Young lovers *still get together in traditional ways—in the park, on the farm, in the woods, or even on a surfboard.* The majority of noncollege as well as college youth accepts the new morality; only 34% view premarital sex as wrong. But when they first meet there is still a reserve, a desire to get to know each other by sharing everyday experience. Those who reject the puritanical moral code of earlier generations consider themselves neither immoral nor amoral. They are trying, with some difficulty, to work out personal moral codes they can live with in an era that offers many options.

235

An enduring relationship is still the goal of most young people and most still believe marriage is the best way to achieve this goal. Liberated college women want to combine marriage with self-fulfilling careers and expect husbands to share housework and child care. Noncollege women, who get the least satisfying jobs, prefer to stay at home in the traditional way if their earnings are not essential to make ends meet.

"We know that people and movements are fallible. We're afraid to believe too much in anything or anyone," laments one young college student.

Says another: ". . . now we can vote, and we're old enough to attend rallies and knock on doors and wave placards, and suddenly it doesn't seem to matter any more."

This cynicism affects not only political beliefs but also many young people's attitude toward education. The old tenet that higher education will help youth achieve its life goals is no longer accepted without question. An increasing number of colleges have empty seats; the National Association of College Admissions put that negative number at 600,000 in 1973, and growing fast. Blacks as well as whites suspect that education will not fulfill all their needs: after peaking in 1972, the number of blacks entering U.S. colleges has fallen off at a rate between 10 and 15 percent per year.

"English is the best prerequisite for unemployment," said a UCLA student when asked about the applicability of his courses.

Instead, a return to conventional careers (but perhaps for unconventional reasons) seems to characterize the college youth of the seventies. Among young women, for example, the service-oriented career of a nurse appeals to 3.7 percent more than it did in 1968-69. Among men, 2 percent more want to be farmers; at the University of Connecticut's College of Agriculture and Natural Resources, enrollment increased 31 percent in 1974 over the previous year. Both men and women are flocking into schools of journalism, dentistry, veterinary medicine, optometry, pharmacy, and allied health service. Engineering is returning as a popular career choice; the engineering school of the University of the Pacific has grown more than 300 percent in the last five years.

By far the most popular career choices among college students, however, are business, law, and medicine. Business schools describe their enrollments as "explod-

ing," while law and medical schools are receiving thousands of admissions for openings that number only in the hundreds.

In their world philosophies as in their college courses, young men and women seem to be shunning abstract and radical ideas. Whereas 32.6 percent of college freshmen called themselves liberals in 1973, the group dropped to 28 percent in 1974; meanwhile the percentage of conservatives remained constant. The growing group consists of "middle of the roaders." A senior at Boston University comments on the lack of interest in causes: "Students can't afford to waste their time and money. They are seeking tangible, not spiritual returns for their investment in a university."

Even sexual liberation has ceased to cause a stir. Boy-girl dormitories on many campuses appear to have produced a tolerant attitude toward sex rather than a compulsion to indulge. At Berkeley, of all places, the number of single-sex fraternities is rising (from twenty-four in 1971 to twenty-eight in 1974). A reporter comments that

> there is a waiting list of 800 students who want to live in the dormitories where it is easier to be a serious student and not bother with cooking and living in one of the formerly glamorous off-campus apartments. Most dorms are, of course, co-ed.

But no one should conclude from this conservative trend that American youth has lost all inclination to dissent, to suggest alternate ways, indeed to pull all of society along with it in new, reformist directions. Said a student quoted by *Fortune*: "College means for me something intangible, perhaps the opportunity to change things rather than to make out well with the existing system." Young graduates entering careers in business and law are quietly acknowledging that their prime purpose is not to win high stakes but to bring

238

Recreation tends to be less structured than it once was. Dancing to rock and country music doesn't involve learning "steps"— it is a form of spontaneous, vigorous, and uninhibited self-expression. In California, they invent new games—whoever manages to sling a 60-lb. bale of hay (left) over the highest string wins. But in Vermont young people still hurl themselves into the icy waters of the same abandoned quarries their fathers once used. There was a time when parents were afraid television would turn their children into zombies. But this generation, the first to be brought up on the tube, can take it or leave it alone. TV is something they fall back on when there's nothing better to do.

about a readjustment of the establishment game. Legal firms are being organized in both urban and rural locations with that activist, socially conscious objective. Staffed by earnest young attorneys, they generally call themselves "public interest law firms."

Asked about the toning-down of present students and recent graduates, Paul Soglin (a former radical who is now the young mayor of Madison, Wisconsin) said:

> I disagree totally with anyone who says this group of students has lost their ideals. I know many people from my college days who are turning around the policies of major corporations, who are making changes as lawyers and journalists, and who are taking active roles in community organizations.

Olympics contestants, who have already won top honors in local and state events, compete in carpentry (above), drafting, and bricklaying (below). Medals are given to winners of 22 job-skill and 8 leadership-skill events.

Indeed the college youth of today seem to want it both ways: to work within the system but also to reform it. With quiet, steady persistence, today's students are stressing new objectives, the objectives of what sociologists call the postmodern age: ecology, purer food, equality for women, as well as political reform and minority rights.

Even among the vast and often noncommittal majority of America's youth—those who go to work instead of college after high school—a distinct change in values and objectives has taken place. A 1974 Yankelovich survey of more than 3,000 young people revealed that most noncollege youths, "just like their college counterparts," have started to "go beyond good pay and economic security, toward other values." Many young workers are becoming increasingly dissatisfied and frustrated with their jobs. They want interesting and challenging work—work that offers opportunities for further education and training and for personal expression. In fact, among young blue-collar workers, job security, which was important to 51 percent of those inter-

Vocational students cheer winners of gold, silver, and bronze medals at the annual U.S. Skills Olympics of VICA—the Vocational Industrial Clubs of America. The organization, with 6,461 clubs in 45 states, stresses craftsmanship, good citizenship, and leadership. It instills pride in vocational students—most of them in high school—who once tended to feel inferior to classmates planning to go on to college.

The work ethic still seems to be built into most young Americans—farm youngsters still help feed the animals, city children still earn money delivering newspapers. But there have been changes. Increasing numbers of young people—like the suburban hospital orderly (above, right)—take a year off after high school to earn money for college. And women's liberation has given girls the confidence to tackle jobs once reserved for the opposite sex. The young Radcliffe graduate at left is a skilled mechanic, earning money for med school in a Cambridge garage. The Kansas teen-ager below spends college vacations helping her father—a custom harvester. When rain threatens, she can cover and tie down the heavy tarp that protects a truckload of wheat and drive the huge rig to the grain elevator as skillfully as a hired hand twice her size.

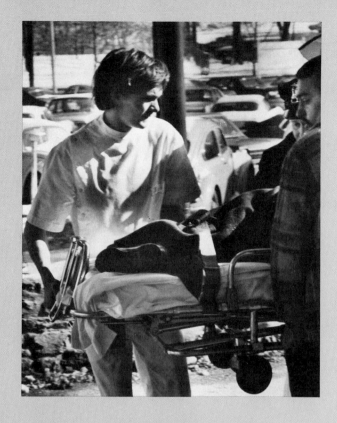

viewed, ranked fifteen percentage points below interesting work as a job criterion; while the chance to make a lot of money was among the bottom ten on a list of thirty-five job criteria.

Among many college youths also, the urge to make a lot of money, to be successful in the traditional sense of the word, seems less strong. Many college students are inclined to drop out of school, out of the slots predetermined for them in corporate offices of the future, into a contemplative life on the farm or ranch or waterfront. As expressed by one young writer: "It almost seems as if a switch were thrown somewhere a few years back, and a great majority of America's talented and thoughtful youth swung off on a track to another kind of maturity." Elaborating on this thought, another writer commented: "These people have not lowered their aspirations but are aspiring to something else. . . . The numbers are not great, perhaps no more than 10 percent in a class. But they are significant and I think they are growing."

Remarking on the youth of the sixties, social scientist Daniel Moynihan has said: "Suddenly a new social class was created in the U.S., so large in its number that it was fundamentally isolated from the rest of society. . . . At every level there emerged a sense that 'we are alone and separate from them.' " Today the youth culture is no longer as hostile or private, no longer as mysterious as portrayed in Dustin Hoffman's The Graduate. Now less isolated from the rest of society and less divided from each other, young Americans are pulling together even as they seek different ways. Their generational views are strikingly similar. The Yankelovich survey highlights this confluence of social class attitudes: whereas there was a wide difference between the two major youth groups in 1969 on the subject of whether big business should be reformed (37 percent of the college population thought it should be while only 24 percent of the noncollege population agreed); by 1973 the

243

difference in opinion on that subject had shrunk considerably (54 percent as opposed to 45 percent).

Common Cause, the citizens' group for governmental reform, has observed a dramatic increase in its young and involved members despite the fact that the youth population has stabilized and become "more pragmatic." On some 135 campuses in nineteen states, a Ralph Nader-originated organization called PIRG (Public Interest Research Groups) has launched a veritable youth crusade. They have investigated such social problems as lethal toys—finding in Michigan that 40 percent of the state's stores put these dangerous items on the shelves—and have brought about effective, sidewalk-level reform by releasing the information. Across the land other, isolated examples bloom of concerned and contributory youth: 180 girls at a school in Connecticut sought to preserve a tidal marsh threatened by oil spills; to the amazement of their elders they eventually succeeded in getting a bill through the Hartford legislature that would save the wetland.

Among both major youth groups, a strong concern today may be an urge to keep the population down. Of young women between eighteen and twenty-four, more than half were unmarried in the mid-1970s, whereas only 42 percent were unmarried in 1960. Though the American mother bore an average of seven children in 1800 and more than three in the baby-booming 1950s, she now produces less than two in the course of her life.

Yet concerns come and go. American youth remains constant, constant in its challenge to the rest of society. The perennial concern of young Americans—each in his or her own way—has been to cross a certain boundary line from the old situation to the new expectation. It's a line not recognized in static societies where the next generation must follow in the steps of the one before, where the woodcutter's son becomes a woodcutter's father. But it's a line that youth can see—and across which they may eventually carry the rest of us.

244

A teen-ager's crusade against the inertia of bureaucracy and the indifference of polluting corporations has led to a project to save California's beautiful San Bernardino National Forest. College student Andy Lipkis, knowing that 40,000 trees were being killed by smog each year, wanted to replant with smog-resistant varieties. The State Division of Forestry refused to give him seedlings they were plowing under and corporate executives refused to give him the money to buy them. But when the local press took up the story, Andy was inundated with small donations. The embarrassed foresters and corporation executives quickly saw the error of their ways; stores and small firms in the area asked what they could do to help. Andy has now planted thousands of seedlings with the help of college friends, Boy Scouts, and youngsters from surrounding summer camps.

Mountain West – Legendary Land 5

The boys did not know that to build a fence in the West the rocks have to be pried out with a crowbar. Then when the hole is dug, the post has to be tamped into place with smaller rocks and earth. The boys were from Indiana, part of the new youth migration to the Rocky Mountain West, and like so many of their contemporaries, they wore long hair and jeans. After a while they took off their shirts. In the noon heat, the pines smelled of resin and a haze hung over the mountains.

"You provide the know-how," they told the woman who hired them, "and we'll provide the brawn. Jobs are hard to find in this country."

The woman did not tell the boys that men experienced in building fences were even harder to find at prices that she, and other landowners, could afford.

As the boys were spiking rails to the posts, a neighbor drove up in a truck, the back of which was littered with fencing and irrigation tools. A rifle hung on brackets over the rear window, partly to use against coyotes, partly to prove the westerner's right to bear arms.

The rancher wore a broad-brimmed hat, and his eyes squinted against the sun. Regarding the boys, he spat without changing expression. Boys with long hair are not popular in many parts of the West.

"I see you got your ten acres."

"Yes," the woman said, "and I paid as much for it as my Dad did for his 2,000-acre ranch in the thirties."

"Won't be long before all the ranches in this valley are subdivided," the rancher said. "Heck of a thing—all these people coming in and buying our land."

He did not object to the woman having bought a small place. Her family had lived in the state since the gold rush. In his opinion she was entitled to live on as much or as little acreage as she pleased.

In the case of newcomers, like the boys, however, the rancher felt differently.

Picking up their chain saw, the boys told the woman:

"We're quitting for today, okay? We're going into town to buy a cowboy hat, and then we're going swimming in the river. It's too hot to work."

The rancher looked at the sky. Hot or cold, he worked from dawn until dark and barely made a living.

As the boys drove off in their battered truck, the woman explained apologetically: "The boys like this country. They want to buy land and live here."

"Yeah?" The rancher's tone expressed skepticism. "Give 'em a winter and they'll go back where they came from."

This opinion is heard at intervals in rural areas of the Rocky Mountain West and was first expressed 150 years ago by the fur traders who saw the emigrants jolting over the prairies in covered wagons. In the early part of the nineteenth century, there was sound basis for such an opinion. To some extent, there still is today. For the competitive, the ambitious, the status-seekers, the Rockies do not offer the opportunities found elsewhere. Still people come.

In the six Rocky Mountain states, the area of which is well over 600,000 square miles, there were in 1970 only four cities with populations of more than 100,000 —Denver, Salt Lake City, Las Vegas, and Colorado Springs. The political, financial, and cultural centers of America are not in the Rocky Mountain West. To realize why this is so, look at a map. Better still, look at the country itself. Even in this day of shopping centers and air-conditioned condominiums, the environment of the mountain states influences the people as do few other areas. To understand the people, it is necessary first to understand the land. See it, feel it, listen to it.

It frightens some. A woman on a bus tour of retired Civil Service employees who had never been west exclaimed: "I think the country's beautiful, but I'm afraid the bus will break down and we'll be stranded in a desert or on a mountain pass."

Visitors are often impressed by the immensity of the

country. The most northern of the Rocky Mountain states, Montana, is larger than Denmark, Belgium, the Netherlands, and Great Britain combined, but the population of the state in 1970 consisted of only 694,409 inhabitants. Of that number, 27,130 were Indians. With the exceptions of the Chambers of Commerce and hard-sell merchants, Montanans favor a small population, as do most people in the Rocky Mountain West—a new and radical departure from the tradition that progress is equated with growth.

A knowledgeable person traveling through the region would not be surprised at the smallness of the population. Indeed, he might be amazed that people live in some places at all. The Rocky Mountain states of Montana, Wyoming, Idaho, Utah, Nevada, and Colorado are isolated on the east by the Great Plains and on the west by the ranges of the Sierras. The high peaks of the Continental Divide lift against the sky on the Canadian border in northern Montana and continue down through the Wind River Mountains of Wyoming to the San Juans in Colorado. Flying west, a traveler can see the gradual lift to the high plains and then the mountains, split by great gorges and rivers and forested ridges. Flying east to the Rockies from the lushness of the West Coast, he sees the Great Basin of Nevada and Utah—arid, grey desert in which the naked rock casts no shadow.

Except for a few fertile areas, the land is harsh in the Rockies: the soil poorly fitted for agriculture; the climate cold in the winter, hot in summer. The region includes most of the United States that lies west of the area of twenty-inch rainfall and a great deal of desert with less than ten inches of annual precipitation. The great rivers—the Missouri, the Colorado, the Clark Fork, the Snake—are the arteries that pump the life blood of irrigation to the West—rivers fed by silver veins of water that trickle from the grey rocks above the timberline.

The mountains affect winds and rain, as well as the flow of rivers. The average elevation of Nevada is 5,500 feet. Utah varies from 4,000 to 6,000 feet, except in the southwestern corner, while Wyoming averages 5,000 to 7,000 feet above sea level, with mountain ranges lifting to 11,000 feet. In Colorado, fifty-four mountain peaks are 14,000 feet or higher.

In the winter, blizzards howl down from the Canadian barrens across eastern Montana, Wyoming, and Colorado. Despite barbed wire fences and modern ranching methods, a hard winter means that hundreds of cattle freeze to death. They drift before the wind to huddle by a fence or in a gulch, and there the rancher finds their frozen carcasses. One often hears the comment that the weather is "ten months winter and two months darn poor sledding." This is partly a complaint, partly a boast, for westerners know they must be tough to survive.

In the summer the sun bakes the empty, treeless miles; the earth cracks into clay. Poplars planted as windbreaks stand like tattered sentinels around the few ranch houses. The towns, which are often 100 miles apart, are a shabby combination of the old West and the new—a Victorian brick bank next to a Penney's plastic store front. The vitality of these towns has been drained by new highways to larger urban centers.

And yet at times the heart soars. The sky is infinite; the air as clear as spring water. In the autumn the land

Distances in sparsely populated
Montana are calculated by the
hour rather than by the mile.
Travelers fill their tanks before
heading out on roads like the one
at left. It may be hours before
they see a man, a house, or a
crossroads settlement.

tarnishes to ochre with purple shadows on the hills. In May the meadowlarks sing above the greening earth.

The geological wonders of this vast land encourage exaggeration. At a truck stop recently, in Buffalo, Wyoming, a lean cowboy was overheard telling an easterner:

> Yes, sir, I was ridin' one day; it was getting along about supper time and I was mighty hungry. Danged if my old cayuse didn't throw me. First he drug me through a huckleberry patch, and then a raspberry patch, and then he drug me through a crick so's I could have a drink a' water.

From the beginning the West has been obscured by a rainbow of myth, colored by personal ambition, political necessity, greed, and the dream in every man's heart. Frederick Jackson Turner, a noted historian, believed that "the existence of an area of free land, its continuous recession, the advance of . . . settlement westward, explain American development. . . ."—that is to say, the growth of American democracy. The West was the refuge for the oppressed and the exploited. Other historians differed, pointing out that more midwest farmers went westward than poor factory workers from eastern ghettoes and that industrialization and social advances in Europe also contributed to American progress.

Historically the frontier ended in 1890, but few would deny that it continued to exist in a diluted form in isolated areas until World War II. In the early thirties, many families still lived on homesteads in log cabins insulated with newspapers. They used outhouses, hauled water from the nearest creek, and lived lives little changed from pioneer days. Their manner of speech reflected their ties to the land: "He had to stand twice in the same place to cast a shadow." . . . "Fat? Say, he's prime for shipping." . . . "She's as thin as the running gear of the katydid." In rural areas today, oldtimers still express themselves in such graphic terms.

The frontier traditions of comradeship, courtesy, and openhanded hospitality also live on. In many small western towns, it is possible to roam the streets late at night or to find a welcome at the nearest house in case of emergency. Yet how much longer the rural westerner will continue to extend hospitality to strangers is difficult to say. Carolyn Wolfinbarger, who lives in the isolated country north of Grangeville, Idaho, says: "It isn't like it used to be. When we saw tracks in the trail, we knew whose they were, and we left our door unlocked and wood on the porch. Anyone was welcome to come in, cook a meal, and spend the night if we weren't home. Now I don't know."

In metropolitan areas, such as Denver and Salt Lake, rural traditions tend to linger among first generation city-dwellers but to lose strength among later generations—a tendency accentuated by the recent and continuing influx of newcomers. Generally, the more urban the population, the weaker the western tradition, which might loosely be defined as the social mores of the nineteenth century modified by the harshness of living on the frontier.

But in the Rocky Mountain West, the term "urban" can be deceiving. More than two-thirds of Nevada's residents live in Las Vegas and Reno; one out of every four Coloradans lives in the metropolitan statistical areas of Denver and Colorado Springs. Thus, Nevada is classified as 80 percent urban and Colorado as 78 percent, but none of the mountain states is urban in the same sense as Illinois or New Jersey. Even Denver, the mile-high Queen of the Rockies and one of the most cosmopolitan of the western cities, is within a short drive of wilderness and vast cattle ranches.

Distance from civilized centers and the vastness of the country helped to create the myth of the Rocky Mountain West. From 1804-1806, Lewis and Clark explored the northwest, bringing back valuable maps and scientific data. In the mid-1800s Senator Thomas Hart Benton extolled the doctrine of Manifest Destiny, while his son-in-law, John Charles Frémont, fired the public's imagination with his explorations. The fur traders added to the myth, although not as much as is often thought, for the fur trade flourished for only a brief time—from 1810-1840. Nevertheless, Hugh Glass's struggle with a grizzly and Jedediah Smith's trip across the arid Great Basin grew into epics. The fur trader became a legendary hero clad in buckskin who could perform superhuman feats of strength and who roamed the West because he yearned for a free life.

The romance of these western legends still has its appeal. Young men in homemade moccasins and leather-fringed jackets are an increasingly frequent sight on the streets of western cities like Jackson, Wyoming, and Aspen, Colorado. The ideal of these youthful adventurers, and that of the girls who accompany them, is a log cabin or a tipi, home-baked bread, homemade clothes, and venison. Few of the young men trap, since it's difficult to obtain a permit, something Jedediah Smith didn't need to have, and beaver are no longer as plentiful. Still trapping is by no means a lost art. In 1974 the Nevada Fish and Game Department listed one man who made a profit of $17,000 after trapping for only three months.

Despite outward similarities between the life style of many of today's youthful western immigrants and that of the adventurers of the past, there are important differences in their goals. The fur traders of the 1800s went west to make enough money to return home and buy a farm or become a rich merchant. Dr. David Abrahamsen, author of *Our Violent Society*, believes that this dream, which was shared by trapper, prospector, and pioneer alike, contributed to violence. The transition from a familiar life to a precarious existence in a

The beautiful main campus of the University of Colorado at Boulder covers nearly 600 acres along the Front Range of the Rockies.

The Will Rogers Shrine overlooks the Broadmoor Hotel in Colorado Springs. The old Broadmoor, fronting on its own private lake, is one of the most elegant hotels in the country—known for impeccable service and superb accommodations.

hostile land forced people to learn to defend themselves, to become aggressive and egocentric, to exploit the resources around them in order to survive. Men like Hugh Glass and Jedediah Smith developed extraordinary courage, daring, and resourcefulness as they coped with the wilderness; they were men of great vitality who relieved the tensions of a dangerous and lonely existence by periodic and often violent roistering.

The modern immigrants—young, middle-aged, and elderly—are generally better educated than their historical counterparts, and many are seeking an escape from what Dr. Rollo May, an eminent psychologist and author, calls "the anonymity of people; the loneliness and alienation of cities."

A young doctor practicing in Twin Falls, Idaho, says, "I came here because it's a good place to raise my family. The schools are good, and my wife can go to the supermarket without being mugged."

In Colorado Springs, a grey-haired couple cited their reasons for moving west: "We couldn't take the traffic any more or the smog or the crime. Here we've found it easy to make friends, and the country is so beautiful."

The couple were lunching at the Broadmoor, one of the few remaining elegant old hotels in Colorado Springs. From the window of the Broadmoor, the plains fall away to the east; Fort Carson lies out there. NORAD (North American Defense Command) has its headquarters deep in the grey stone peaks behind the town. A few miles north is the Air Force Academy. Colorado Springs, carefully zoned, is a city of today—pines and rocks, sunlight and endless distances.

Some of those who come west to "slow down" end up doing the opposite. An ex-football player, Norman Dacus, became so intrigued with Nevada's possibilities after he moved there that he developed a $25 million oasis on the desert near Las Vegas.

Not all the social and economic change in the West is being brought about by newcomers.

John Talbot, publisher of the *Missoulian* in Missoula, Montana, says, "There are enclaves of liberalism around the universities. Kids are influenced by the professors and their peers."

The liberalism seeps, sometimes slowly, into the rural areas. If students take over the family ranch or establish a business in a small town, they are apt to become conservative; but if they go to one of the cities—Boulder or Denver, for example—they are apt to remain liberal.

Whatever happens, westerners support the institutions of higher learning, which have grown considerably in the last few decades and are having an enormous cultural, as well as social, impact on the Rocky Mountain region. The University of Wyoming exemplifies the new pride in education. For many years after it was founded in 1886, it was awarded a smaller budget than that allotted for coyote and wolf control. Today it has a physical plant valued at more than $13 million and colleges of agriculture, engineering, and nursing, as well as fine arts.

One problem that students, native-born and non-resident alike, face after they graduate is finding jobs. In 1970 per capita income in Colorado ($4,574) and Nevada ($5,078) was above the national average, but the per capita income of three other states was below average. Montana ranked 35th, for example; Idaho 38th; and Wyoming 29th.

In the growth areas of the Rocky Mountain states, federal money feeds the prosperity. The U.S. Government is the largest single employer in the West. This, in addition to millions in federal funds that have been, and still are, poured into railroads, highways, reclamation projects, the administration of public lands, defense installations, and farm subsidies is some compensation for the large amounts of federally owned land that are exempt from taxes. In Nevada, for example, 86 percent of the land is federally owned; in Colorado, 36 percent; in Utah, two-thirds; in Montana, 30 percent of the land is under federal jurisdiction; in Wyoming, 50 percent; and in Idaho, more than two-thirds. Public ownership of these vast areas is of enormous cultural and economic significance.

In some parts of the Rocky Mountain West, the employment picture is not very bright. Many of the jobs are seasonal, highway construction and farming, for example. The recreation areas of Aspen, Colorado; Sun Valley, Idaho; and Jackson Hole, Wyoming, however, are beginning to publicize year-round activities.

Still there are other problems. In Montana, Wyoming, and Idaho, as well as in certain regions of the other states, the distance from markets, high freight rates, and cold winters discourage manufacturing and encourage the exploitation of natural resources.

Ignorance of the problems of earning a livelihood in

the West is nearly as great today as it was 100 years ago. The two boys who dug the post holes provide one example:

"I'd sure like to stay here," Jim told the woman who hired him. "In Indiana where I lived all you could see were mobile homes—thousands of them."

The boys had driven to Montana in a car. If they failed to find jobs, they could turn to food stamps, relief, and vocational rehabilitation.

"They got it too easy," the rancher snorted to the woman.

But the rancher felt that all the new immigrants have it too easy—the retired school teachers, civil servants, midwestern farmers, the professional men and women, the young people who know little about the immigrants of the past who made the West what it is today. If they did know, they might understand the rancher's resentment. On the other hand, the rancher was guilty of forgetting the dream that drew his grandfather to the Rockies.

During the gold rush, Joe Meek, the scout, was reported to have said: "It's not the high mountains ner great rivers ner hostile Indians that'll give us the most grief; it's . . . every day, rain, hail, cholera, breakdowns, lame mules, sick cows, prairie fires, lost horses, dust storms, alkali water. Seventeen miles every day. . . ."

Seventeen miles a day in a wagon for nearly 2,000 miles. Some immigrants walked. Many of the Mormons pushed hand carts, but they made it because of their trust in God and Country and the strong men who led them.

The pioneers followed the prospectors, who established a tradition of mobility and exploitation of the land. The cattleman and the sodbuster carried on that tradition. Free land was the prize, encouraged by the Homestead Act, enacted in 1862 to provide a market for the growing industrialization of the East. After conducting a topographical study, the explorer and geolo-

gist Major John Wesley Powell told the politicians that 160 acres was insufficient to grow crops in the arid region; as a result the homesteads were enlarged to 350 acres. Ranchers hired cowboys to sign up for homesteads and then bought the land for next to nothing to add to their own holdings. The same deceit was practiced under the Desert Land Act, passed in 1877, which allowed a man to purchase 640 acres for $1.25 an acre.

The lumbermen profited similarly under the Timber and Stone Act:

"Sure," George Weisel, a lumberman, said several years ago: "We all had our men (lumberjacks) prove up on a timber claim, and then we bought it for a dollar an acre and logged it off."

In the early 1900s, the railroads promoted dry land homesteads. More people meant more crops to haul;

253

more timber meant more lumber for freight. So they plowed up the grazing land, until the drought and bank failures of the 1930s slowed the frantic pace. The homesteaders who survived grew strong and silent, sometimes bitter, marked forever by fear of want and determined to guard against it.

One man who remembered those times said, "Ma and Pa had $6,000. When it was over, all they had was a covered wagon and eight kids."

Newcomers often fail to notice the gaunt shells of the sodbusters' homes or the windowless cabins in the mountains. Many do not realize that they are participating in one of the periodic migrations to the Rocky Mountain West. Government census estimates for 1990 predict that only Nevada and Colorado will have appreciable gains in population, with Nevada showing the larger. Utah is expected to gain less than 15 percent; Montana, Idaho, and Wyoming will gain only 5 percent. What the statistics do not show is that the high plains of Montana and Wyoming are expected to de-

Students at the Aspen Music School come from many countries. Between 1945 and his death in 1960, industrialist Walter Paepcke turned Aspen into an international cultural center, founding both the prestigious Aspen Institute for Humanistic Studies and the Aspen Music Festival.

crease in population, while the scenic recreational country west of the Continental Divide in those two states will have an increase. The same might be said for the more fertile areas of Idaho, as compared to the arid, sagebrush country.

One explanation for the census estimates can be found in the sources of income for the Rocky Mountain states, as compiled by the Department of Commerce in 1970.

Colorado is one of the most prosperous of the mountain states. In recent years tourism has developed into a major industry, annually bringing in more than $600 million. Colorado is not only blessed with some of the most spectacular mountain scenery in the United States;

Denver citizens are proud of their colleges, symphony, theaters, and art galleries—including the new Denver Art Museum at right.

it also has a splendid location, which gives the state an economic advantage over other parts of the Rocky Mountain West. Its capital, Denver, is the hub of the railroads, highways, and airlines that spread throughout the region.

Denver has grown from a frontier town of log cabins in the 1860s, when hardly a day passed without a shooting, to a sophisticated urban metropolis. Its buildings are new and modern: the Denver U.S. National Bank Center with its fountains and trout pool; the steel and enamel annex of the historic Brown Palace Hotel; the Civic Center; and Larimer Square, once a ghetto, now a charming area of brick shops, art galleries, and restaurants. A visitor sitting in the lobby of one of Denver's hotels might not see any difference between Denver and other cities—until a man in a big hat and high-heeled boots appears in the crowd.

Denver is like that. It does not pretend to be intellectually avant garde like San Francisco or to be a cosmopolitan giant like New York, but neither is it stodgy. It retains a small-town atmosphere of friendliness and a certain touching naivete that is perhaps left over from the days when mining magnates and cattle barons pursued European titles and rococo architecture.

Denver's citizens are fiercely loyal. John C. Davis, a third generation Denverite in the wholesale drug business, says, "I remember when the Denver Country Club was in the country; now, it's in the middle of the city. We have problems: smog, traffic, but I'd rather live in Denver than anywhere else. Denver is an exciting city; things are happening."

Mr. Rex Jennings, president of the Chamber of Commerce, who lives with his wife Betty in southeast Denver and whose grown children make the city their home, said:

> Denver is a good place to live. It's as simple as that. It's big enough to offer the pleasures of city living—we have a first-rate symphony orchestra and a fine NFL football team. We can watch our own national hockey, baseball, tennis, and basketball teams. Our museums are first-rate, and we have a good theater. At the same time, Denver is still small enough to be pretty informal. It is also small enough to avoid some of the big city problems other cities have. I think that we, as citizens, can guide the direction our community is taking. It all adds up to that indefinable thing called "a good quality of life."

Defense installations and other federal enterprises sparked Denver's growth; among others there is Lowry Air Force Base, the U.S. Mint, Atomic Energy Commission offices, and the Air Force Accounting and Finance Center. In 1972 Denver reported retail sales of $6.3 billion. Texas money promoted the city's real estate. The *Denver Post*, one of the most widely read newspapers of the West, also helped; but the greatest credit must be given Denver's citizens who are both progressive and independent. What other group of people would have turned down the Winter Olympic Games on the grounds of ecology?

In both Montana and Idaho, agriculture brings in the largest share of income. But while agriculture perpetuates a traditional way of life, it cannot support high employment or high wages. This has led to the exploitation of natural resources. A visitor to Butte, Montana, can see immense machines gulping earth in open pit copper mines. In addition to copper, Montana has important reserves of coal, oil, lead, and other minerals. Idaho is another storehouse of natural riches: it leads the nation in the mining of silver, is second in lead, and third in zinc. Both states are important sources of lumber.

What does this mean in terms of people?

A big diesel thundering down a mountain trail with

twenty-five tons of logs, the driver in a hard hat, a new folk hero—skillful, physically able, fearless.

A ranch woman with astonishing blue eyes who hays, fences, helps to calve, breaks horses, cooks, and in the autumn gets her elk for the winter's meat. Her grandson, riding his horse down a steep bank into a stream, slides forward onto the horse's neck:

"What do I do now?"

"What would you do if I weren't here?"

"We're an independent people, a proud people," said a president of the University of Montana.

Wyoming, pictured by myth as the cowboy state, lists mining as its largest source of income; oil and gas, that is, followed by agriculture. In Casper, the sun reflects on the silver tanks of Texaco and cattle graze on the bare, windswept hills. Oil and cattle barons? The inquiry is received with a shrug. Perhaps the explanation lies in Jackson Hole, where the blacksmith's wife rides with the millionaire on a ridge in the Tetons, both contestants in a Competitive Trail Ride. If a horse stumbles, money will not prevent the rider and his mount from plunging over the cliff. Skill as a horseman will, and in that respect, the blacksmith's wife is equal to the millionaire.

Westerners like to believe that all men are equal and that all have equal opportunity.

One young westerner, a thin young man with horn-rimmed glasses, graduated recently from the University of Colorado. During the Depression his grandmother dug potatoes while pregnant with his father. Now the boy plans to be a doctor. He intends to practice in a small town in the West, although he might make more money in some other region of the country. To him, however, the way of life is more important than large fees. There are others who feel as he does.

In Utah there is pride, too. Utah is a manufacturing and mining state with agriculture listed third as a source of income. A visitor, driving through Utah with a van-

load of horses, asked the driver: "Why do Mormon farms look so prosperous?"

It was August and cherries and apples hung red in the orchards along the base of the Wasatch Range. There were melons in the gardens and cattle grazing in honey-colored meadows.

"I guess it's because we're taught to be proud of the land," replied the driver.

Salt Lake City, Utah's capital and Denver's rival as a magnet for job seekers, is more than just western; it is unique as the Mormon capital. Founded by Brigham Young, who cajoled, threatened, and personally assisted hundreds of Latter-Day Saints across the Great Plains, the city retains to this day the mark of that astounding man. Young designed Temple Square to be the city's center. There stand the immense dome of the Tabernacle, the Gothic Assembly Hall, and the sculptures of the Mormon pioneers. The Church of the Latter-Day Saints owns bookstores, mercantile establishments, the Hotel Utah, and many other enterprises.

A visitor can feel the city's vitality. Salt Lake might have remained a religious shrine to the past; instead it has become a center for aerospace firms, for the production of antiaircraft missiles and aircraft navigational systems, for warehousing and distribution, and for medical research at the University of Utah.

Salt Lake, like Denver, has experienced the migration of a new type of businessman who appreciates the quality of life as much as financial opportunity. Gene Gerek is one of these men. In his late thirties, he is president of EPPCO, which produces a new polymer powder coating for food and beverage cans. Mr. Gerek says:

> After traveling extensively throughout the United States, Canada, and Europe and living in Detroit, Pittsburgh, and Chicago, there is no doubt that Salt Lake is the place to live and enjoy life. The excitement of a growing city coupled with scenic beauty that is unbelievable in proximity and variety make a combination that's hard to beat. For example, in April I cut

The Sunday morning concerts of the internationally acclaimed Mormon Tabernacle Choir have been broadcast coast-to-coast from Temple Square in Salt Lake City since 1929.

my lawn, and twenty minutes later, I was skiing on twelve feet of snow. Salt Lake City is an easy place to love.

Nevada, which is predicted to have the Rocky Mountain West's greatest gain in population, lists tourism as its major source of income, most of which is derived from gambling. There is hope among Nevadans that the mining of precious metals will be revived and that great strides will be made in shipping, industry, and outdoor recreation, but in the early 1970s Nevada remained essentially a one-industry state. Some 60 percent of the state's residents make their living off the gaming business.

Nevada, however, is not all slot machines and showgirls and the biggest hotel in the world. There is also the University of Nevada at Reno, which maintains a Desert Research Center; the verdant farmlands between Reno and Carson City; the glittering waters of Lake Tahoe. And there is the Nevada of small communities—mining towns like Ely and Yerington, cowtowns like Elko and Winnemucca, isolated ranches, deserted ghost towns, and violet shadows that lengthen across the lonely miles.

In 1973 the economic picture in the West changed, perhaps as drastically as when gold was discovered in the last century. America now faces an energy crisis, and in the West there are vast reserves of coal and oil that can help solve the problem. In Colorado, Utah, and Wyoming there is enough oil shale, government experts predict, to provide 3 million barrels of oil a day for 600 years; in southeastern Montana and Wyoming there are reserves of low sulfur coal. Colorado also has an $80 million geothermal potential in the San Luis Valley, and the National Science Foundation is already drilling through superheated rock near Helena, Montana.

"The Rocky Mountain states," *Colorado Business*

Magazine reported in the summer of 1974, "are among the hottest in the nation in relation to potential energy development."

Development produces jobs. Workers swarmed into Colstrip, Montana, for example, when Western Energy Corporation began building a coal-fired generating plant. Trailers, mobile homes, and bars quickly appeared.

William Coldiron, vice president and general counsel for the Montana Power Company, one of the principal utilities developing the coal generating plants at Colstrip, pointed out certain advantages of the development: "For many years, raw materials have been taken away from Montana and manufactured. The construction of the coal-fired generating plants will give the state an opportunity to manufacture raw materials here and to export the surplus. It will broaden the tax structure, increase job opportunities, and provide economic advantages."

But Montana ranchers are concerned. According to a study made by the University of Montana Institute for Social Science Research, the ranchers, in academic language, "are disturbed by a shift in the established power structure from the ranchers to the new mining industrialists."

"Newcomers," the report says, "have not been accepted into the established social structure."

It is the old distrust of the trapper for the pioneer, the cattleman for the sodbuster, the modern rancher for long-haired boys who quit work to go swimming. The ranchers feel their way of life is being threatened. Throughout the West ranchers are fighting to maintain their independence in the face of fluctuating cattle prices, inflated operating costs, and shortages of materials.

"People have the wrong impression of ranchers," said Melvin McDowell. "They think all we do is sit on the front porch and watch the money roll in."

McDowell runs 2,000 head of cattle on 15,000 acres of rich bottom land in the Big Hole Valley of southwestern Montana. The Big Hole averages 6,000 feet on the level. In the late autumn sunlight, it is a wide, fawn-colored valley rimmed on the west by the Continental Divide.

"We get a frost nearly every night in the summer," McDowell said. "In the winter it can get down to fifty below zero. We feed from December until the first week in May."

McDowell is lean and dark-haired with the weathered skin and direct eyes of a man who has spent his life outdoors. His wife, Joyce, has modernized their Victorian-style ranch house; an antique walnut rocker sits in the living room by a television set. The kitchen, with all the

Workers are pouring in to build power plants (below) and the boom is on in Wyoming's Sweetwater County. People throughout the Rocky Mountain West fear the boom-and-bust effects of uncontrolled development and are fighting plans of a consortium to exploit vast areas with coal deposits so shallow they could be stripped off in 20 years.

The soil is stripped to expose a 70-foot coal seam in Wyoming. Coal underlies 40% of the state. Area residents have gone to court to reverse federal sale of water rights to utility developers because the water is needed to irrigate rich wheat fields like the one being harvested below in Montana.

latest equipment, opens to a family room. When a visitor walks in, he is greeted with traditional western hospitality: "How about a cup of coffee? Won't you stay for supper?"

The ranch house is surrounded by corrals, barns, sheds, and a bunkhouse. McDowell estimates that he maintains nearly 100 miles of fence and that he puts up 3,000 tons of hay.

"We eat breakfast at 6:30 A.M.; usually it's dark by the time we're finished for the day. Calving time, it's all night for six weeks."

"When we have a real sick calf," Joyce McDowell adds with a smile, "I take it in the truck sixty-five miles to the vet in Dillon."

On a ranch a wife is a working partner.

McDowell calves in April because of the late season in the Big Hole. There are four "hospitals" on the ranch; they have holding corrals, sheltered pens, and a shed with water. Pulling a calf is dirty, bloody work. So is treating a cow with sore teats or handling a critter who won't claim her calf.

Three hired men help McDowell and his son Jock, who is a graduate of Montana Agricultural College and was twice National Intercollegiate Bronc-riding Champion.

McDowell is proud of Jock, who is the third generation of the family on the ranch.

"You have to give kids an incentive," said McDowell. "I've made over a share of the business to Jock." Guiding his pickup over the meadow, he pointed to some fat healthy heifers—Hereford and Hereford-Angus cross: "Those ear tags are Jock's idea; each color means the type of vaccine given to the animal."

"The only way kids can get into ranching today," observed McDowell, "is the way Jock's doing it. If he had to buy land and stock, he'd need half a million just for land and another quarter million for stock and machinery. Then he would need operating capital."

Wagon driver hauls fodder for the cattle at the Snake River Ranch in Wyoming.

"The rancher's caught in a price squeeze," McDowell continued. "For example, barbed wire that cost $12 a roll last year costs $38 now. That big machine that we use for feeding: it cost $22,000 a couple of years ago. It's gone up $5,000 or $6,000. Wages are up, but even so you can hardly get a man. A young fellow who was helping us quit to work for a construction firm. Know what he's getting? Eighty dollars a day and $100 a day on weekends. Ranchers can't compete with that kind of money."

At the end of October, 1974, McDowell sold 900 head of steers and heifers. He was lucky that year; he saw daylight while many ranchers suffered losses.

Asked the reason for the low price of cattle and the high price of meat in the supermarket, McDowell replied: "Two things, as I see it. There are too many cattle. A lot of business and professional men have bought cattle and land, which has driven up the price. When times get tough, they unload the cattle and the price goes down. People like that shouldn't be in the cattle business. Another reason for high meat prices—one for which the rancher is not to blame—is the high cost of feed and transportation."

As McDowell looked across the meadows tufted with willows where the cattle shelter during winter storms, he shook his head: "I don't know. We were lucky when

Cattle drive in Montana moves Herefords to new pastures. The short, sun-cured grass on the seemingly barren land of the Rocky Mountain West once supported millions of buffalo. Today, ranchers, environmentalists, and new political leaders are fighting to preserve some of the country's richest grazing land.

our Dad died. He had made provisions to pass the ranch on, but times like this are more difficult. Jock, as a working stockholder, will be able to carry on, but there are ranchers in other parts of the West who are less fortunate. With inheritance and gift taxes so high, the younger generation often loses its incentive."

McDowell was silent for a moment; then he said: "I'm not good with words, but what I'm talking about is more than money. This ranch and the way we live—we want to keep it."

Ranchers are proud men, independent, sometimes intolerant. They distrust not only the coal and oil companies but also the ecologists who are helping them preserve their land against strip mining.

Ecologists are new to the Rockies, and while their aim is to protect the land, they threaten one of the most valued traditions of the West: the belief that a man has a right to do what he wants with his property. To the westerner the building of dams, the blasting for ore in the belly of the mountains, the cry of "Timber!" as a tree crashes in the forest is man's victory over nature; it is a symbol of his virility.

This attitude on the part of native westerners has been as much to blame for abuse of the land as exploitation by out-of-state corporations. Newcomers who have seen what has happened in other parts of the nation have sounded the alarm against the evils of unrestricted development and have lobbied for legislation to protect the environment. Aided by the Sierra Club and the Wilderness Association, they have worked for the curtailment of clear-cut logging, which leaves forested mountains gouged to raw earth, eroded, treeless. The Forest Service lists timber as a crop and speaks of harvesting—a euphemism, since it takes a pine 150 years to grow to a decent size in the arid Rockies, as compared to 75 years on the Pacific Coast. But when logging is curtailed, the schools and roads receive less tax money from timber sales; unemployment rises in the forested

regions; and the wood products industry brings pressure to bear on the Forest Service.

Conservationists have also worked for land use planning, which, like logging, has an economic impact on the region.

"People are looking for cheap land," said a real estate agent who works in Hamilton, Montana. "They start in Colorado and come north, but there's no cheap land left. An acre that sold for $150 ten years ago now sells for $1,500."

Ecologists claim that good land use policy is economically advantageous, especially in regard to tourism, which is growing in importance. As the population expands in the United States, the unspoiled areas of the West attract increasing numbers of people. They come to ride the wilderness trails along the snow and rocks of the timberline; to feel the tug of a cut-throat on a line cast into a pool as green as a zircon from glacier snow; to thrill to a rubber raft tossing in white water.

Westerners who once thought of the land solely in terms of its capacity to produce today are finding more enduring values in their region and are discovering a pride in their heritage. They are building museums, such as the Museum of the Plains Indians in Browning, Montana, which has outstanding dioramas of the Blackfeet, and the Whitney Museum of Western Art in Cody, Wyoming, that displays paintings by Charles Russell and Frederic Remington. They are restoring ghost towns and frontier army posts and encouraging regional crafts and literature.

Until recently, westerners displayed their art at country fairs, and there the visitor can still glimpse the rural West in the displays of preserved fruits, angel food cakes, fancy quilts, watercolors, and flower arrangements. At the same time, young artists are winning recognition for working in new mediums. Grants for the arts have helped to fund symphonies in towns such as Missoula, Montana, and Laramie, Wyoming, while

repertory theaters bring Genet and Arthur Miller to high school gymnasiums. The Utah Symphony has played in Carnegie Hall, and the University of Utah has an outstanding ballet and modern dance program. Still, most westerners prefer Charlie Russell's cowboys to modern art. As for literature, the books of Bernard DeVoto, Wallace Stegner, and A. B. Guthrie, which depict the Old West, remain best sellers.

New fads are not of great importance in the West. The westerner, if asked, is apt to reply that he likes Frederic Remington, not as an art expert once said, because of a "sick nostalgia for the past" but because Remington knew how to paint a horse.

As for Indian crafts, they are not as important to the culture of the northern tribes as they are to the Navajos of the Southwest. The northern Plains Indians excelled in basketware and in bead designs on buckskin. Such work, however, requires more skill and patience than many young Indians are willing to give.

"Culture?" said Gary Kimball, a young Gros Ventre lawyer and a member of the Montana legislature. "The Indians have no Plains culture, only a reservation culture."

Historically, the greatest foe of the Indian has not been the military but the federal government, which in the late 1800s succumbed to railroad, cattle, and mining interests and ordered the Indians confined to reservations. There, robbed of their identity as warriors, they lapsed into objects of charity, subject to government subsidy.

Not until the late 1960s did the western tribes, inspired by the civil rights movement, seek to reassert their pride as Indians—no easy task, for the tribes in the old days fought among themselves oftener than they fought the whites; and jealousies disrupted attempts at organization.

In the six Rocky Mountain states, there are twenty-one reservations, excluding the Nevada colonies, which comprise only a few acres. These reservations have problems in common—high unemployment, as much as 57 percent at Fort Belknap, Montana, among the Assiniboin and the Gros Ventre. Indeed, according to Alvin M. Josephy, Jr., author of Red Power, the annual income for Indians is a thousand dollars lower than that of the average black family. Life expectancy is sixty-three years, as compared to seventy years for other Americans. Alcoholism is acute. The school dropout rate is 50 percent.

The Indians of the Rocky Mountain states want self-determination; they want to bring industries to the reservations, to update the tribal courts, and to clarify rights to timber, minerals, and water.

Slowly but surely, the Indians' situation is improving. Through federal grants, new houses and schools are being built and public health facilities expanded. At the University of Montana, as well as other institutions in the West, Indian Studies programs, which provide scholarships and counseling, have been instituted.

Thus in many ways the Indians of the Rocky Mountain West are at last regaining their identity. Still they have a long way to go. One major problem, which affects blacks and Mexican-Americans as well as Indians, is that they form only a small minority of the region's population.

The majority of the Mexican-Americans in the Rocky Mountain West live in southern Colorado, and like the Indians, most are in the low income group. Recently, however, there have been attempts to provide them with better schooling, housing, and job opportunities. This is also the case in regard to the blacks. In 1970, Colorado had 66,411 blacks, the majority of whom lived in and around Denver. On the other end of the scale, Wyoming listed only 2,130 blacks.

In the rural areas there are few blacks. In Fairplay, Colorado, there was only one black family, and the woman was elected mayor. When reporters interviewed

New faces in Colorado politics include (at left) Governor Richard Lamm, the 40-year-old environmentalist who defeated the incumbent Republican, and (at right) 36-year-old Senator Gary Hart, who was George McGovern's campaign manager in 1972. Hart also defeated an incumbent Republican.

the townspeople about the election, most replied that they did not think of the mayor as a black but as an individual who could do the job.

This does not mean that westerners are more tolerant than people in other parts of the United States. It means that minorities have not been a problem and, more important, that westerners tend to vote for the person, not for the party. This confounds pollsters and results in surprising bursts of liberalism, such as the first law for women's suffrage, passed in Wyoming in 1888; the election in Montana of the first congresswoman; and the legalization of abortion in Colorado. Environmentalists have also won an increasing number of victories in the Rocky Mountain states; in 1974, for example, Colorado elected Richard Lamm, who led the campaign against bringing the 1976 Winter Olympics to that state, as governor and sent another liberal conservationist, Gary Hart, to the U.S. Senate.

In all but the heavily populated areas, the constituents know the candidates for office. Thus a senator is greeted on the streets with "Hi, Mike" or "Hi, Frank."

Candidates running for office still make door-to-door calls, shake hands at the Post Office and supermarket, attend coffees at suburban homes, and give talks in high school gymnasiums.

The familiarity with candidates results in the assumption that the people have a say in what goes on at the state capital. During legislative sessions, which are annual in all the states except Wyoming, Nevada, and Montana, people will visit the capital to express an opinion to a representative, to testify before a committee, or merely to watch. Legislators may introduce constituents. "Mr. Speaker, we have with us today the junior class of ———."

Traditionally, the West has elected conservatives to local offices but sent liberal Democrats to Congress on the basis that Democrats are more proficient at acquiring the federal funds necessary to the western economy.

This is a delicate matter, since the West lacks influence in Washington. Altogether, the six Rocky Mountain states have only thirteen representatives in Congress, while California alone has forty-three. For this reason, Dr. Frank Jonas of the University of Utah feels that the West does not have the vote to determine its own destiny. On the other hand, the energy crisis, which has focused attention on the West's reserves of oil and coal, may bring about a change. As former Governor John Vanderhoof of Colorado said at the Western Governors' Conference in 1974: "I think we'll begin to play a much more important role on the national level than we have. They've got to listen to us."

The same reasons that prompt westerners to participate actively in politics prompts them to take part in community affairs—schools, cultural activities, conservation, zoning, crime prevention.

Dale Dye, Ravalli County sheriff in western Montana, said, "If people see a crime being committed in rural areas, they'll try to prevent it, or they'll report it. They aren't afraid of becoming involved."

"I think people are tougher, more stoical in the West," said a medical student. "They don't expect much, and they don't complain."

Few people born in the Rockies want to live elsewhere. Dee Park, the cowboy foreman of the Bitterroot Stock Farm, expressed his feelings about the crowds of New York after a brief visit to that metropolis: "I'd rather be home in a corral full of cows."

Sometimes, as people grow older, they move to warmer climates; but on the whole, westerners' roots go deep. They have grown up with, accepted, and modified the American Dream. As for the new immigrants, the myth of the Rocky Mountain West is as bright as when the first wagons rolled across the plains. The West offers what they are seeking—freedom for the individual and yet the feeling of belonging to a community.

—VIRGINIA WEISEL JOHNSON

The Cowboy:
American folk hero

It takes a rugged, independent sort of man to ride the range in a snowstorm. There is little romance and less glamour in the cowboy's job—and there are many easier ways to earn a living. But there is still a special breed of men who wouldn't trade the hardships of life in the big country for the comfort and confinement that is acceptable to the rest of us. It's a matter of simple, basic values. The cowboy derives a certain satisfaction from the fact that he copes with the elements in a hard land, with nothing more than a horse and a rope to help him. And above all else, it is probably a matter of pride—pride in doing a tough job skillfully and well.

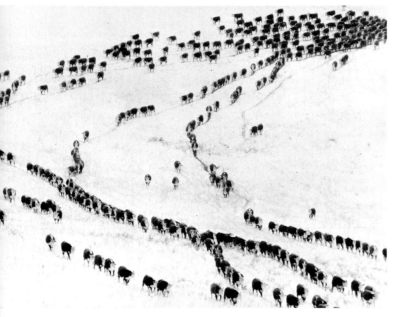

Hunched against the snow in his slicker, the rider at right drives a Montana herd 12 miles to the nearest shipping pens.

Ranchers in Montana (above) and Wyoming (below) get supplementary food supplies to their cattle—using horse-drawn sleds when trucks can't get through.

The cattle must be fed during periods of heavy snow because they will starve rather than paw through the snow to get at the grass. Ranchers try to harvest enough grain and hay—it takes at least a ton of hay in reserve per head—to carry their herds through until spring. Thirty-foot drifts sometimes isolate ranches and stock; people in Wyoming and Montana still talk about the blizzards of 1887, which wiped out 90% of some herds. In late March, with snow still blanketing the drop pastures, cowhands at the Padlock Ranch in Wyoming work 14 hours a day for up to six weeks without a day off. They ride hourly patrols to drive two-year-old heifers into the calving sheds and to pick up calves dropped in the snow before they freeze to death.

Weary cowboys warm up around a small fire while eating the hot stew brought to them by a pickup truck from ranch headquarters.

Rounding up the cattle and branding the calves is a dusty, sweaty job. Each one-to-two-month-old calf is roped, wrestled to the ground, branded, inoculated, and dehorned; the males are castrated. Some of the big ranches still run horse-drawn chuck wagons and provide tents for their hands at branding time in the spring. Others do their branding at ranch headquarters.

A thin wisp of smoke (at left), the acrid smell of burning hide—and another bawling calf is marked with the distinctive brand of its owner.

The Nevada cowboy (at right) hunkers down for a mug of coffee. Old hands say the brew should be tested with a horseshoe—it isn't fit to drink unless the shoe floats.

The days of the great trail drives are past
and even the cattle are gentler than the self-sufficient longhorns that once roamed the unfenced countryside. Cowmen on
modern ranches head for the roundup in trucks, towing their
saddled mounts behind them in trailers. Piper Cubs, helicopters,
motorcycles, snowmobiles, and the ubiquitous pickup
speed the work—and cut the need for skilled hands in half. But
the cowboys who work the cattle today, like the old-timers, are
proud, tough, and self-reliant. Most of them work for wages and
a few own spreads like the one at right, in the shadow of Colorado's
Sangre de Cristo mountains. But all of them share a way of
life that remains unique—a life that has stamped their weather-
beaten faces with the mark of individualists and free men.

Western Wonderland: adventure for all

For millions of urban Americans who prefer doing to viewing, a vacation in the Rockies is the fulfillment of a long-held dream. Whole families take to the road in summer with their campers and tents. In winter, the experts schuss the deep powder that blankets the heights, and visiting easterners—accustomed to well-packed "boiler plate"—lose their dignity but not their good humor on their first runs down the mountain. Nearly 8 million ski buffs lavish more money on skiing than is spent on any other sport. For travel agents, clothing designers, equipment manufacturers, real estate speculators, and resort owners, skiing is big business. The great ski resorts—such as Aspen, Vail, and Snowmass in Colorado; Sun Valley in Idaho; Alta and Snowbird in Utah; Jackson Hole in Wyoming; and Big Sky in Montana—are mainstays of the economies of the mountain states.

Hot-dogging—the "in" thing for young skiers—is a new form of stunt skiing that sometimes results in serious injuries. The trio below actually holds hands during an unbelievable back flip.

Summer visitors explore the mountain states in search of high adventure—or simply to escape the confinement of teeming cities. Experienced hikers in sturdy boots shrug into their backpacks and head for the wilderness in twos and threes. City folk in city clothes band together by the busload to tour the mountains in air-conditioned comfort. The weary crowd trudging down the trail (facing page) look somewhat out of place in Utah's Bryce Canyon National Park, but at least they are getting a glimpse of a world they would never have seen on their own. For those who have more time—and more money— there are dude ranches where suburban youngsters brought up on TV westerns can try their hands at something resembling the real thing. The food served after a trail ride at the Lazy U Dude Ranch in Colorado (top right) is something to write home about. Privately owned vacation resorts siphon off some of the summer visitors, but not enough to ease the jam in the country's 38 national parks. The park system is currently fighting a losing battle to accommodate 217 million vacationers who clog roads and crowd facilities which, in 1960, attracted only 79 million.

Adventurous visitors ride the rapids of the Colorado with professional guides, buoyed by huge rubber pontoons—the type used by the army to build pontoon bridges. Most trips last a week or more and the passengers make camp every night by the water's edge.

Legalized casino gambling is the biggest attraction for most of the 20 million tourists who visit Nevada every year. Luxury hotels on the Strip at Las Vegas can afford to offer big-name spectaculars (below) at reasonable prices because they recoup their losses in casinos that never close. Proper housewives of uncertain age (at left, above) tend to prefer the slots. They sit for hours, pumping coins into two machines at a time in the hope of hitting a jackpot (at right, above). Their husbands usually congregate at the crap tables or try their luck at blackjack. Gambling odds are better in Nevada than in states where games are illegal and unlicensed, but few visitors manage to come out ahead.

Minimum bets are lower in the downtown Casino Center (above) than on the Strip. The play at the roulette table (below) is heavy, with most of the stacks of chips bet straight up for possible payoffs of 35 to 1.

Rodeo—the most American of sports—has come a long way from its beginning in the days of the open range when cowboys would get together at the end of the roundup to show off their skills and place a few bets. Working cowboys still compete but most champions are professionals who spend their young lives on the circuit. The 3,500 members of the Rodeo Cowboys Association risk their necks in some 600 rodeos, held in 42 states and Canada and attracting more than 10 million spectators. The 1974 All Around Champion was Tom Ferguson, a 24-year-old star who earned his spurs in the Intercollegiate Rodeo Association.

Fence riders (at left) are dressed to kill, as is the contestant adjusting his boots (above). The bareback bronc rider in Red Lodge, Montana, (at right) clings to the flank strap in an effort to stay on for the required eight seconds.

Danger is the common denominator in rodeo—a sport that is harder on men than on animals. Broken bones and cracked vertebrae are routine— Larry Mahan, All Around Champion more often than anyone else, rode in one event in a plaster cast after having broken his foot in another. The rider sent crashing to the ground by the angry saddle bronc below might have broken his neck—in 1974 one contestant died and 260 were seriously injured in the arena. But there is never a shortage of rodeo entrants—in recent years there actually have been too many seeking to ride in the bigger rodeos. Danger poses an irresistible challenge to such men—they become almost obsessed with doing what other men cannot or dare not do.

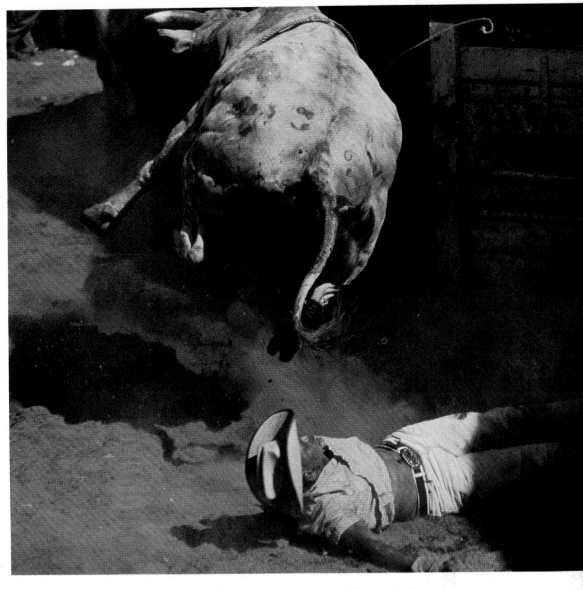

The bucked-down bull rider (above) has only seconds to get up and dive for the barrier. Brahmas are the most dangerous of rodeo animals because they usually try to gore and trample fallen riders.

The bulldogger (below) is attempting the final maneuver in steer wrestling—the art of leaping from a galloping horse, hooking an elbow around the horns of a half-ton steer, and digging in boot heel to stop the animal before wrestling him over onto his side.

Southwest – Cultures in Contrast 6

The Southwest is a land of extremes. In many ways the most American of all regions, it is yet the most alien. Somehow, one's first impression of the Southwest is that it has not fully joined the rest of the nation: it seems to have retained a separate character, to have somehow resisted complete assimilation. And yet despite its "foreignness," the Southwest is intensely, indisputably American. The residents of Texas, Oklahoma, New Mexico, and Arizona are proudly patriotic—proud of their heritage, proud of their country—and brashly confident about their importance to America's future.

Still the Southwest *is* different. We find there not leafy woodlands and green grass watered by ample rainfall but red and tan landscapes blasted by sunlight and etched by wind. Not towns lining roads that give way finally to concatenated metropolises but vast and open space out of which burst immense cities with the passion of an oil strike or a newly bloomed oasis. Not a diversity of cultures struggling to function as one but three coexisting peoples each of which asserts its own character.

Perhaps the land has shaped the people. Or perhaps the intensity with which the people have developed their own strengths and resources has been forced upon them by the intensity of the land. Either way, any artist desiring to portray the character of the people—from the hogan-dwelling Navajo to the Chicano farmer and the wheeler-dealer in Houston's Astrodome—could do so only against a canvas of canyon-creased outlands and turquoise sky.

Northern New Mexico is one place where the region's three cultures meet. Here in the course of a single memorable day, a visitor may go from the beam-and-adobe serenity of a Pueblo Indian village to the Hispanic grandeur of the Palace of Governors built at Santa Fe in 1610, then to the dramatic flame-out of the New York-owned natural gas company near Gallup.

One might also hear the oft-quoted answer of an Indian who was asked if he spoke Spanish and English as well as his own language. "You know what we say?" he replied. "When we're friendly, we speak Indian. When we're a little mad, we speak Anglo. And when we're angry, we speak Spanish!"

Indeed the three ways of life dance together in the sun, but they don't mix. And they suffer in different ways from the explosions that have rocked the land in the three decades since World War II: the scientific explosion triggered by the testing of the atomic bomb in New Mexico in 1945; the population explosion brought about by the millions who moved to the oil-rich territory for jobs; and the cultural explosion of the southwestern spirit as it has flowered into diverse life styles and art forms. Suddenly the region, once dismissed as irreclaimable desert, has the allure and vitality to attract executives to Houston, physicists to Albuquerque, ballet stars to Tulsa.

In popular eyes, it has been a change from Cowtown to Glamour City. In the minds of writers and intellectuals, the change has been rather more profound. Dreading what might happen to *Our Southwest*, Erna Fergusson wrote in 1940:

> The arid Southwest has always been too strong, too indomitable for most people. . . . Those who can stand it have had to learn that man does not modify this country; it transforms him, deeply. Perhaps our generation will come to appreciate it as the country God remembered and saved for man's delight when he could mature enough to understand it. . . . The Southwest can never be remade into a landscape that produces bread and butter. But it is infinitely productive of the imponderables so much needed by a world weary of getting and spending.

More than oil or minerals or gas, sunlight is the

Southwest's true wealth, just as water—or the lack of it—is its scourge. As a matter of scientific fact, the high altitude and pollution-free air makes the atmosphere of the Southwest more receptive to solar rays. But clean air draws tourists, and tourists force change.

The English visitor, J. B. Priestley, bore poetic witness to that change. At first, after exploring the "wonderland" of northern Arizona ("the Grand Canyon, the Painted Desert, and all the rest, not excluding the remote Rainbow Bridge"), he spoke of the "perfect winter climate, sunlit and warm all day, cool at night, under a blaze of stars." He pictured the saguaro cacti, which dominate the desert hillsides, as "visitors from some other planet"; he hymned the pure, magical air, "the amethyst peaks" of the mountains, the "dark canyons and rocks fantastically colored by sunlight." Then, returning thirty years later, in the 1970s, he saw the great changes tourism had caused: "It is southern California and Florida all over again, if on a smaller scale." But ultimately he perceived that the Southwest remained unique in form and in spirit: "There was too much defiant wilderness for it to be ruined yet or for a long while to come."

The changing and the unchanging coexist not only in the dramatic contrast of "defiant wilderness" next to burgeoning cities but also in the deeper, philosophical differences that separate the cultures of the region. Of the triad of cultures that have shaped the Southwest, two are on the side of conservation and continuity: the Spanish and the Indian. The "Anglo" preference for swift action and for experiment prevails beyond contest in Oklahoma and Texas. These two states pair in similarity against the twin states of New Mexico and Arizona, where one can see the undeniable truth of Frank Waters's observation that just as the Atlantic Seaboard acknowledges English culture as its mother symbol, the Southwest acknowledges Mexico as its fatherland. For their part, Arizona and New Mexico tend to shun any sense of brotherhood with big, boastful Texas and its friend, Oklahoma. "Go home, Texas" is still a standard greeting to visitors with a Texas license plate when they cross over into "The Land of Enchantment" or "The Place Where the Sun Spends the Winter."

In a sense, dramatically opposed contrast is the real signature of the Southwest: desert and oasis, flat plains and towering mountains, subhumid and arid land blooming into gardens thanks to great dams and underground artesian wells. A country in which space used to seem even the poorest man's wealth, it has now become so cluttered with tourist resorts and new residents that land prices in certain areas have increased a thousandfold in less than two decades. An inland, water-deprived territory in the past, the Southwest now sparkles with large and beautiful lakes and has converted landlocked Tulsa into a port with ship channel and river traffic operating down the Arkansas and Mississippi rivers 900 miles to the sea.

What the three contrasting cultures in the Southwest have in common—after sunlight—is a land that conditions life more decisively than is generally true of the rest of the nation. It is usually thought of in terms of sun and space and silence. But it is also a harsh and rugged land, intermittently beautiful, a land that, to quote Texas's Brush Country philosopher J. Frank Dobie, "you often curse in presence and bless in absence."

It is a land whose subterranean wealth, in oil and gas, uranium and coal, has greatly benefited the ambitious, energetic, aggressive Anglo culture (and also fortunate Indian tribes in Arizona and Oklahoma) far more than the surface wealth has benefited the region. Outlanders tend to think in terms of "cattle kingdoms," and these do exist; but small ranching, farming, and sheepherding have been the major economic life styles of the southwestern population throughout history, of the Anglos as well as the Indians and the Spanish-Americans.

"The moment I saw the brilliant, proud morning shine high up over the deserts . . . something stood still in my soul and I started to attend," wrote British author D. H. Lawrence, describing the mystic hold the American Southwest exerts over the millions who visit the region each year. They come to see magnificent natural wonders such as the Grand Canyon, viewed through Limestone Arch at left, to cavort in dazzling sunlight and warm water at winter resorts like Camelback Inn near Phoenix (below), or to try ski resorts only an afternoon's drive away from scorched desert.

Living in harmony with nature has long been the Pueblo way. As author Paul Horgan notes: They "ordered the propriety of life to the landscape that surrounded them. Their sacred beliefs . . . recognized the power, nearness, and blaze of the sky; the colors of the earth; the sweep of the mountain; the eternity of the river." Kachinas, or spirits (symbolized by the dolls below), helped guide them.

It is the Southwest's vast surface space that has been the real wealth of the Indians who settled the area centuries ago. The traditional Indian religious feeling, in which a unitary sense of spirit animates everything contained in earth and sky, binds the believer into a natural rhythm with his universe, into harmony with the land, no matter how arid and difficult it might be. Once holy places to the gods were built on high mesas and mountains; dwellings were carved out of the cliffs on the way up to the places of worship; farms were cultivated in the valleys below. Corn was life's principal nourishment. It became a fetish in the religious sense, and so remains. As the infant Indian is laced to his cradle-board, giving him forever a flat head structure in back, an ear of corn is placed beside him, a symbol of life's continuity and of its source in nature. In this ritualized worship of a fundamental harmonic rhythm in tribal life, the Indian is a philosopher of the eternal and the unchanging and the basically religious core of all life. He has the serenity and the strength of an individual who finds meaning in living, a meaning shared by the whole community.

The Indian religious spirit seeks harmony and identity with the processes of nature—in sacred masks and dances and rites, as well as in daily life. The religion nurtures a society in which each individual is "absorbed" into a communal and collective pattern.

The Pueblo Indians' sacred kivas, where their reli-

Once they were cliff-dwellers like the people who lived in the caves (below) along New Mexico's Gila River; now they live in man-made villages (left). But the change in setting matters little; in most Pueblo villages, the old ways still prevail.

gion is handed down from old to young, symbolize the womb of the universe. From the union of the Earth-Mother and the Sun God emerged the Indian race. Within the kiva are kept the sacred truths, guarded as the eternal source. From the kiva emerge the male dancers for the great ceremonies to induce rain, fertility, and harvest. Their trained fleet feet beat symbolically the seeds of growth and life into the welcoming and passive earth. These religious dances have the sanction and structure of immemorial tradition, transmitted from generation to generation.

No matter how desperate his economic situation, the religion-sustained Indian has a survival strength that has been astounding. Consider this Navajo prayer:

> Now with a god I walk,
> Now I step across the summits of the
>   mountains.
> Now with a god I walk,
>   Striding across the foothills.
> Now on the old age trail, now on the
>   path of beauty wandering,
> In beauty—Hozoji, hozoji, hozoji-i.

Of course, many of the Indians have discovered other kinds of beauty, the kinds the Anglos seek, material beauties in general. And not merely the individuals who leave the tribes but, of late, leaders within the Tribal Council. The Navajos, for example, have produced expert bankers, and they own possibly the largest bank in Phoenix. In many other ways, they have "gone modern." Once impoverished, living on land nobody else wanted (but finding it beautiful nonetheless), the Navajo tribe is today learning lessons in Anglo enterprise and the use of power.

The Navajos number about 140,000, living on 25,000 square miles in Arizona and a part of New Mexico. It is still conventional for small family hogans, or mud-brick and stick dwellings, looking like adobe

igloos, to house three generations of a family. Thus it has been for a thousand years and more, each family with its little herd of sheep, each family surviving on its own (with perhaps a small subsidy from the Bureau of Indian Affairs).

A few signs of modern life are evident: organized schooling in usually distant schoolhouses, modern stoves, pickup trucks, even coin laundries scattered here and there. Yet the food staple remains "fry bread" (or "squaw bread" as Texans call it). Made from flour and water with a touch of baking powder and salt, it is fried in heavy, sizzling lard. Despite the mode of preparation, fry bread is unbelievably light.

Corn is the staff of life of the rural Navajo sheepherders. Unlike Anglo consumption of corn, the Indian use of the plant, the whole plant, starts soon after its springtime sprouting. It is eaten green, after the plant is boiled, whenever it reaches stripling size—about two feet. Soon after that, the stalk must be discarded, being too tough to taste good. The Navajo still cooks or roasts the corn ears in an earthen pit, whose interior is first warmed by a fire that heats the earth thoroughly. The corn-filled pit is then covered with hot earth and another fire is built on top of that. Corn ground on the *metate* (usually a lava-rock bowl with shallow rim) is used in many ways, as bread in the form of *tortillas* or as "sandwich bread" in the form of *tamales*. The rich hot seasoning of chile peppers offers a range of strength to the point where, according to the old saying, you eat the pepper and then "vice versa."

The Navajo pantry is usually an earthen storage pit; for winter needs it is stocked with dried corn, dried melons, dried squash. When possible, peaches from the orchards are dried and conserved (Indians also love canned fruit, when they have enough money ahead to afford it). They value goat meat as much as mutton, and run goats with their sheep herds. When deer can be had, venison is a favorite food. The Indian shares a worldwide enthusiasm for one Anglo-American specialty, bottled drinks or soda pop, bought at the trading store.

The New York Times recently interviewed a Navajo woman, Alice B. Yazzie, about her family's food and health ways. She replied that they ate one big meal a day—beans, rice, and meat (lamb or mutton from their own flock, or pork or beef from the trading post). The food is cooked on an iron stove whose exhaust pipe juts out through the mud roof of the hogan. In that single room Mrs. Yazzie keeps house for a family of twelve. Four people sleep on the two beds; the others sleep on sheepskins thrown on the earth floor at night.

"Indians use sagebrush to treat colds," the translator reports after talking with Mrs. Yazzie. The herb smells like mentholatum when pinched. Sickness may also prompt a 100-mile drive to the particularly powerful medicine man at Window Rock, Arizona, where the Navajos have a hospital. Medicine men nearer the family's mesa dwelling may use a combination of herbs and native psychiatry. Their role as religious leaders continues to give them an important place in modern Navajo society.

Like the Indians, the Spanish-Americans, who began entering the territory in the late 1500s, were profoundly religious and appreciative of the land. These settlers in the communities of New Spain were isolated in time and space from the mother culture; they retained much of it, but they enlarged it, too, with Indian lore and knowledge. Today the temptation to adopt the speed and convenience of Anglo ways entices many of their descendants, but others refuse to change basic values.

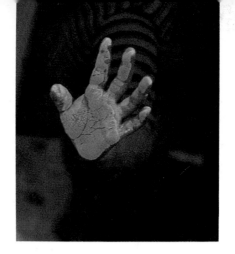

Half of all Mexican-Americans, the second
largest minority group in the U.S.A., live
in Texas, New Mexico, and Arizona. Their
culture has made a lasting imprint on the
Southwest, but a large percentage of the
people earn less than $3,000. Recently, however,
Chicano activists have made some headway
in gaining more political power, better
education and income for their people.
Right and left, Mexican-American father
and son try their hands at carpentry.

The refusal, because of an innate love of manners and
ceremony, remains polite but is still stubbornly strong.

A great difference, however, between the life of the
rural Spanish-Americans and the Indians concerns the
role of women in the culture. Indian custom is matri-
lineal; Spanish-American is patriarchal. Family continuity in Indian life is preserved through the mother's
name, and the rules of inheritance operate through her
rather than through the father's line. Her relatives take
over the education and upbringing of the children. In
the Spanish-American tradition, male, or machismo,

ways still prevail; the man is treated as a lord, at least
officially.

"She always defers to her husband," the psychologist
Robert Coles, author of *The Old Ones*,[1] writes of an
old Spanish woman whom he met in rural Cordova,
New Mexico, and whom he admired for her distinctive
and noble way of life. "She will not speak until he has
had his say. As the two of them approach a closed door,
she makes a quick motion toward it, opens it, and
stands holding it, and sometimes, if he is distracted by a
conversation and is slow to move through, one of her
hands reaches for his elbow while the other points. 'Go
now,' is the unstated message, 'so that I can follow.' "

The woman, Mrs. Domingo Garcia, told Coles of the
quiet perseverance with which she and her husband
lead their humble lives. She also described the difficulty
of maintaining their own way in the face of the all-
pervasive Anglo culture.

> You bend with the wind. And Anglo people are
> a strong wind. They want their own way; they
> can be like a tornado, out to pass over everyone
> as they go somewhere. I don't mean to talk out
> of turn. There are Anglos who don't fit my
> words. But we are outsiders in a land that is
> ours. We are part of an Anglo country, and that
> will not change.

She prefers not to think of herself and her family as
"Chicanos," which is the term used by the youthful
activists of her people. She feels that the term seems to
make her belong less to this country. And that it encourages divisiveness. Instead she emphasizes that she
and her husband "belong to this country and to no
other, and we owe allegiance to the State of New
Mexico."

Most of all she belongs to the land and to the daily
round of her farmer's work. Collecting and arranging
the eggs, smelling the earth scents carried by the wind,

Preserving traditional ways, a Mexican-American family in
Glen Dale, Ariz., breaks the piñata, a decorated pottery
jar filled with fruits, candies, and gifts, as part of the
Christmas festivities.

[1] From THE OLD ONES (Univ. of New Mexico Press) by Robert Coles. Originally in *The New Yorker.*

working the dough for her hot bread—those are the tasks that tax her strength and that return strength to her. The constants in her life are the church and the hills:

The mountains, our mountains—I look at them when I need an anchor. They are here. They never leave us. Birds come, stay awhile, leave. The moon is here, then gone. Even the sun hides from us for days on end. Leaves don't last, or flowers. We have had a number of dogs, and I remember them in my prayers. But those mountains are *here*. They are nearer God than we are. Sometimes I imagine Him up there, on top of one or another mountain, standing over us, getting an idea how we're doing. It is wrong to think like that, I know. But a poor old woman like me can be allowed her foolishness. Who is without a foolish hope? Who doesn't make up dreams to fit his wishes? Sometimes I walk up toward the mountains. I can't go as far now as before. I don't tell my husband I'm going; he would worry that I'd lose my breath completely

and no one would be around. But I go slowly, and, as I say, I have to be content with approaching those hills.

Going slowly is not the Anglo way. From the "roughnecks" on the Texas oil rigs to the intense astronomers at Kitt Peak awaiting the latest word from outer space, the most newly arrived denizens of the Southwest like their action fast as a rodeo and big as the Astrodome.

Of course not all of them actually make it big, rough and ready though they may be. Travelers tell of finding a left-behind prospector near Tombstone, Arizona (that haunted town whose lively newspaper was called *The Epitaph*); when his teeth began to rot, he pulled them out himself one by one with mechanic's pliers. They also tell of Widow Schubert who built a new house west of Canyon City, Texas, in President Lyndon Johnson's Baptist-churched countryside. Long past eighty and still working hard on her old farm nearby, she thought she'd better move away from the place when her husband died. Away from the chickens—for whom she would regularly collect slop from the town's

Lawless Tombstone, the Arizona town they said was "too tough to die," lives on in the memory of tourists who come to see the O.K. Corral (left), scene of the controversial battle fought by the Earp brothers and Doc Holliday against the Clanton gang, and Boot Hill Cemetery (right), end of the line for many gunslingers, gamblers, and outlaws.

(on grave marker) HERE LIES LESTER MOORE FOUR SLUGS FROM A .44 NO LES NO MORE

restaurants—away from the weedy cotton patch, and away from the sagging old porch and the yellowed wallpaper. Into the new house with its all-electric kitchen, wall-to-wall carpets, and central air conditioning. But then she decided not to move. She'd rather sweat and live with the memories in each creaking board.

Lots of the Anglos do make it, however. That's why they ventured into the Southwest in the first place. Traditionally they came in order to forget a failed past or to find Eldorado. On the crest of "manifest destiny" the early settlers moved into the vast territory, brushing aside the weak government of Mexico and ignoring the old doctrines of Spain. It was soon all theirs by right of might. Even the red men, even those herded into what was first known as "Indian Territory" (but subsequently rechartered as the State of Oklahoma), finally had to cede that the English-speaking white men ruled the region.

Today some of the rulers try to shield themselves from the sun and the natives and to live in artificially moistened and cooled isolation. The suburbs of Houston, where the rich and near-rich live in self-conscious splendor, deserve special comment. Of them, Larry L. King wrote as follows in *The Atlantic Monthly*:

> West Houston—River Oaks, the Rice University Section—has preserved a restful greenbelt pleasing to the eye, a great swath of trees and grasses which, when viewed from a downtown skyscraper, appears to be Central Park ten times over. These privileged enclaves, however, do not fall under the gaze of the incidental tourist. One is more likely to remember fake Tudor and baroque semi-mansions rising out of the coastal plain as far as thirty miles out from the city, $90,000 homes astonishingly built cheek by jowl, looking like a Levittown for bankers who probably collect bullfight paintings superimposed on silk.

Not all Anglos seek to isolate themselves from the realities of the land, however. A memorable and true son of the Southwest was Everette Lee DeGolyer, who became the prototypical pioneer geophysicist. Like Sam Houston (who had lived with the Cherokees for a time as a boy in Tennessee and later as a man in Oklahoma Territory), DeGolyer was fascinated by Indian life. He loved the "red-earthed" landscape and the two original cultures he found there when he and his family arrived from Kansas. At age twenty-three he made the greatest oil strike in history up till that time (1909); eventually he founded Amerada and the gigantic corporation which ultimately became Texas Instruments.

DeGolyer was a man of brains and generosity, giving his enormous private library to Southern Methodist University and his science collection to the University of Oklahoma (so that its science library now stands as the equal of Harvard's). His is a desert-to-skyscraper career; his story of technological daring and civic conscience must be included in the lusty song of southwestern civilization. He always thought of himself simply as an "oil man."

Out of the vast expanse of "sky, sunlight, and solitude" that is the signature of the Southwest rise the glittering skylines of the region's major cities—symbols of Anglo innovation and determination. Once considered an impossible area to develop—a government surveyor sent back this report to Congress in 1858: "The region is altogether valueless. After entering it there is nothing to do but leave"—the Southwest today has two of the nation's "ten biggest" metropolises, Houston and Dallas, and at least twenty cities with populations of more than 100,000.

The rapid growth of cities and the dominance of urban living over rural life is typical of the nation as a whole, but in the Southwest the speed of urbanization in this century has been staggering. In 1950, for exam-

*Windmill and oil derricks
rise from rolling plains in
Beaver County, Okla.
The Sooner State ranks fourth
among oil producing states.*

ple, Houston's population was less than 600,000; today it is nearly 1,300,000. Dallas has grown from 400,000 in 1950 to nearly a million. The population of Albuquerque, New Mexico's largest city, increased 600 percent in thirty years: from 34,000 in 1940 to 250,000 in 1970. Other southwestern cities including Phoenix, Tucson, Tulsa, and Oklahoma City have grown in similar proportions.

The Southwest's phenomenal growth over the past thirty years can be attributed largely to one major factor: modern technology. Man's inventions have made this harsh and arid land livable on a large scale. Diversion and storage techniques have brought water to the thirsty land. Modern methods of transportation—from the railroad to the airplane—have lessened the region's dependence on the few existing water routes and made it more accessible. And then there is that miracle of modern comfort—air conditioning. David Nevins, author of *The Texans*, writes:

> I've often suspected that it is no coincidence that the rise of the south accompanied the perfection of commercial air conditioning. After all, it is hard for people who are melting to compete . . . . Now air conditioning has conquered climate in automobile, home, office, factory, church and even, in Houston, the ballpark, and it changes the very style of living. . . . clothes are heavier and more formal, people go outside less often and with less pleasure. Far from giving a strictured feeling, however, this only seems to enhance the psychic charge of the cities . . . .

A Phoenix editor voiced the same thought in a conversation with writer Neal Peirce: "Without air conditioning we might still be a winter resort. . . ." Instead Phoenix is America's twentieth largest city, a metropolis dedicated to growth, sometimes at an almost frenetic pace. "Phoenix is wrenched with change," observed reporter John Barbour, continuing with this description of the dizzying pace of the city:

> In less than ten years, 500 industrial plants have moved into town. Manufacturing now outsells the tourist trade four-to-one. Now people come to Phoenix for jobs more than for the sun. They have built a city on wheels, built around more than 100 bustling extravagant shopping centers, a city of near strangers where six out of ten families moved into new homes in just six years.

Perhaps because of the rapidity of its growth—from 65,000 people in 1940 to 581,500 in 1970—Phoenix has retained little of the unique flavor of the Southwest. It has been described as "spread city" and dismissed as a "bland, mercantile center." But there is no denying its vitality. In the words of Neal Peirce: "No American city today is more replete with . . . vibrant, ambitious young people who by pluck and luck and daring have come and made their fortunes. . . ."

As is true of all major cities, Phoenix has problems, but it also has a concerned, innovative populace. Like the pioneers who settled this land before them, the citizens of Phoenix seem determined not only to succeed but also to solve whatever problems confront their city.

Tucson, Arizona's second largest metropolis, is less aggressive than Phoenix, more traditional, and more liberal. First settled by the Spanish in 1776, this oasis city has retained a sense of history, preserving the Spanish style of architecture in many of its buildings and keeping to a slower pace of life. And as home of the University of Arizona, Tucson has become one of the major cultural centers of the Southwest, attracting artists and intellectuals from all parts of the country.

Despite its slower pace, Tucson is as much a part of the new Southwest as Phoenix. The postwar industrial boom, triggered in Tucson by the wartime establish-

ment of air force bases near the city, has brought more than 200,000 new residents to the area. The income from manufacturing and processing, primarily in the electronics, aviation, and communications industries, has surpassed that of tourism, long the backbone of the city's economy.

Erna Fergusson once wrote of her native city: "Albuquerque has never struck a bonanza or known a boom. Little gold has been discovered in its hills, no oil nor artesian water in its subsoil. The fertile Rio Grande Valley produces less nowadays than it did before the building of the modern town." When she wrote those words, in 1940, Albuquerque was a sleepy little city of perhaps 30,000 people. Lying in a valley along the banks of the Rio Grande, shielded on the northeast by the rough peaks of the Sandia Mountains, Albuquerque existed primarily as a health resort, known for its Spanish atmosphere and its warm, dry climate.

Today all but the Spanish architecture has changed. The nuclear age has transformed life in Albuquerque. After the exploding of the atomic bomb at Los Alamos in 1945, scientists and technicians poured into New Mexico to man atomic research laboratories. Scientific installations such as Kirkland Air Force Base, which operates a nuclear effects research laboratory; Sandia Corporation, a nuclear weapons center; and White Sands Proving Ground have attracted numerous electronics and other industries, along with thousands of new residents to the Albuquerque area.

Despite its population and industrial booms, Albuquerque, like Tucson, has retained some of its Spanish heritage. The city's "Old Town," along the Rio Grande, takes one back to the days of the original Spanish settlement, with flat-roofed colonial buildings and a plaza ringed with restaurants and small shops. The University of New Mexico helps perpetuate the state's past by the use of old architectural styles for its new buildings and, more importantly, by its press, which publishes at least a dozen books a year, most dealing with regional culture.

Oklahoma City's transition from tent-and-clapboard town to modern metropolis was less spectacular than that of Albuquerque or Phoenix, but no less impressive. "The City of Tomorrow," as its boosters call it, rises sharply from the rolling plains, its sparkling skyline visible for miles. Its new downtown boasts acres of wide streets, plazas, malls, a convention center, theaters, new homes, and apartments. Tulsa, its friendly rival and the second largest city in Oklahoma, is equally beautiful, fresh and clean and modern.

Both cities were built by oil: Tulsa for years called itself the "Oil Capital of the World"; Oklahoma City, not to be outdone, drilled an oil well directly in front of the State Capitol. And both cities, when many of the state's oil fields began to run dry, set out to attract new industry. Tulsa is now headquarters for American Airlines and a center for other aerospace and aviation firms. Oklahoma City is the site of the FAA's Aeronautical Center and Aeromedical Institute and of Tinker Air Force Base, the world's largest air depot, as well as a center for electronics, transportation, and oil supply firms.

Explosive growth is the trademark of all the major southwestern metropolises, but the biggest "boom-towns" of them all are in the Lone Star State.

Dallas, second largest city in Texas, is a mystery to

Oil and aerospace are two industries that have helped bring fabulous wealth to Texas. Oil derricks (far left), 1,100 of them, sprout all over downtown Kilgore, center of the vast East Texas Oil Field. Discovery of the field in the early 1900s recast the economy of Texas. NASA's Manned Spacecraft Center (left) sprawls over 1,620 acres southeast of Houston; at the height of the Apollo program, it employed more than 10,000 people.

some observers of the Southwest. In his book *Dallas Public and Private*, Warren Leslie wrote: "The truth is, there really isn't any reason for Dallas. It sits in the middle of nowhere and nothing." It has no port, no oil resources, no rice fields, no wealth of cattle. Yet somehow Dallas has always attracted the go-getters, the ambitious we-can-do-it breed that settles frontiers and builds great cities.

Modern Dallas is a financial and insurance center, commercial capital of the entire Southwest. A sophisticated, cosmopolitan metropolis, Dallas is the least southwestern of all Texas cities. Its citizenry identifies with the East and takes pride in its fashion—Dallas is the third most important fashion center in the United States—and cultural achievements.

But it is Houston that sets the pace for all of the Southwest. Twenty-five years ago, Houston was a one-note metropolis, what Houstonians themselves called a "whiskey and trombone town." Now it is one of the most "internationalized" cities in the nation, thanks to its position as Space Flight and Energy Capital of the world, thanks to its vast petrochemical wealth, thanks to the bold leadership of some remarkably imaginative civic leaders.

To the onlooker, Houston seems to have annexed the future. The present changes so rapidly that one is hardly aware of it in the face of the dizzying future prospect. Not all of Houston's achievement is due to modern technology, but much of it is. NASA's choice of Houston for the Manned Spacecraft Center catapulted the city to the fore as a capital of science. Oil technology has brought the national headquarters of Exxon, Shell, and Tenneco to Houston, making it the hub of the energy universe. These and other developments have brought a phalanx of superb scientists, technicians, and financiers, a whole new non-southwestern-oriented population to this, the nation's sixth largest city.

*Often called Children of the Sun,
southwesterners are addicted to the
outdoor life. Golf (right) is a year
round sport in the region, even in
arid New Mexico and Arizona (below),
where rainfall averages less than 20
inches a year and water must be pumped
in to keep the courses green.*

As it has grown more sophisticated, Houston has tired of its reputation as the domain of the bigger-than-life, free-spending wheeler-dealer. As one resident told writer Stuart Jones: "Frankly this city is trying to shed that brag label. . . . We've adopted the British style of understatement. We simply state the facts, and if they *appear* extravagant, it isn't our fault."

Despite this recently acquired cosmopolitan attitude, "big deals" remain a staple of economic life in Texas, from Houston's winning of the location of the $400 million dollar NASA Space Center (later named the Lyndon B. Johnson Space Center) to Dallas's license to create jointly with Fort Worth the "world's biggest

airport," the D-FW, as it is known, bigger than Manhattan island. (Naturally, since Houston's most recent airport, the International, covered ten square miles.)

Big deals, or transactions as the rest of the nation insists on calling them, profit from a theatrical setting. Both Dallas and Houston provide opulent private clubs, where transactions may be sealed over lunchtime martinis and deluxe gourmet food, and country clubs which offer golf as the catalyst for many a business agreement. But these are standard, and the Texans have dreamed up something else, a stage setting, in a way, to yield the maximum mingling of business with pleasure. Two such arenas of business wheeling-dealing are Houston's

celebrated athletic stadium, the Astrodome (which has an immensely successful Disneyland-type annex, the Astroworld) and Dallas's rival sports center, the Cowboy Stadium (named not for the western folk hero but for the Dallas professional football team, the "Cowboys").

The relatively new Cowboy Stadium features an array of "boxes" paralleling the privacy and elegance of the European opera houses and theaters of *La Belle Epoque*, so expensive that one justification of their existence lies not in the comfort of watching the game as though in one's living room (with bar attached) but in the virtue of making business deals with guests.

Says one owner of such a box: "It's a fun private way to have a party." But says the banker of this oil man: "There are probably more deals cinched in those boxes than on all the golf courses in all the country clubs of the city." The boxes cost $50,000 each, seating only twelve guests; and the owner must pay for twelve tickets set aside for each game, whether the box is used or not. Adds the banker: "And when you consider the figures involved in some of these deals, the $50,000 is more than worth it."

Since this is Texas, the initial $50,000 is only part of the outlay. The proper decorating and furnishing of the box may well run to a matching sum. In general, the wives determine the interior decoration; the men set the style in dress. So, cowboy boots and ten-gallon Stetsons consort with lavender upholstered chairs and Grecian decor that includes gold-leafed mirrors, columns, and draperies.

The Astrodome and Cowboy Stadium rank as supremely ironic examples of Anglo innovation, bringing traditional outdoor activity indoors. Nonetheless, one of the distinguishing traits of southwestern life is the fact that so much of it, during so much of the year, can be lived outdoors. At heart, southwesterners remain Children of the Sun; and of course with their usual

exuberant, experimentive energy, Anglos have found
ways to exploit that.

Consider, for example, that amazing modern phenomenon near Phoenix: a city for the "elderly," a
retirement community where neither children nor
grandchildren are welcome, the much-publicized and
immensely successful "Sun City."

Sun City is an experiment in geriatrics, a luxury sub-
urb specifically designed to insure the happiness of the
"elderly." Launched in 1960 by Del Webb, a former
owner of the New York Yankees, Sun City has now
filled its original 9,000-acre "city," developed from cotton fields twelve miles north of Phoenix, with a population of 30,000. Available lots are nearly exhausted,

but developers still have another 11,000 acres in the
present tract. They estimate that Sun City will have a
population of 50,000 by 1980 and at least double that
after its second twenty-year period. These figures refer
to a population in which the average age of the individual citizen is sixty-seven.

To qualify for admission to Sun City, a prospective
purchaser must be at least fifty and relatively wealthy.
A one-bedroom apartment without extras starts at
about $30,000; a plain two-bedroom house sells for
nearly $70,000. For another $3,000, new residents can
get the Eldorado, which has a sunken swimming pool
in the living room.

Some people have the wickedness to call this and
similar suburbs "geriatric ghettos." But the elderly who
have what it takes delight in the luxuries of Sun City—
the golf courses, shopping centers, recreation centers,
shuffleboard courts, bowling alleys, amphitheaters, sta-
diums, lakes. The only thing they do not find is the
presence of childhood and youth. For many oldsters,
this is great. They love being pampered in a way that
removes them from the vital rhythms of life, that in-
sulates them from much of "nature."

Another sun culture development has been taking
place along the seacoast of Texas, the third largest
coastline of the continental United States. Often called

Sun City Stadium (above) serves as spring headquarters for
Milwaukee Brewers, then becomes "home field" for the Sun
City Saints, a women's softball team, and the Sun City Raiders,
the men's team.

the "Golden Crescent," the Texas Gulf Coast curves from semitropical Brownsville and the Magic Valley up to Corpus Christi (which calls itself the "Texas Riviera") and on to Galveston Island near the Louisiana border. It nourishes and sustains and often threatens with hurricanes the greatest concentration of chemical plants in the nation. Half of the U.S. petrochemical industry is located in the Golden Crescent. One-fourth of the refinery capacity of the nation neighbors the Texas coastline. In fact, about one-third of the Lone Star State's economic power springs from this ocean-front area and its environs. Every day its importance in shaping the life of the state, and indirectly of the Southwest, visibly increases. And part of the reason is "tourism." Believe it or not, Texas's State Land Commissioner Robert Armstrong states categorically that "Texas has passed Florida in the total number of tourists. The coast draws a large percentage of them. . . ."

The winter haven and the number one current tourist attraction is that part of the Gulf Coast that, if not for Key West, would be "the southernmost point of the United States," the palmy and citrus-rich Rio Grande valley. The Texas coast also has a long string of thin barrier islands stretching all the way along the Golden Crescent. The longest of these is near Mexico, Padre Island, almost a hundred miles in length but

only a few miles wide. Both at its northern tip near Corpus Christi and its southern boundary near Brownsville, Padre Island is undergoing a fantastic real estate development (by far the greater action is on the southernmost end of the island) that many claim to be a "rerun" of the spectacular development of Florida earlier in the century.

It won't be Florida by a long shot, however, because there isn't enough beach area available to private interests. The United States government, realizing the minimal portion of seashore in the nation available to all the people, several years ago designated nearly seventy miles of the Padre Island stretch as a "National Seashore," forever accessible for beach use to all. Thus private ownership is limited to a dozen or so miles at each tip. The success of the privately developed portion, especially at the southern tip known as "South Padre," has been phenomenal.

The Anglo spirit of inventiveness has often been brash, uncontrolled, perhaps too concerned with constant growth and the fulfillment of personal ambition. But there are increasing signs that this is changing, that the Anglos of the Southwest are searching for a different type of fulfillment. There is, for example, the hunger for cultural betterment that marks so many of the new southwestern cities: the symphonies, the civic operas, the ballets, the art museums. And along with this desire to experience more than just growth, more than just wealth, may come a new interest in the region's other two cultures. In time, the Southwest's now dominant Anglo culture may offer the rest of the nation a special kind of excellence, a fusion of the old and the new, a workable equilibrium that preserves the past while discovering the future. Someday there may be a true "confluence" rather than "clash" of three cultures, each enriching the other, all enriching the nation.

—LON TINKLE

Affluent Texans: "the biggest and the best"

The lavish elegance of Houston's Jesse H. Jones Hall for the Performing Arts (at left and below) symbolizes the metamorphosis of Texas from cattle kingdom to oil kingdom. The legend of cowboys, longhorns, and the open range still influences the attitudes of the Texan, but the reality has changed since the Spindletop gusher blew in at Beaumont in 1901. Oil money has built most of the cultural monuments and skyscrapers that sprout all over the Texas landscape today. And oil has created most of the multimillionaires who dominate the life style of this affluent society. Until very recently, growth—unplanned and unregulated—has been almost a religion in Texas. But as 80% of the population has crowded into the cities—and from the cities to amorphous, sprawling suburbs—many Texans have begun to have second thoughts. The affluence is there for all to see, but its spread is narrow and per capita income remains well below the national average. Texas ranks first in the production of oil, gas, cotton, and cattle but 42nd in per capita expenditures for public education. Most of the state's revenue comes from a regressive sales tax and corporations pay neither income nor profits taxes.

The activist millionaires of Houston have turned their city into the corporate capital of the Southwest and are determined to turn it into the cultural capital as well. The three ladies pictured below are among those who have contributed much to the city. Miss Ima Hogg, an able businesswoman who helped increase the family's oil and real estate fortune, is—at 93—the beloved "first lady of Texas." She has spent a lifetime of effort and millions of dollars in support of the arts, restoring and endowing historical landmarks and founding a child guidance center and a mental health foundation. Mrs. Oveta Culp Hobby, as publisher of the Houston Post, has long been active in civic affairs. Mrs. Dominique de Menil, chairwoman of Rice University's Department of Art History and a knowledgeable collector, was a moving force behind Houston's great new Mark Rothko Chapel.

Helicopters and Lear jets simplify life for Texas executives. Houston traffic jams are no problem for the helicopter, above, piloted by Tenneco board chairman, N.W. (Dick) Freeman.

Ima Hogg, at left; Oveta Culp Hobby, above; Dominique de Menil, at right.

Houston's Galleria complex, linking an office building and a luxurious hotel (below) with a spectacular mall, features the air-conditioned, glass-roofed, 80-by-170-foot ice skating rink at left. Three levels of plush specialty shops—including Tiffany, Mark Cross, Parke-Bernet —overlook the rink, which is open all year.

The flamboyant opulence of the Astrodome—particularly the private quarters of its promoter, Judge Roy Hofheinz—reinforces all the clichés ever written about brash, free-wheeling Texas millionaires. To the decorous "old guard" of Houston society, it is an anachronism, but to the judge—posing at right with the local Sheriff's Mounted Posse—it has meant a bonanza of welcome publicity. His own rags-to-riches story is as improbable as his surroundings. Arriving in Houston as a penniless orphan from Beaumont, he worked his way through college, studied law at night, passed the bar exams at 19, was elected to the state legislature at 22, and—at 24—became the youngest person ever elected judge in Houston's Harris County. Hofheinz quit politics long enough to make his first million, then served two terms as the city's mayor—a post held by his son today.

The $38 million Astrodome (at left, above) is connected by a $1 million bridge to the $26 million Astroworld—the judge's answer to California's Disneyland. His suite includes a rococo barbershop (left) and a puppet theater for his grandchildren and guests (below).

Hofheinz built a railroad
at Astroworld and a sumptuous
private car for himself that
includes the Gay Nineties bar at left.
His Astrodome suite includes
a pool room, bowling alley,
and putting green.

The finest art collections in Texas probably still hang in the private homes of wealthy collectors, but several outstanding new galleries have recently been built. The neoclassical Houston Museum of Fine Arts, the first in Texas, was opened in 1924 thanks to the efforts and contributions of the oil-rich Hogg family. Its new wings (at left), designed by Mies van der Rohe, were also financed by wealthy individuals and foundations. Another famous architect, Philip Johnson, designed the new Art Museum of South Texas (at left, below) on the banks of the harbor channel at Corpus Christi. It provides a handsome setting for traveling exhibitions but has no sizable permanent collection of its own. Fort Worth has been more fortunate. Its new Kimbell Art Museum, designed by Louis Kahn, has been endowed with an estimated $75 million. The Kimbell's permanent collection, including the fine 12th century French frescoes pictured below, is being rapidly expanded. Fort Worth also has the Amon Carter Museum of Western Art, with a fine historical collection that attracts visitors in Stetsons and boots like those at right, who are admiring an exhibition in Fort Davis.

The good life in Dallas
(at right) includes Neiman-Marcus,
the posh department store that
advertises—and actually sells—
such Christmas specials as His
and Hers airplanes and submarines.
Stanley Marcus (below), a millionaire
and the most successful merchandiser
in the Southwest, is a collector of
pre-Colombian sculpture and has
served on the boards of almost every
cultural institution in the city. In
historic San Antonio (facing page),
the "old rich" live graciously, dress
for dinner, and entertain each other
at lavish house parties. The city has
beautified the Paseo del Rio, where
visitors may enjoy fine wines and
mariachi music at riverside cafes or
dine by candlelight on a riverboat
that meanders through the center
of town.

The LBJ Library at Austin
houses millions of presidential
documents. It is Texas-sized
—the biggest and most
expensive monument of its
type ever built in the U.S.

Dignity and
strength mark the
face of this proud
and beautiful
matriarch. Property,
including land,
is traditionally
owned and passed
on by Navajo
wives; income is
shared among
members of the
family group.

Navajo girl (below) cooks fry bread at a temporary camp in Arizona's Monument Valley
Tribal Park. Sheepherder (at right) drives his flock down to water across the valley's golden
dunes. Water and vegetation are so sparse it takes 65 acres to support a single sheep.

The Navajo: "with beauty I walk"

"With Beauty before me I walk, with Beauty behind me I walk, with Beauty above me I walk, with Beauty all around me I walk." These words from a Navajo prayer express the love of a proud and ancient people for their traditional lands —25,000 square miles in northeast Arizona and small areas of New Mexico and Utah. The 140,000 Navajos are the largest of the Indian tribes and settled here —according to archeologists—around 1500 A.D. Almost half the population speaks no English and about a quarter of Navajo households still lives in timber and mud hogans, earning a meager living by herding their sheep across the dry and sparsely vegetated—if awesomely beautiful—land.

To live in harmony with nature— this is the core of Navajo religious philosophy. Modern Navajos have adopted Christianity and the white man's medicine, but most also continue to believe in their traditional gods and in the intricate rituals of their medicine men. Illness and misfortune strike, according to the Navajo, when there is disharmony, and there are hundreds of long-established rituals to restore harmony between man and nature. The medicine man leaning over a ceremonial sand paint-

The Monument Valley weaver (at right) works without a pattern; she shears, cards, and dyes her own wool to produce a unique product. A 3-by-5-foot rug that takes up to 350 hours to make may bring less than $100 to the weaver, though the eventual retail buyer may pay $2,000 or more for it.

ing (top left) works with an assistant to create a semi-abstract design with such materials as red sandstone, yellow ochre, white sand, and charcoal. When the young patient sits in its center she is supposed to absorb its power and be drained of illness. Herbs and chants will complete the ritual. The Sweatbath Ceremonial (at right) is used to cleanse both mind and body. A tiny hogan is built of cedar logs, covered with sand, and lined inside with heated rocks. Ritual chants are sung and the Indians emerge—shining with sweat and purified.

313

Bulldozer operator works at Black Mesa coal strip mine, where the average wage for Navajos is $11,300. Traditional Navajos see the earth as a gigantic female figure—they speak reverently of "Mother Earth and Father Sky." Strip mining to them is the rape of the sacred earth.

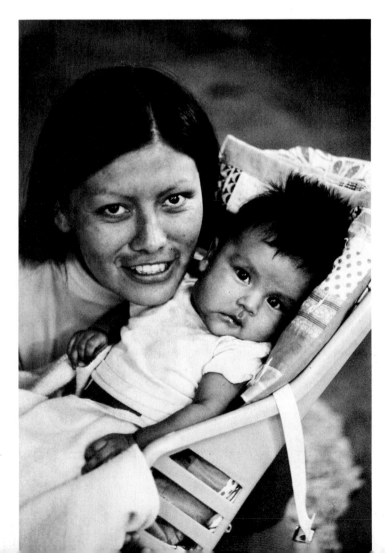

Sonny Jim (above) and Jessie Whitesheep (at right with her baby) belong to a new generation. Sonny is a hero to children when he rides the bulls at the Rough Rock Rodeo, and Jessie—a teacher's aide—still lives at the camp centered in grazing lands owned for generations by her mother's family.

Education and economic developments have sparked a resurgence among the Navajo, who are no longer willing to put up with poverty, an unemployment rate of 65%, and an average annual income of $300 per year per person. Almost every Navajo child goes to school today, compared with only 10% a decade ago, and even the older people (at right) are beginning to learn to read and write. The democratically elected Tribal Council is now led by the first Navajo chairman to hold a university degree— 45-year-old Marine veteran and former electrical engineer, Peter MacDonald. Long-range road-building programs, with the help of federal funds, began to open up the reservation in the 1950s; and rich deposits of coal, oil, natural gas, and uranium were discovered. The Tribal Council wisely decided that, instead of dividing royalties and income from mineral leases among the people, they would invest them in job-producing factories and public works. They built a factory for lease to Fairchild Semiconductors at Shiprock, which now employs more than 700 Navajos for the exacting work of wiring miniaturized circuitry. Hundreds of other Indians strip mine coal, market timber, and work in new power plants.

The General Dynamics plant at Window Rock (below), which produces electronic components, employs 75-100 Navajos.

West Coast–
Restless Region

At a fork near the Snake River in southeast Idaho, the Oregon Trail divided and wagon trains parted. Those who rode on over the Cascade Mountains into the rich Willamette Valley of Oregon were typically merchants and farmers. To the southwest, over the Sierra Nevada, gold hunters moved toward the Mother Lode. With them went thousands who sought their fortunes not in the gold camps but on the fringes of the ebullient society that sprang up there and in San Francisco. They, and not the miners, were the shrewder opportunists of the gold rush. They laid the foundations of the present California society, one that is quintessentially American in its drive for innovation and for freedom from restraints; in its adventuresome mobility; its restless, putty culture; and its easy, casual style.

The California gold rush is the only one in our history that laid the basis for the genesis and virtually uninterrupted growth of a substantial society. The mo-
tives which have led to a subsequent century of migration to California, making it the most populous state in the Union, have been mutations of those which brought the rush for gold. The Forty-Niners were generally single young men from the eastern seaboard. With some notable exceptions, the succeeding waves of migration to California have also been led by independent young people seeking more money, more pleasure, and more freedom than they have found in the rooted, traditional regions of their origin. California remains a relatively young and mobile society with high rates of suicide, divorce, alcoholism, drug addiction, and crime, traits associated historically with mining camps.

There was scant gold in Oregon and Washington. The people who settled that area were of different temperament. Many of the Oregon settlers were from the Northeast; they named their towns Portland, Salem, Albany, and Springfield. Their trim white farm houses

San Francisco's beloved century-old cable cars continue to operate because indignant citizens have frustrated every effort by economy-minded transportation experts to abolish them.

318

Fog rolls in over the Golden Gate Bridge when inland temperatures soar and dissipates when the land cools.

and church spires, more like those of an older America, contrasted with the early towns of California—where the frenetic settlers requisitioned what they liked of California's Spanish panache and fleshed out their own boisterous image in the saloons and bordellos and opera houses of San Francisco. To the seashores and valleys of the far Northwest, in the land that was to become Washington, went many Scandinavians and Germans; they found much to remind them of home in the climate, the sea, the forests, and in the farming valleys.

Despite the homogenizing effect of fast transport and communications, regional characteristics along the Pacific shore have tended to grow sharper in the intervening years. Styles of speech and economic and family patterns will not vary as much between Los Angeles and Seattle as between Boston and Savannah along the Atlantic coast, but those sensitive to social mores find many contrasts in outlook and aspiration. The voice of Seattle, for example, is less shrill, its hunger for motion and glitter less marked. The people of the Northwest are more rooted than the residents of the California metropolises. They are bound to their land, not urban drifters like so many Southern Californians. On weekends they take to their boats, their ski slopes and hiking trails, not to long motorized processions of escape.

The Northwest remains apprehensive of the raw,

almost undefinable vigor and transitional force that California exerts on American society. It is not alone. California has long been a highly visible target. Its natural scenic wonders provide a Bunyanesque stage that encourages uninhibited individualism. Californians are prone to try anything that has not been tried before. In this they differ from people in older regions of the United States, and as a result they have given California its unique role as an early-warning system for American change. Along the way they have been part of the largest migration in history, the climactic phase of a 200-year westering epic that has seemed at times almost a mystical part of the American experience.

The men and women who settled America when it was a remote wilderness continent were searching for freedom and prosperity; they sensed fewer impediments than most in continuing across the Alleghenies, the Great Plains, and finally the deserts and mountain ranges of the West to find land and gold and open space. As they moved westward, the pioneers also sought escape from the inhibitions of older societies, and finally there evolved the boisterous blending of American exuberances that is California.

Like other convenient idioms of American regionalism, the words *West Coast* are seldom used by those who live along it. Nor does the phrase suggest any common image to the people of the Pacific shore. Only with the veil of distance does the West Coast become

The 2,000-year-old coast redwoods in northern California have been decimated by loggers, but 86,700 acres are now protected in state and national parks in response to intense citizen pressure that began in 1918.

The 2,400-mile Pacific Crest Trail, extending along the mountains from Canada to Mexico, appeals to hikers of all ages. The young couple at left, Will and Linda Gray, stop to rest and study the map at 7,620 feet in Washington. Franklin Blocksom, age 76, is a retired government engineer who worked in Alaska. He and his 75-year-old wife, Hildur, (at right) often hike the trail in September when they can collect huckleberries for canning.

320

an entity and then because it is blurred by astigmatism. The television producer flying from Manhattan to the West Coast sees his destination as that bleak sprawl between Los Angeles International Airport and the Beverly Hills hotels, restaurants, and offices which become his circuit. The eastern banker thinks of the coast in terms of San Francisco's Montgomery Street, and the youthful rebel heads toward Berkeley. Those who traffic in timber and fish know the forests and seaports of Oregon and Washington.

Perhaps only to the geographer and the demographer does the West Coast assume some intactness as a region.

The geographer knows this Pacific coastline as that remarkably varied and often dramatic shore, 1,700 miles in length, lying between San Diego Harbor and the northern reaches of Puget Sound. From Mexico to Canada the coast is an outthrust arc, more precipitous than the Atlantic coast, with mountains rising sharply behind the shore. East of the highest of these ranges, up through California, Oregon, and Washington, are the quiet lands, sparsely settled and usually arid because the mountains have sucked the prevailing ocean winds dry.

Most urban centers in these three states lie along the coast or close behind. About 1,200 miles of this West Coast shoreline are Californian. The state spans about the same ten degrees of latitude as that from Cape Cod to Savannah on the Atlantic coast. It ranges from the fog-shrouded redwood forests of the far north to the golden, subtropical shores of Southern California.

The demographer is able to see the West Coast as the recipient—in varying degrees at different locales—of a vast and relatively recent migratory phenomenon, the destination of pioneers and, more recently, of millions who have followed their westering urge to this far continental shore.

Where the demographer's narrow discipline ends and others begin, the West Coast fragments again. Northwest politicians make capital of their pledges to halt the "Californiazation" of Oregon and Washington. In their booster years of runaway growth, now ended, California communities from San Diego to San Francisco bulldozed and filled, paved and littered, annihilated and uglified much of the natural majesty that helped to lure Californians westward. In the process they spilled over state lines to clog the campgrounds and fishing streams of Oregon and Washington, less explosive regions where concepts of progress have been less allied with compulsive numerical growth.

In the personalities of its cities, this Pacific shore best reveals its history and its current thrusts.

Seattle is one of the most gently beautiful cities in the United States. Set on hills and lakes beside Puget Sound, it lies between the rugged Olympic Peninsula on the west and Mount Rainier, an exquisitely formed mountain, to the southeast. It is the largest city for 700 miles in any direction, but it is notable for its easy pace. The Scandinavians and Germans who helped settle Seattle have contributed to its image as a haven of homebodies. Seattleites like to tell about a visiting writer who excused himself from a party one evening.

An hour later he was back. "I just took a stroll around downtown," he said. "Aren't you folks just a mite short on sin?" The sale of whisky by the drink was not legalized in the state of Washington until 1848, and Sunday blue laws have been relaxed only in recent years. A Seattle restaurateur grumbled: "The only trouble is that this town is full of Scandinavians who eat and make love at home."

The city has long been whiplashed by the industrial dominance of the giant Boeing Co., with the feast-or-famine economy that is inherent in the aerospace business. Pushed to its knees in the 1950s, Boeing revived with the success of its 707 jetliner and Minuteman missile. By 1970 the company, always Seattle's largest employer, was in another trough. The local depression that resulted seemed catastrophic, but a pessimist's highway billboard—"Last One Out Turn Off the Lights"—became the rallying cry for yet another civic renaissance of the kind that has characterized this city and its people. Washingtonians appreciate the livability of their state and, when necessary, sacrifice to remain there.

South of the mighty Columbia River lies the Willamette Valley and Portland, the dominant city of Oregon. It is a busy river port, conservative in its affairs. Portland has had wide economic swings between its shipbuilding booms and lumber recessions. Its people appear demure when contrasted with the residents of California cities or even Seattle. There is a continuing rivalry with Seattle, for both cities are larger than any other in the Northwest and dominate the affairs of their respective states.

The Oregonian has acquired a reputation for his support of liberal legislation, partly because of a reform leader, William S. U'Ren, who campaigned across the state in the early days of the century for what came to be known as the Oregon System: the initiative, referendum, and recall. Half a century ago Oregon voters set aside substantial amounts of their coastline as state parkland. The state's antilitter law in 1971 was an early example of the legislative victories of environmentalists over business interests—in this case, banning the sale of throwaway cans and bottles.

As one travels south from Portland, berry fields and fruit orchards give way to forests which dominate the land for 600 miles, most of the distance from Portland to San Francisco. The vast and virile California that lies north of San Francisco seems more attuned in mood to the Northwest. Here stand the redwood and rain forests, volcano and glacier, still unsettled miles of stormy coastline, and behind the coastal mountains, barren highlands. Were San Franciscans forced to accept some rural allegiance, they might choose to be a part of this northern shore instead of the more cluttered metropolitan coast that extends southward from their city.

Among the caveats decreed by the noted San Francisco columnist, Herb Caen, is one that Southern Cali-

A folk festival draws a huge crowd of people to this beautiful site on the Big Sur overlooking the Pacific.

fornia begins at San Jose, a city with precipitous growth tendencies just south of San Francisco. But Caen's image of San Francisco, an enchanting fluff of sepia and red flock, has submerged under the weight of California's new role as the most populous—and in certain odd ways the most influential—of the fifty states. San Francisco, with all its dazzling beauty, increasingly finds corporate headquarters defecting to more populous Los Angeles.

Despite her worsening urban crises, San Francisco remains the narcissus among American cities, feeding on her own image, always her own best audience. Unlike other California metropolises, she looks like a city, densely settled and compacted in an area no more than seven miles across. Even the honeycomb of new skyscrapers fails to destroy the magnificent vistas of fleeting cloud and windswept bay, linked by the steel bands of the city's great bridges.

San Francisco's tradition of open-minded tolerance has made it the spawning ground of social movements, especially among youth. Its North Beach is the Greenwich Village of the West. San Franciscans worship the gospel of *laissez-faire*. Its campus movements and youth cults move on and off stage, but in them America often

has seen a foretaste of trends that have later swept the nation.

In densely populated Southern California lies the megalopolis of Los Angeles, which first began to outgrow San Francisco after its complex water supply system and its artificial harbor were assured just before World War I. It is the center of gravity in the American West. It seethes with change and bulges with the strengths of its diverse people: their hunger for innovation and their high state of technology—most apparent to the casual visitor in an astonishing network of fast, multi-lane freeways. Technology and the pursuit of leisure often appear to be the twin gods of the citizens of Los Angeles.

The Los Angeles metropolitan area stretches 70 miles from north to south, a bewildering expanse of coastal plain cluttered with squat skyline and occasional clusters of tall buildings. Unlike San Diego, a gentle, clean, and leisurely city 100 miles to its south, Los Angeles appears to have run amuck. But it works. Its population is about 3 million, and that of Los Angeles County has passed 7 million. The ethnic mix is complex: Mexican-Americans are the largest non-Anglo minority, but blacks take a more active role in public affairs.

The significance of Los Angeles is not its size but its innovations in coping with size. These are vital because Los Angeles is a fragmented city, spun out into unrelated nodules which become communities of strangers. Theirs is a vagrant society that lacks any sense of unity, one blighted with anomie. But it is an inquisitive, open-minded city, where new patterns in living are being tested, abandoned, and adopted.

All along this Pacific shore, author Carey McWil-

liams wrote, the only thing that seems to remain constant is "rapid, revolutionary change." Its people like to believe they have achieved technological marvels through their wits alone; but they have also been aided by rich natural resources, the vagaries of history, and the federal budget. Yet Californians in particular have

Smog chokes freeways although California emission standards are the nation's toughest. New freeways are being built every year with highway user funds constitutionally assigned to road-building. The powerful highway lobby has defeated all efforts to divert funds to pollution control or public transportation.

324

displayed a rare degree of economic self-reliance since the state's earliest days and have contributed such diverse items to the national scene as branch banking, the ranch house, casual sportswear, the massive and diverse agriculture of its factories in the fields, political management firms, and the Frisbee.

The distinctiveness of the western style is its immoderate blend of buoyancy and despair based on a hungry, energetic drive to have more, move more, and do more. The critic Clifton Fadiman once described Californians as being in the "vanguard of American social development," but they are not yet a settled society. A climate of change tolerates mediocrity, worthlessness, and ugliness. The most critical lack of California's society may be its absence of restraints and commitment to any common heritage. It rushes at a sometimes dizzying pace toward a future that is not yet charted. In recent years more and more Californians have begun to sense that after years of excessive expectation, this far shore lacks the momentum to glide forever above the rubble of unrealized dreams.

By 1970 the soaring migration rate that had made California the most populous state had slowed. Both Los Angeles and San Francisco began to go through periods of population decline as citizens fled to the suburbs to escape urban crises. For seventy years California had grown at least twice as rapidly as the nation; suddenly it was growing no faster. The California juggernaut had mastered desert and rivers and moun-

tains, but grave doubt began to emerge in the seventies about man's capacity to intrude into his environment without destroying it. By 1974 there were 14 million registered motor vehicles in California, a state with 20 million people; and this symbol of frenetic mobility was being challenged by environmental and fuel crises.

Among the major California cities, only San Jose and San Diego were still growing in 1974. With the unique process of acceleration which has always characterized it, California moved rapidly toward zero population growth. Its people espoused the cause of the environment through a landmark law regulating use of coastal lands. This new obsession has brought Californians from behind their patio walls and has begun to reverse their materialism and privatism.

The characteristic penchant for impermanence so associated with the Californian has been under siege by millions of young California-born citizens. They are not hobbled, as were their fathers, by the excesses and instability of the frontier, with its allegiances "back home" to distant kin and farms, schools, banks, and businesses. California is their birthright. In a sense they are the state's first generation, the first true Californians. There is evidence that they are putting down roots as they hike over mountain trails and spread their sleeping bags within sound of the Pacific surf.

The frontier dreams that came with the gold rush have grown obsolete. But even as those dreams are swept away, the people of this West Coast cannot resist dreaming. The energies and innovative skills that brought California so rapidly from gold camp to superstate have not been lost. Its people are uniquely aroused by issues involving man and his environment, as are the residents of the quieter Northwest. A sense of place seems dearer to oncoming generations of Californians than to some earlier migrants. They move, as Californians always have, toward new dreams.

—NEIL MORGAN

Californians: exuberant and energetic

The pursuit of happiness is almost a compulsion in California, where the "leisure class" is everybody and nature provides the playgrounds free of charge. As a result of the benign climate, Southern Californians do most of their living out-of-doors. Sun-drenched beaches are only minutes away for many; mountains and desert can be reached by most in two or three freeway hours.

Backyard swimming pools dot the landscape around Los Angeles. In Southern California, one family in 16 has its own pool.

In the never-never land of Southern California, oil derricks are camouflaged as skyscrapers, and ski areas—a three-hour drive from the beach—are filled to capacity by noon.

California is probably the world's leading center of innovative technology, with one complex near Pasadena's California Institute of Technology and a smaller one developing near San Diego. But the most dynamic complex in the state is in Santa Clara County, with some 800 pioneering technological companies clustered around Stanford University. The area now surpasses the famous Harvard-Cambridge complex, which declined primarily because of overdependence on government contracts. In Santa Clara, the primarily consumer-oriented industries are based on components and technologies that did not even exist a few years ago. They manufacture semiconductors, lasers, electronic items, and other sophisticated technical products. New industries formerly had to locate near transport and raw materials, but the high-technology industries of today depend only on brains. They are founded near educational centers, preferably in areas where climate and the natural beauty of the land add to the quality of life. Santa Clara has everything, including proximity to San Francisco and an influx of talented and highly educated young people—what has been described as a "high-voltage population." The technological entrepreneurs in the area are extraordinarily successful—at least a hundred (many in their early thirties) have become millionaires.

Young scientists at the Xerox Research Center near Stanford sprawl on "bean-bag" cushions in conference room. Research directors have found that such informality improves communication and creativity.

328

The General Atomic Company near San Diego (above) is a world center of research efforts in controlled thermonuclear fusion for power production. It is also involved in nuclear instrumentation and solar energy. Scientists here and at Salk Institute (upper left) are only a few yards from two public golf courses bordering the Pacific.

Phenomenally successful Intel Corporation of Santa Clara makes semiconductor memory chips for computers. At right, a stylus cuts finished memory chip from three-inch silicon wafer. Each chip is roughly the size of two letters in this sentence and holds 4,000 transistors. Immaculate lab is essential since a speck of dust can ruin a chip.

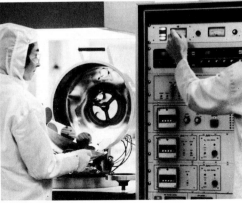

Sproul Plaza (top) at the University of California at Berkeley was the center for demonstrators in the 1960s. Students at the Los Angeles campus (center) and at San Diego (directly above) are casual in dress and life style but very serious about their studies.

The University of California—with nine campuses, 120,000 students, and a $1 billion budget—is one of the world's great universities. Only the top 12% of the state's high school graduates are accepted; the rest must at least begin at state or community colleges. UC leads the nation in the number of National Merit Scholars in its student body and in the number of Nobel Laureates on its faculty (14). The American Council on Education rates Berkeley as "the best balanced distinguished university in the country," with 32 top-ranked departments compared to Harvard's 27.

At the beautiful oceanside campus of Santa Barbara (top), students take their exams indoors, but like those at left, do much of their studying outdoors.

Dropping out of suburbia, for the Crowleys, has been a rewarding experience. Lynn quit his executive job and bought 30 acres on the Big Sur coast. "Nothing I did really had any meaning," he explains. "I just couldn't cut it any longer. The work was so high-pressured I had no time for my family. Also, I was worried about the school atmosphere —the dope scene and the whole bit—that my kids were in." It took him a year to build the house, and Theodora still commutes to a part-time job to help earn the cash income the family needs. Eventually, they hope to support themselves with a tree nursery on the property and by selling vegetables.

The Big Sur is a ruggedly beautiful 90-mile stretch of coastline 150 miles south of San Francisco.

Lynn and Theodora milk the recalcitrant family goat.

Vegetable plot (at left) and chickens help reduce the family's need for cash income.

The Crowley daughters love their new outdoor life in spite of the fact they must commute 40 miles to the nearest school.

333

Ten curves
in one block
on Lombard
Street.

San Franciscans have what has been described
as "a lovely sense of the absurd." They love the ding-
dong of their cable cars and the siren song of their
foghorns. They delight in "the artful foolishness of old
Victorian houses" and in the improbable curves of
Lombard Street—"the crookedest street in the world."
Some of the Brahmins collect antique cars; others park
racy motorbikes on the streets of the financial district.
Their women are among the best dressed in the world,
and everyone eats superlatively well—in 26 languages.
William Saroyan said of the city: "If you're alive, you can't
be bored in San Francisco," and Somerset Maugham
applauded it as "the most civilized city in America."

Antique shop in a restored house on Union Street.

Victorian row houses on a peaceful Sunday morning.

Executives confer on Montgomery
Street in the financial district.

Picnic lunch at the Concours d'Elegance auto show
at fashionable Pebble Beach.

University of Oregon (left) at Eugene attracts many young Californians.

Northwesterners: a farsighted people

Oregon, where public officials say "you're welcome to visit but please don't stay," is trying to discourage migrants from polluted and overdeveloped states. Residents happily mail out cards produced by the Ungreeting Card Company—"People in Oregon don't tan in the summer . . . they rust!" or "Last year in Oregon 677 people fell off their bikes . . . and drowned." Oregonians have an impressive sense of collective responsibility: their magnificent 360-mile coastline has been closed to developers; billboards have been purchased and cleared from the highways, and 1% of highway funds are invested in bicycle trails; pop-top cans and nonreturnable bottles were banned in 1972. The Willamette River, which flows through the valley where 70% of the state's people live, was an open sewer in 1966. Today it is once again a spawning ground for 30-lb. salmon. Oregon is an inspiration to people in other states who doubt their ability to influence their own lawmakers.

The lights of Portland sparkle in the foreground as dawn colors the sky behind Mt. Hood.

First prize for painting at the Oregon State Fair.

337

Washington, dominated by the megalopolis on Puget Sound, is an outward-looking state. Because of its burgeoning trans-Pacific trade and its position as the "gateway to Alaska," the value of Washington's exports is the highest per capita in the U.S. Until a few years ago, the residents of the state's leading city—Seattle—were exponents of uninhibited growth, but these sentiments have begun to change. Developers appear to have lost the battle for "urban renewal." Instead of being torn down, buildings in the raunchy, dilapidated sections of the city—dating back to the gold-rush days at the turn of the century—are being faithfully restored, refurbished, and reopened as restaurants, shops, offices. An abandoned 12-mile railroad right-of-way through the most scenic parts of the city has been developed for the exclusive use of bikers and hikers. Plans are even being drawn to build a 4.5-acre park over the freeways that currently divide the city.

Floating homes on Seattle's urban lake are on platted, submerged lots. Sewer connection is mandatory; utilities and city services are available.

Seattle, bordered on three sides by water, is reversing the flight to the suburbs by restoring and revitalizing its downtown areas.

A quiet street in one of the older, middle-income sections of Seattle.

Thousands commute by ferry (at left) to jobs in Seattle.

339

Steel transmission towers carry power from Columbia River hydroelectric projects.

Wheat is harvested in eastern Oregon. To insure better crops, planted fields are alternated—the field above is fallow.

The Northwest leads the nation in the production of hydroelectric power—the Columbia River and its tributaries create a third of U.S. capacity. The area also has a strong agricultural base, producing and processing quantities of fruits, vegetables, and wheat. Almost half the country's lumber comes from the West Coast, and Oregon—where plywood was invented in 1905—produces more than half the nation's plywood and nearly a fourth of its softwood lumber. In Washington's Puget Sound area, Boeing has built more commercial jets than the rest of the non-Communist world combined. When Boeing prospers, half the manufacturing workers in the area are on its payroll. When orders dwindle, unemployment rises as high as 15%— as it did in 1971.

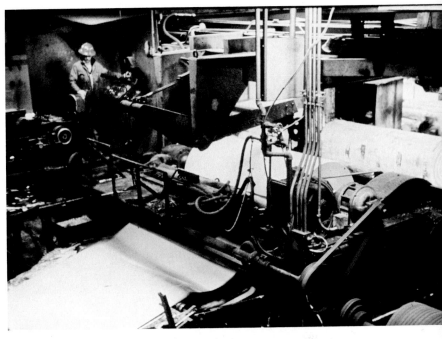

Thin ribbon of plywood is peeled from solid block as a first step in the production of plywood at this Washington plant.

The Boeing 747 plant at Everett, Washington, is as big as 10 of Houston's Astrodomes— so big that clouds form inside and, on occasion, it may even rain.

Hawaii – Paradise in Transition

"The old Hawaiians knew all there was to know about islands," says a modern-day Hawaiian whose home high on the mountain slopes of rural Oahu looks out to the ocean.

He is right. But it is also true that his ancestors knew nothing but islands.

The origins of the Hawaiian people were in the Polynesian archipelagoes of the southern Pacific. In the course of hazardous exploratory voyaging over unknown seas, they discovered and settled a small uninhabited group of islands north of the equator, in the latitude roughly of the Tropic of Cancer.

Planting themselves there, they shaped their culture for centuries in virtual isolation from the rest of the world. There was no other inhabited island group closer than 1,900 miles, and the continental land masses were farther away still.

For the Hawaiians, Hawaii became the world—a small world, less than 6,500 square miles of land in more than 70 million square miles of water. As their distant descendant says, they were, quintessentially, islanders.

"Think about what that means," he goes on. "Asians and Africans—they had continents to play with. Westerners, especially Americans and Australians, people like that—if things got too bad or too crowded where they were, they could move on. Or even if things just looked better somewhere else. But once the Hawaiians got here, they were here to stay. There was nowhere else for them to go. They lived with what they had and took the consequences of what they did. That's what being an islander means."

In other words, the Hawaiians had to arrange their lives to take into account the very real environmental constraints of their situation. It was the gods of the Hawaiians who spoke authoritatively on these matters. There were divine prohibitions against exhausting natural resources—the fish of the sea, the coconuts of the shore, the taro of the valley. There were dark and awful supernatural punishments that might follow the pollution of a village water supply by human excrement. And because the gods of the Hawaiians spared them population control by total war or epidemic disease or prolonged famine, there was cultural permission to practice abortion and infanticide, so as to keep population in line with resources.

It worked. The Hawaiians stabilized their population at a level of nutrition which kept them healthy and which permitted their food supply, carefully managed, to renew itself.

The population level was also one at which man did not dominate the landscape. Again, the gods were responsible for this. Reverence for nature was an article of faith at the same time that it was a condition of survival.

In human terms, the Hawaiian environment was—and still is—a marvelously healthy and benign and life-enhancing one: blue skies, warm sun, cooling trade

Ancient City of Refuge, with its towering wooden images, was restored by U.S. Park Service. For 400 years it was a haven for lawbreakers, defeated warriors, and for those who had violated the rigid taboos of a feudal society.

At left, a fisherman uses a six-to-seven foot spear in shallow water, attracting the fish with the light of his kukui-nut torch.
Older natives are still skilled at tossing a net (below) to trap fish.

winds, a serene climatic constancy tempered by changes in elevation and aspect from windward to leeward. And yet the Hawaiians could find as well, among their small islands, the variety of experience offered by snow-capped mountains, barren lava fields, broad open plains, waterfalls hundreds of feet high, rain forest, melancholy swampland, reef-protected shallows, and the excitement of high surf.

Today, there are more than 900,000 people in the islands. Perhaps one in ten of the inhabitants has any Hawaiian blood. Hawaiians are overwhelmingly outnumbered in their homeland. Hawaii has become another kind of place altogether.

The isolation that was so decisive in giving ancient Hawaii its special character was broken irreversibly in 1778, when the islands were located for the West at large by the celebrated British explorer, James Cook. In the almost 200 years which have followed, however, the dominant influence on Hawaii has been not British but American.

"Some simple matching up of dates demonstrates this," says one historian of the islands.

> Hawaii was brought to the attention of the West just after the American colonies declared their independence. By 1820, while the new American nation was still establishing itself, New England whalers and missionaries came to Hawaii. By the late 1840s, there was a strong economic connection between Hawaii and the California gold-fields. One hundred years after American independence, in 1876, there was an economic treaty locking Hawaii's principal product, sugar, into the American market. In the 1890s, when the United States was getting ready to play an imperial role in the Pacific and in Asia, there was a revolution in Hawaii, led by Americans, which overthrew the Hawaiian monarchy and prepared the way for annexation by the United States.

This came in 1898, the year in which the American nation clearly announced itself as an imperial power. Hawaii officially became a territory of the United States in 1900 and, more than half a century later, in 1959, became the fiftieth state of the Union.

The contrasting great influence in the making of modern Hawaii is Asian. At the beginning of the twentieth century, Caucasians, mostly Americans, outnumbered a sadly diminished Hawaiian population. But over the same years Caucasians and Hawaiians together were being outnumbered, and increasingly so, by Asians—Chinese, Japanese, Koreans, and Filipinos.

They were sugar and pineapple workers, brought in

Tourists in an outrigger canoe ride a wave at Waikiki.

344

Tourists—3 million a year—outnumber residents three to one. Wall of high-rise hotels at Waikiki boasts 22,000 rooms. In August, sunbathers have less room on Waikiki Beach than at New York's Coney Island.

by the thousands and then by the scores of thousands to work the flourishing plantations of the islands. Hawaii, all through its history under the American flag, has been a place where most of the inhabitants have been nonwhite, a sizeable proportion of them born somewhere else or at least the children of immigrants.

"Of course, this is the melting pot all over again, isn't it?" remarks a local politician. "Very American. Immigrants making good. Except that here, most of those in the pot have been nonwhite."

The turning point in the assimilation process was World War II, which began for the United States at Pearl Harbor. Hawaii was put under martial law for the duration of the war. A volunteer unit raised from among Hawaii-born Japanese, the 442nd Regimental Combat Team, fought with great distinction in the European theater. And in the postwar period, Hawaii's people began to talk in terms of statehood for the islands—first-class American citizenship for themselves.

The decade that followed statehood, the 1960s, saw another decisive stage in the breaking down of the relative isolation that had continued to characterize Hawaii throughout the territorial period. "Partly it was statehood itself that did it," says the politician. "There was a tremendous surge of interest in the islands, as really a part of the United States for the first time. But of course that interest wouldn't have been maintained without the possibility that mainland Americans could come and see the place for themselves."

It was the passenger jet that accomplished this, delivering large numbers of people to the islands quickly and cheaply all through the sixties. "Somewhere in the middle sixties," says a woman very successful in the tourist business, "I felt a kind of tip-over. Every year from then on, the islands were housing more tourists than residents. One million by 1966, 2 million by 1970, 3 million now and still rising."

Aside from expenditures for military and civilian government personnel, tourism is the biggest element in the Hawaiian economy. Islands once characterized by deep isolation are now as deeply committed as any place in the world to making themselves known everywhere.

"There's no doubt about the influence tourism has had on life locally," says a successful businessman. "Look at employment opportunities here now, per capita wealth, disposable income. It's been a real economic revolution. We can't do without it."

True enough, especially as the bases of the old plantation economy, sugar and pineapple, encounter increasingly hard going on the world market. In fact, the five major companies (C. Brewer & Co., Theo H. Davies & Company, American Factors, Castle & Cooke, Alexander & Baldwin) which steered Hawaii through the plantation era are now diversifying. They are taking their agricultural interests overseas where land and labor are still cheap and developing their choice Hawaiian real estate for tourist resorts.

And for urban subdivisions. It has become clear that tourism has stimulated growth in the total resident population and will go on doing so. Hawaii has one of the fastest growth rates in the nation, and it is not natural increase that pushes population figures up so sharply; it is in-migration. Part of this flow of people comes from Asian and Pacific sources—the Philippines, Japan, Hong Kong, Taiwan, American Samoa—but the most significant migrants, in number and influence, come from the American mainland.

For the first time in Hawaiian history, Caucasians—haoles is the local phrase—are the largest single group in the population. They number about 40 percent now, and given present trends, it is possible to look ahead to a time when they will have 51 percent or more of the population—an absolute majority.

"This is momentous," says a sociologist, herself a relatively new arrival from the mainland, "and I don't

know if anyone here—myself included—quite understands what it might mean."

One thing it certainly means is that Hawaii will never be the same again. The islands have had a reputation—for the most part deserved—for tolerance and ethnic harmony. This was the case even when ethnic background might automatically have meant economic and social advantage or disadvantage. There is a phrase to cover this gentle human generosity—"the aloha spirit." It has consisted of many things, largely unspoken, tending to disappear when described or examined.

Often enough, it has just been a matter of letting people be themselves, live their own lives, a matter of not leaning too heavily on homogenization as a social principle. Modern times continue to do a great deal of homogenization to be sure: of all the temples in Hawaii, the one with the most worshippers by far is a vast edifice at Ala Moana in Honolulu, a shopping center ranking with the biggest in the world, never more thronged than on Sundays, a cathedral of consumerism. People buy color televisions there, and between commercials they watch themselves and their islands on "Hawaii 5-0," just as others do around the world. But despite this remorseless socio-economic shaping and mediating of the notion of the good life, there are all sorts of islands of ethnic variety in Hawaii. The camera-store owner, catering largely to tourists, is in private life a knowing and sensitive fancier of *haiku*, a classic form of Japanese poetry. The Harvard Ph.D. turned hard-driving businessman puts a lot of his drive to work reviving nineteenth and early twentieth century Hawaiian music. Another Ph.D., this one from Yale, is a superb Chinese cook. The high-ranking woman civil servant is a judo black belt. The islands as a whole are sports crazy—everybody bets on football and basketball matches, yet a good many also bet on cockfights.

"One element in the aloha spirit that hasn't had much attention," says the sociologist, "is that *everybody*

in Hawaii in modern times has been a member of an ethnic minority. There has always been the big racial division between white and nonwhite, *haole* and local. But beyond that, there are all sorts of distinctions made between various kinds of locals, between Hawaiians and Orientals and between Orientals of different backgrounds. And so on and on. There has always been a separate, more or less private place for people to take a stand, an identity that they could maintain."

Negative aloha, as this might be called, is remarkable enough in itself. The positive side, even more remarkable in relation to the United States and to the world at large, is that people of so many different ethnic backgrounds have been so ready to intermarry in the islands.

In this kind of society, entering *haoles*, arriving in relatively small numbers, generally managed to identify with some local attitude. Now, increasingly, through sheer weight of numbers, it is possible for new arrivals to treat Hawaii as just another version of the place from which they came.

As the principal island of Oahu has become more and more urbanized, references to the aloha spirit have tended to retreat to the outer islands. Yet for the rest of the century, the outer islands, where the plantation society and economy persisted longest, will be the area most affected by the new tourist-resident society and economy. The population base on any outer island is small, and one big development project can create irreversible change.

"Take Maui County," says an environmentalist who is watching the process with dismay.

> Three islands, Maui, Lanai, and Molokai. Maui has a population of around 42,000, mostly locals. There's one resort and condominium development planned to add 30,000 to that—the size of another Waikiki. Molokai has only around 5,000 people, mostly working in pineapple, an industry which is in bad trouble. The proposed economic

*Container fleet servicing
Hawaii is one of world's most
modern. The state's cost of
living is high because almost
everything must be imported.*

*Gov. George Ariyoshi (right)
and Sen. Daniel K. Inouye
(far right) are two of Hawaii's
dominant political figures.*

salvation of the island is a huge resort and second home complex for 30,000 people. This will attract the same sort of new resident that has sharply raised the *haole* proportion of the population statewide. When it's in place, Molokai's locals will be outnumbered six to one on their own island. The same thing on Lanai, only more so—population of locals, pineapple workers mostly, about 2,000, and an islandwide urban development planned for 15,000. Whatever the right proportion of *haoles* to locals for maintaining the aloha spirit, this isn't it.

There are indeed any number of signs that the aloha spirit is wearing thin. By the time of the bicentennial of Cook's discovery of the islands, 1978, just two years after the nation's Bicentennial, it might be necessary to start thinking about the aloha spirit as part of the past, a casualty of the present and a certain victim of the future, killed by numbers.

Pressures on the environment—the human environment as well as the strictly physical world—are beginning to be felt all over the islands. This is something new for Hawaii, and no one has developed satisfactory ways of talking about it.

The political rhetoric of the state is still that of the open society, and certainly this has been an invaluable notion over the past generation, which has seen the establishment of a multi-ethnic democracy that works as well as anything in American politics. In 1974, for example, George R. Ariyoshi became the first man of Japanese-American ancestry to win a U.S. state governorship, succeeding John A. Burns who had been elected to the office three times. Hawaii's delegation to the U.S. Congress has included Hiram Fong, the first Oriental ever to be elected to the U.S. Senate; Daniel K. Inouye, who served with great distinction in the 442nd Regiment in World War II; Patsy Takemoto Mink; and Spark Matsunaga.

Openness as a philosophy has also suited the great years of the tourist business. A willingness to encourage almost unrestricted growth has been good for all sorts of economic indices in Hawaii.

The question is whether openness and growth are the best watchwords for Hawaii in the years beyond the Bicentennial, given that those years are likely to be marked, worldwide, by population explosion and by food and energy shortages. On close inspection, Hawaii turns out to be vulnerable on many counts. It has no energy sources of its own. It runs on oil, which has to travel thousands of miles of ocean to reach the place where it is burned. It grows only about a quarter of the food it consumes (not counting the specialized crops of pineapple and sugar, which are for export). The rest of its daily bread is imported, again across thousands of miles of ocean. The islands live at an American standard of consumption, in the middle of the biggest ocean in the world. This gives rise to the staggering figure recently generated by a geographer who did an energy budget for the island of Oahu: per capita energy consumption in Honolulu and its surroundings is one-third higher than on the American mainland. And in absolute terms, consumption is rising rapidly, as more and more mainland Americans decide that the stresses of urban living on the continent are too heavy and come to seek a smaller-scale alternative in the warm-weather, blue-sky islands.

They may imagine that they are getting away from it all. But this is a fantasy. The reality is that Hawaiian life has ceased to be island life. The place now functions as an extension of the continent. Beyond that, Hawaii is in the world market: the food market, the energy market, the capital market, the real-estate market. As a result it responds to strains and pressures wherever they are generated worldwide. The irony is that the Hawaiian Islands have become inextricably part of the world just at the time the world has become an island.

—GAVAN DAWS

Aloha Spirit:
warm and welcoming

Aloha means love, compassion, hello, goodbye—a spirit that has been described as a "benign contagion" which spread from the original native Hawaiians to the many ethnic groups living in the Islands today. In the words of one Hawaiian writer: "Hawaii alone has what the French call, with exquisite expressiveness, a douceur, a certain sweetness, a smoothness, a fragrance, a softness. It is not only in the air, it is in the people."

Lumahai Beach on the lovely island of Kauai.

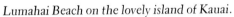

Leis of plumeria, jasmine, vanda orchids, and a hundred other fragrant blooms are given to celebrate arrivals and departures, graduations and weddings, christenings and burials. Even longshoremen on the picket line wear leis around their necks.

Shoppers stroll through Waikiki's Ala Moana Shopping Center, the world's largest.

State legislature (at right) opens a new session with music, dancing, and flowers on every desk.

The island of Oahu, some 40 miles long and 30 miles wide, is the most populous of the islands. With Honolulu as its urban center, it houses almost 80% of the people of the state. The frenzied building boom around Waikiki—which was recently described as "overbilled, overbuilt, and overpriced"—finally aroused local citizen groups, which have had some recent success in curbing the excesses of the developers.

Modern Honolulu, with Diamond Head in the background, is the state capital, business center, and tourist mecca of the islands.

On Kamehameha Day, the statue of the Hawaiian king who unified the islands is hung with 40-foot leis.

Below, a tourist couple ponders the purchase of a hula skirt.

351

Wages for farm workers like those tending pineapple field below rose from 19¢ an hour to minimums well over $2 in 1970. Workers were organized in the 1940s by the longshoremen's ILWU. Taro is planted (above) on a plantation on the island of Hawaii.

Hawaii is "the loveliest fleet of islands anchored in any ocean," wrote Mark Twain. When the original Polynesian settlers reached the islands in their canoes, probably in the 5th Century, they brought with them carefully wrapped seedling plants—sugar cane, coconut, taro, bananas, breadfruit, and many others—to insure their future food supply. For years taro was the principle staple crop—the beautiful heart-shaped leaves (at right) were steamed and eaten as greens; the roots cooked and crushed to be eaten as poi. Taro plants were also used in religious ceremonials and are still used by natives for a variety of medicinal purposes.

The love for children among Polynesian Hawaiians is proverbial. No matter how large their own families, they still follow the ancient hanai tradition of adopting—and even favoring—the children of friends and relatives. The schools are managed by a single statewide board of education, and all schools are funded on a per capita basis. A child's opportunity to learn is neither enhanced nor diminished by the fact that he lives in a rich or poor neighborhood nor because his ancestors are Chinese, Hawaiian, Japanese, Caucasian or—as is more likely—a glorious mixture of racial strains.

Family group of Hawaiians of Samoan descent enjoy singing at a picnic at Queens Beach on Oahu.

Singing and playing their traditional instruments, these ladies celebrate Aloha Week—held annually in October.

356

Descendants of Polynesian settlers, dressed in colorful aloha shirts and muumuus, enjoy their classic native feast —a luau.

The easygoing life style of the islands survives, although there are only about a thousand pureblood descendants of the Polynesian settlers, and only 9% of the population has any Polynesian blood at all. The social environment is outgoing and informal. The Polynesians are untouched by the competitive spirit of Chinese and Japanese immigrants, just as they never adopted the Calvinist work ethic introduced by Caucasian missionaries. With no sense of guilt, they simply enjoy their leisure, their incomparable climate, and the indescribable beauty of their islands.

Leis—fragrant and colorful—are the symbol of the aloha spirit.

Alaska-
Pioneer
Society

"**W**ild and wide are my borders," said Alaska in a poem written during gold rush days, and that description still holds true today. We've all read that Alaska is twice as big as Texas, but its size is difficult to comprehend until you have bounced over its vast expanse in wind-buffeted planes. From Ketchikan to Attu is as far as Jacksonville to San Francisco; Kodiak to Barrow is Oklahoma City to Winnipeg. The very name Alaska means "The Great Land" in Aleut. And as for being wild, where else in the United States can you find temperatures of seventy below, hear the howling of the wind and the wolves, and look *south* to the northern lights?

Within these wild wide borders live some 320,000 people, hardly enough to populate a medium-sized city in the Lower Forty-Eight. If they were to spread out, every Alaskan would have almost two square miles all

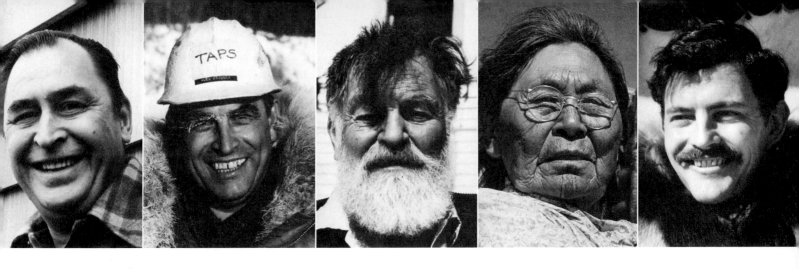

to himself. (In New Jersey he would have to share that space with twenty other people.) And, more than the people of any other state, Alaskans venture out into their breathtakingly beautiful wilderness. Even city dwellers hunt and fish, if only for the very practical reason that meat has to be shipped in and it's cheaper to shoot it than to buy it. A common greeting in Alaska, whether in a native village or at a symphony concert in Anchorage, is—"Did you get your moose?"

Alaska is where civilization and wilderness meet—and both win. Far up in the bush a native trapper runs his line on a snowmobile with a transistor radio in his pocket; in town a housewife goes to the store wearing parka, down-filled pants, and mukluks. The air is filled with excitement, from the midnight sun of summer to winter's twilight at noon. It's the last frontier, the place where anything can happen.

Just going to work in the morning can be an adven-

ture. Take Ed Merdes, a big, likeable guy who would be a typical Alaskan except that there isn't any such thing; in the Great Land people just don't fit into molds. Ed was a poor boy from a Pennsylvania mining town who played football at Cornell to get an education. With the ink barely dry on his law degree, he and his wife Norma took off for Alaska to find challenge and opportunity under skies untouched by factory smoke. Now he has his own law firm in Fairbanks, a big comfortable house that costs a fortune to heat, and six kids.

On a January day when it's fifty below and dark until eleven in the morning, Ed starts the car and lets it run for ten minutes or so. The kids bundle up for school; cold-weather clothing can easily amount to $150 per child. When everyone is in the car, Ed tightens up his parka and opens the garage door. Norma whizzes out; Ed shuts the door, jumps in the car, and off they go.

But they'd make better time on snowshoes, for they

Oil rig rises above the arctic wilderness of the North Slope at Prudhoe Bay, where Alaska pipeline begins. Rigs are moved to new sites when drilling is completed. Above, a solitary Eskimo hunter traverses the frozen Bering Sea at midday near Nome.

Boomtown Anchorage, a tent city for workers on the Alaska Railroad in 1914, now boasts 40% of Alaska's population. It is brash and new and bursting with energy, and—as the only truly modern city in the state—is its political, financial, and business center.

can barely see beyond the hood of the car. At minus thirty-five degrees, moisture in the air freezes and hangs there, becoming ice fog. When this fog covers the city, people go for days, sometimes weeks, without being able to see across the street. At school, Norma reminds the children: "Keep moving, but don't run." Breathing deeply might freeze the lungs.

Ed gets out at his office, and Norma goes on to the store. If she's only going to be a few minutes, she leaves the engine running. For a longer stop she finds a car plug, which looks like a parking meter. She takes the short length of wire that dangles from under the hood of the car and plugs it in. This turns on three heaters: one for the radiator, one for the battery, and one for the interior—not for comfort but to keep the vinyl from cracking.

That's the way you go out in Fairbanks. And if you live a mile or so out of town, you keep a camp heater and sleeping bags in the car, just in case.

Why do people stay on under such conditions? Ed Merdes looks back to the year he was president of Junior Chamber International and visited sixty countries. "No matter how warm the welcome or the climate," he recalled, "I was always glad to get back to Alaska. Do you know what living in a cold country does? It brings out the best in people. When we see a car stopped, we stop too, to see if we can help. We're less selfish, we're more open, we're all together, we're interested in one another. Then summer comes, with its twenty-three and a half hours of sunshine and the flowers and our own vegetables and water skiing on the lake and playing baseball at midnight. Oh, this is wonderful, wonderful country, America at its finest and truest. God, how I love it."

Not everyone shares this enthusiasm. In January, the longest, coldest month, both liquor consumption and the suicide rate go up.

Actually most Alaskans do not experience as severe winters as the inhabitants of Fairbanks. The first white settlements were in the southeastern Panhandle between Canada and the Pacific, where picturesque towns nestle on the edge of blue water under green mountains. Today about 50,000 people live comfortably in this small coastal area, some 13,000 of them in the vicinity of the state's capital, Juneau. The rest are scattered throughout small fishing and lumber towns such as Sitka, Ketchikan, and Skagway. After fishing and lumber, the scenic Panhandle's major industry is tourism.

More than half of all Alaskans live in an even smaller area, clustered around Anchorage on the south central coast. Thanks to the Japan Current, the Anchorage climate is wetter than it is cold.

In many respects Anchorage is just like any other urban complex—there are banks and stores, restaurants and office buildings, crowded schools and crowded streets. Yet even in the midst of a five o'clock traffic jam, you still know you're in Alaska. The jagged peaks

Ice fog shrouds Fairbanks, Alaska's second city. Water was still sold door-to-door in the early 1950s in this rugged frontier town perched at the edge of the Arctic wilderness, but today its University of Alaska is a world center for Arctic research.

Juneau, the capital, (above) is isolated by towering mountains and far from Alaska's population center. Last year voters decided to look for a more accessible site where a new capital may one day be built. The Eskimo village of Kotzebue, below, lies above the Arctic Circle and can only be reached by air for most of the year. Tourists from Outside come to hunt polar bears and see the Eskimos.

of the Chugach Mountains, spotted with glaciers, stand out against the eastern sky, reminding you that in their lower valleys just twenty miles or so away rabbits and foxes, porcupines and weasels are moving through the high green grasses. And on a clear day you can see, some 150 miles to the north, the glistening snow-covered peak of Mount McKinley, America's highest mountain.

North of McKinley and the Alaska Range lies the interior of this great land, so huge that the borough of Fairbanks, which is the size of New Jersey, looks like a snowflake on an otter's back in comparison.

The Arctic Circle is about 100 miles north of Fairbanks, but Alaska stretches still further northward, over the sinister brown-stained peaks of the Brooks Range and down the barren North Slope to the Arctic Ocean. The Eskimo communities of Barrow, northernmost settlement in the United States, and Kotzebue are the major towns in the Arctic region, each with some 2,000 people.

West of Anchorage lies another huge chunk of mountains and muskeg, which trails off into the foggy, treeless Aleutians.

Thus the great majority of Alaskans, including many of the 55,000 natives, live in urban centers. The rest are sprinkled sparsely along the coastlines and rivers in native villages, ghost towns from gold rush days, and trading posts. You can fly over Alaska for what seems like hours without seeing so much as a wisp of smoke in the lonely land beneath.

All this wilderness gives even the most urban Alaskan a symbolic foot on the last frontier. What other state has a congressman who lives in a log cabin with an outdoor privy, north of the Arctic Circle? That's Don Young, of Fort Yukon, population 700. Young's unsuccessful challenger in the 1974 election was Willie Hensley, an Eskimo from Kotzebue. Hensley grew up in a sod hut with windows made of walrus gut.

"We went downstream for the salmon in summer,

361

Bush pilots are the only link with civilization for thousands. They land anywhere—on floats, skis, or wheels—haul freight and passengers, transport the sick to hospitals. Don Sheldon (left) prepares for takeoff; Stanley McCutcheon (right) brings supplies, including fresh oranges for delighted Eskimo children.

upstream for the muskrat in winter," he said. "That's what we did then, and that's what we do today."

With the exception of the natives, few of the people who live in Alaska were actually born there. The sourdoughs, as the whites born in Alaska are called, make up in interesting background and personality what they lack in number. Grace Berg, for example, is a pretty blonde who grew up in Juneau. She used to devote most of her letters to pen pals in the States to a description of her white frame house and flower garden. "Everybody thought I lived in an igloo," she said.

Grace spent years trying to get out of Alaska. She saved enough money to go Outside to college, then got homesick and came back to the University of Alaska. Located on a windswept hill near Fairbanks, it is surely the coldest campus in the world. Grace realized she was hooked. "There's something about this great land of ours that captures the imagination and grips the heart," she explained. She went to Yale for a law degree and happily returned to Fairbanks to marry a doctor named Arthur J. Schaible and practice law as Grace Berg Schaible.

Jim Dalton, on the other hand, is so much of a sourdough that he was *not* born in Alaska. Dalton's father landed in Alaska the hard way—his ship was caught poaching fur seals and every man was thrown in jail. He stayed on and started a trading post. It was dangerous work: the Indians whipped inflation by tying a profiteer's heels to his head and tossing him into the woods. Dalton, Sr., was established when, in 1895, the gold rush began and thousands of men—followed by hundreds of women—poured in from all over the world. They starved and froze and dropped with exhaustion, but enough survived to produce $700,000,000 in gold— a hundred times what America paid Russia for the entire territory.

Dalton prospered and wooed a young lady right off her cruise ship. But when it came time for Mrs. Dalton

to have Jim, she went to Seattle for the event—her baby was going to be born in the United States, not in a territory.

Although Jim Dalton missed being a sourdough by a technicality, he has made up for it since. An engineer, geologist, and Arctic explorer who disappears into the wilds for weeks on end, Jim played an important role in the discovery of oil on the North Slope. This billion-dollar bonanza brought in more money than the gold rush in lease sales alone, before a drop of oil reached market.

There are other interesting sourdoughs in the Great Land, but for every home-grown Alaskan there are a dozen *cheechakos*, or newcomers. In 1930 the total population of Alaska was just 60,000, of whom half were natives. By 1959, the year Alaska became the forty-ninth state, the number had quadrupled, to some 225,-000. Even so, when some 45,000 natives and a military population of perhaps 35,000 were deducted, that left a lot of opportunity for newcomers.

Anchorage claims world's largest floatplane base. There is one plane for every 100 Alaskans, and 2 residents out of every 100 are licensed to fly—roughly six times the national average.

One young man who answered the call was a Kansas farm worker named Walter J. Hickel. He arrived in the Great Land with thirty-seven cents in his pocket, but he was fast with his fists and Alaska saloons can always use bouncers. Hickel, however, soon discovered a more profitable way of earning a living. The best way to obtain a house in Alaska is to build it yourself—a house worth $40,000 in Seattle, for example, costs $55,000 in Anchorage, $65,000 in Fairbanks. Hickel built himself a house, then received an offer for it that was too good to turn down. Repeating the process with developments and hotels, he became a millionaire. Next he turned to politics and became governor, then Secretary of the Interior.

Mike Gravel, by contrast, journeyed to Alaska from his native Massachusetts in deliberate search of a faster track for a political career. He drove his brother's car and subsisted for the last five days up the dusty Alaska highway on a loaf of bread and a jar of peanut butter. He arrived in Anchorage on a Sunday night, and by nine a.m. the next day he had secured a job selling real estate. As soon as the three-year residential requirement was up, Gravel began running for office. In 1968 he got 35,754 votes. That wouldn't have won an election for dogcatcher back home, but in Alaska it was enough to put him in the United States Senate.

There is no aristocracy in Alaska, either of family background or wealth. When the wealthy Mrs. Marshall Field of Chicago visited a friend in Anchorage, she found the contrast between directing her household staff at home and the do-it-yourself attitude in Alaska refreshing. She later married a newspaperman named Larry Fanning, and the two bought an Anchorage paper.

"The people who come here are vital and energetic," Mrs. Fanning said. "They want to do things themselves. I go Outside a couple of times a year—but I couldn't stand living anywhere else."

Neither could Lowell Thomas, Jr., and his wife Tay. As a documentary film producer, Thomas could afford to live anywhere; but he and Tay chose Alaska for its recreational advantages and clean air and water. From their comfortable home in Anchorage, it's only a few minutes to their plane, then only a few minutes more to a glacier for skiing, winter and summer, or to a clear pure stream for fishing.

Flying is a way of life in Alaska. Together Anchorage and Fairbanks have nonstop service to the major cities of the world. But there is also regular service to the tiniest village and remotest settlement, even to the North Slope. There is irregular service to nowhere—bush pilots will fly to tops of mountains, to ice floes, to hunting cabins or fishing streams. Planes have pontoons in summer, skis in winter; thus all that's needed for a landing is a stretch of ice, snow, or water. The bush pilots hold Alaska together. There are no roads north and west of the Anchorage-Fairbanks area; it's either boat, snowmobile, or plane.

Brutal cold, howling winds, rain, snow, fog, and high mountains are the obvious hazards faced by the pilot of a small plane. But there are more unusual challenges as well. In the blowing snow condition, for example, a pilot may come down on a perfectly clear day to find himself in a ten-foot-high blizzard that has wiped out all visibility on the ground. In a whiteout there's no difference between sky and ground; in the early days, before instruments, pilots didn't know whether they were right side up or wrong side down.

Oil workers on the North Slope are masked against −42° cold. Exposed flesh freezes in seconds at temperatures that drop to −60°. The men work up to 12 hours a day, 7 days a week, with one to two weeks off after two to four on the job. "No weapons, no booze, no women." But the best men, with overtime, can earn up to $60,000.

"Everybody I know could name several good friends who've been killed in air accidents," commented a young woman whose husband flies his own plane. "But what do you expect us to do, walk?"

Where there are roads in Alaska there are campers, ranging from pickup trucks with homemade bodies to elaborate custom-made vans. Getting outdoors is the major recreation in Alaska—hunting, fishing, skiing, hiking, or simply roaming the wilds. The whole family goes together. This way of life encourages a wholesomeness, a togetherness. It stimulates ingenuity and keeps the Alaskan alert, as when a picnicker is busily picking berries and backs into a bear doing the same thing.

Alaskans seem to have many characteristics in common. For one thing, they're unpredictable. In politics, for instance, Democrats are in the majority, but somehow a Republican is always being elected to some office somewhere. They're independent and self-sufficient, yet always willing to help someone else. Before newcomers abused the custom, Alaskans with cabins in the wilds always left firewood handy in case someone stumbled in half-frozen. People even used to leave their keys in their cars in case somebody needed transportation.

Alaskans are ingenious, always ready to try something new. Despite the existence of day-long sunlight and fertile soil along the Tanana River south of Fairbanks, for example, attempts to grow grain consistently ended in failure. Then one spring Jim Harding, an agronomist, saw barley sprouting in an abandoned field that had been used for snowmobile races. Of course! Sow the barley in the fall so that it sprouts in the melting snow. Fed to pigs in heated sheds, the barley makes it possible for interior Alaska to produce its own meat. And what to do with the carbon dioxide and manure produced by the pigs? Grow strawberries.

Many communities have to double up their crowded schools, but in Fairbanks they've made a game of it. Students in the morning shift go to East Lathrop High School; those in the afternoon shift go to West Lathrop High School. Different bands, teams, school spirit, everything—all in the same building.

Families are close in Alaska; they communicate with each other. This, combined with that utter unpredictability of Alaskans, resulted in national headlines in 1970. Wally Hickel, staunch conservative and loyal Secretary of the Interior, learned from his six children that many American youths disagreed with the Nixon administration on several major issues, including Vietnam. Hickel insisted on explaining their viewpoint to President Nixon, and was fired for his pains. No one in Alaska was surprised at Hickel's stance; Alaskans generally listen to their kids.

For all their talk about escaping the pollution of the Lower Forty-Eight, Alaskans are messy with their land. You can find beer cans miles from nowhere. Nor is this a trait of the newcomers. Native villages, with split salmon and caribou hides drying on top of their log cabins and trash strewn over the dirt streets, offend the eyes and noses of visitors. But to people who have subsisted in this harsh land for thousands of years, there are more important things to worry about.

Great changes are taking place in the Great Land today. The oil rush and the construction of an 800-mile pipeline have attracted thousands of newcomers. And while oil has brought riches to some of Alaska's citizens, it has brought nothing but aggravation to others. Those who have carved out tiny homesteads in the wilderness resent the close pursuit of all they have tried to escape. But of all Alaskans, it is the native population that has been most affected. Civilization has been creeping up on them for a century; now it has pounced.

The Eskimos along the northern and western coasts and the Indians in the interior have traditionally been nomadic peoples, following their food supplies. Then came the impedimenta of civilization—houses with doors and windows, stoves and other modern imple-

Drill rig steams in −53°
temperature at noon in January.
For 56 days a year the sun
never rises above the horizon
at Prudhoe Bay.

ments—making it difficult to move. Once there were many native villages on the North Slope, for example; now there is only Barrow. And while the new, permanent settlements make life easier in some respects—Barrow, for instance, sits on a natural gas formation, which provides free heat for every tarpaper and corrugated tin shack—there are not enough jobs in the villages to replace subsistence hunting and fishing. In many areas, malnutrition and the white man's diseases have narrowed the native's life expectancy to thirty-four years.

With permanent villages have come permanent schools. After completing the primary grades in a one-room village school, native children—and their parents—face the decision of whether to go on. Every fall, all over Alaska, the students who choose a secondary school education are rounded up and flown off, some to boarding schools in the state, some to federal institutions as far away as Oklahoma.

It's a hard life for a village kid thousands of miles from home, but a large number finish high school and some go on to college. Then, for many, the problems begin. Linda Gologergeren, an Eskimo girl from St. Lawrence Island, which is so far from the mainland that they speak a Siberian Eskimo dialect, went through the heartbreaking experience of getting an education far from home. At last report Linda was an airline stewardess with a modern apartment and full social life in Anchorage. When in the city, however, she was always homesick for the gossipy village life on her misty island home; yet when she was home, she missed her job and her social life in civilization.

The Alaskan natives are a race in transition. Fortunately recent events have made life easier for them. Following discovery of oil at Prudhoe Bay on the North Slope, thousands of square miles of land were officially deeded to the natives, along with money from the sale of leases on land currently held by the state. Native corporations were then set up to administer the holdings.

One petroleum expert has likened Alaska's oil reserves to infinite wealth. Furthermore, these oil reserves are coming on stream at a most propitious time: not only does the nation need oil, but the creation of the native corporations will help assure a fair distribution of the income from petroleum and, eventually, natural gas. In the Bicentennial year, America's forty-ninth state can look forward to an income of perhaps a billion dollars a year for at least a decade.

Alaska's oil bonanza comes at a turning point in the history of our planet, a time when man is beginning to learn how to use natural resources without abusing them. In the cruel conditions of the Arctic and sub-Arctic regions men have always had to work together, to trust one another in order to survive. With this heritage, the people of Alaska may well be uniquely fitted to enjoy both the advantages of a civilization enhanced by enormous wealth and the bounties of a rich and beautiful, still wild frontier.

—BOOTON HERNDON

365

The Robinsons—Peter, Harlow, Nancy, and Vin—have been living in the bush since 1968. "Things are easier now that we've learned to handle the basics—food, warmth, and shelter."

Homesteading: life in a rugged land

Pete and Nancy Robinson were 22 years old when they packed themselves, their son Harlow, their dog, and most of their possessions into a 1950 pickup truck and set off for Alaska. "Everyone said we'd never make it in that $200 rattletrap, but we never doubted for a minute that we'd get there. We did—with exactly $40 left in our pockets!" The couple had originally met during mountain-climbing outings at Colorado State University: "We always felt more at home in the mountains than in town and were sure we could create the kind of life we wanted in the Alaskan wilderness." After nine months working in Talkeetna—Nancy as a teacher and Pete as a weather observer—they jumped at the chance to help new friends build tourist cabins and a lodge at Ermine Lake, 156 miles north of Anchorage. They lived there for three years in a 12-by-18-foot log cabin, 17 miles from the nearest railroad section house at Hurricane. Orders for supplies had to be mailed in Hurricane. When an order was ready, word would be sent out over "Northwind," a radio program that sends personal messages to people living in the bush. In midwinter when the snow was deep and temperatures dropped below zero, the trip to pick up supplies—on skis, snowshoes, or by dogsled when the snowmobile was out of commission —could take all day.

Five-room log cabin, built by Pete in subzero weather in 1971, was a necessity after Vin was born in Fairbanks in 1970. It overlooks Ermine Lake (background, at left) and Mt. McKinley—highest peak in North America—and is only a quarter mile from the new Anchorage-Fairbanks road. The family spent seven months of 1970 in town because they were out of money—Pete worked for a lumber firm, Nancy as a teacher's aide.

In winter, water is hauled every other day from an ice hole (above) cut in the lake. "We go back after a crust of ice has formed to shovel snow over it. That helps insulate the ice so it won't get so thick that we have to chisel it open." In background is 20,320-foot Mt. McKinley.

Survival in the bush— simply to keep wood in the stove and food on the table—requires unending hard work. Pete handles the heaviest chores and hunts small game and moose. From June through September there is an abundance of salad greens and berries. But it takes money—about $5,000 a year in high-cost Alaska—to pay for staple foods, winter clothing, and medical expenses. So for part of each summer the family goes wherever Pete can find work. He has built log homes in Palmer and Anchorage, worked as a hunting guide, on bridge construction, and as a laborer on a chainsaw. "But it's frustrating to hunt for work in the seasonal job market and our goal is self-sufficiency. An insurance settlement made it possible for us to buy some farmland near Trapper Creek, 40 miles south of the lake. The new land is fertile enough to provide all our own vegetables as well as feed for the goats and chickens we hope to have. None of this is possible here because of the higher altitude and frequent bad weather in the growing season. We also hope to sell carrots and potatoes and to sell or trade our own lumber for things we need. We'll have to build another house—and the next one will have a well and a hand pump. Eventually, we'll also have electricity from the power lines nearby."

One good-sized moose a year is enough for the family. Nancy always helps with the butchering.

Ten gallons of birch sap boil down into only a pint of syrup. Pete and Harlow (below) use the snowmobile to haul in a felled tree.

Plastic boat and pitcher were used for baths until Pete built a small sauna by the creek. "Now it takes only 10 gallons of water to clean up the whole family!"

"I split firewood when Pete is too busy. It was hard until I learned how to handle a maul and wedge, but now I enjoy doing it— especially when a log needs just one good whack with the axe."

"I make time to share with the children, though it can be difficult with so much to be done. They're always within sight or sound—so much so that it occasionally gets on my nerves."

"Washing clothes outdoors in summer is pleasant —and I don't have to haul the water very far when I set up by the lake."

Housekeeping in the wilderness— without

running water or electricity—is not easy. Nancy grinds the wheat and makes her own baked goods in the uneven heat of a wood stove. "I do three or four tub loads of laundry at a time so I can use rinse water again as wash water. It takes 40-50 gallons for two-weeks-worth of laundry." In summer, Nancy harvests greens and berries, makes jams and jellies, cans berries, and—when the spring thaws come in April— she cans or dries the leftover moose meat.

"Most of our clothes are dried indoors on a rack in winter but in the spring I go back to the line. When the snow melts it will be over my head."

"We usually thaw, butcher, package, and refreeze only one moose quarter at a time because small packages spoil more quickly if there's an unexpected thaw."

The boys help stack and
bring in firewood. "We
need at least eight cords a
year to feed the stove and
keep the house warm, and
it takes Pete two full days
to cut—with a chainsaw—
haul, and stack each cord."
In midwinter the sun is
above the horizon for less
than 6 hours but is visible
for almost 20 hours in
midsummer.

The boys help out in many ways.
Because the nearest school is 35 miles away, Nancy
teaches them with correspondence courses
provided by the state. Assignments and exams are
mailed to teachers in Juneau. "Correspondence
school keeps me in close touch with what and how
the boys are learning. But sometimes the parent-
teacher role becomes strained and I begin to feel
they need other adult authority figures in their
lives—and other children, too." When Nancy and
Pete build their new house at Trapper Creek, the
boys will be able to go to a small elementary school
nearby. Although they miss having friends of their
own age, they do see more of their father than
children Outside. Pete takes time when he can to
show them how to do some of his chores: "Most of
all, I want them to think about what they're doing
so they'll do it rationally and efficiently. I want
them to learn that survival anywhere—in the bush,
in the city, on the farm—depends on thinking things
out for themselves without waiting for someone
else to tell them what to do and how to do it."

Harlow enjoys teaching Vin to handle snowshoes (above),
but is less than enthusiastic about his homework.

Vin helps feed the puppies
as the Husky mother,
Chena, looks on. The boys
also help feed the cat and
a pair of rabbits kept to
provide rabbit meat.

There are neighbors in the valley, and there is a special closeness among the young people who choose to live a simple life far from the trappings of 20th century civilization. Good friends often get together and are always ready to aid each other when help is needed. On Thanksgiving, there is a tradition—begun in 1971—that the young bush families will assemble for dinner at someone's cabin. They arrive on snowshoes, skis, dogsleds, and snowmobiles, bringing contributions for the feast. There is never room in their small homes for such large groups to gather around a table so everyone sits on the floor. One year, in Kathy and Rick Ernst's new home (at left) a table was improvised from boards, plates from cardboard and foil. "There are more and more children at these gatherings," says Nancy, "and we're as glad to be together as any long-separated family of aunts, uncles, and cousins. We actually think of our friends as 'family' because all our relatives live so far away. Although we all came to Alaska in search of a less crowded place, with a flavor of wilderness and pioneer times, we still think including other people in our lives is pretty important."

The young pioneers frequently get together to help each other on the big jobs. Pete (at right) helps a college friend, Dave Johnston, to complete the log work on his new cabin.

Neighbors Betty and George Menard often bring the baby over for a visit and Nancy's brother, Don Child (in background above), comes up occasionally from Valdez.

Picture Credits

Credits from left to right are separated by semicolons, from top to bottom by dashes.

1 Maria Ealand(2)—Paul Seaman; David Muench; Leo Choplin, Black Star—Paul Conklin; Susanne Anderson. 8-9 Bruce Roberts, Rapho-Photo Researchers. 10-11 Bill Weems. 12-13 J. R. Gilcreast, Jr. 14-15 Jim Holland, Black Star. 16-17 Bill Weems. 18-19 Jonathan Blair, Black Star.

Chapter One.
22 Constantine Manos, Magnum; Peter Vandermark, Stock, Boston; Clif Garboden, Stock, Boston; Philip Jon Bailey, Stock, Boston; Jonathan Rawle, Stock, Boston— Fred Ward, Black Star. 24-25 Arthur Griffin. 25 Jonathan Blair, Black Star—Hanson Carroll, Black Star. 26, 26-27 Ted Spiegel, Black Star. 27 Gerald Brimacombe, Black Star. 28 Fred Ward, Black Star. 29 Guy Gillette. 31 Rollie McKenna. 32 Ted Spiegel, Black Star. 32, 33 Gerald Brimacombe, Black Star. 34 Ed Cooper. 35 Christopher Morrow, Stock, Boston; Farrell Grehan, Photo Researchers. 36-37 Nathan Benn. 38 Nathan Benn. 39 Nathan Benn —Clemens Kalischer. 40 Don Morgan, Photo Researchers. 41 Ted Spiegel, Black Star. 42-47 Kosti Ruohomaa, Black Star(all). 48-49 Clemens Kalischer(3). 50-51 Ed Cooper. 51 Hanson Carroll(2). 52, 52-53, 53 Jonathan Blair, Black Star(3)—Ivan Massar, Black Star. 54-55 VOSCAR, the Maine Photographer(4). 56 William Berchen—Hanson Carroll. 57 Hanson Carroll(2). 58 Jonathan Blair, Black Star; (top) Paul Conklin—Jonathan Blair, Black Star. 59 Peter Miller, Photo Researchers. 60, 61-62 J. R. Gilcreast, Jr.(2). 61 Michael Philip Manheim ©1974(2). 62-63 Nathan Benn(4). 64 Maine Dept. of Commerce & Industry—Nathan Benn. 65 Clemens Kalischer; (top) Paul Conklin—Paul Darling. 66-67 Fred J. Pratson(4). 68 Katherine Knowles; Mary Eleanor Browning, DPI—Franz Kraus, DPI; Paul Conklin. 69 Maine Dept. of Commerce & Industry.

Chapter Two.
70 Maldwin Hamlin, Memphis Chamber of Commerce; Paul Conklin(2); Michael Semak, Time-Life Books; Susanne Anderson— Alfred Eisenstaedt, Time-Life Picture Agency, ©Time, Inc. 72 James Pickerell; UPI. 73 UPI; James Pickerell—Wide World; University of Alabama. 74-75 J. Alex Langley, DPI(2). 76 Bruce Roberts, Rapho-Photo Researchers. 78-79 Dan McCoy, Black Star. 81 Brian Payne, Black Star. 82 National Trust for Historic Preservation. 83 John Lewis Stage, Photo Researchers. 84 Ed Cooper— EPA/Documerica, Flip Schulke(2). 86 Bruce Roberts, Rapho-Photo Researchers. 87 Owen Franken, Stock, Boston. 88 Virginia State Travel Service. 88-89 National Trust for Historic Preservation. 88 Henry Groskinsky, Time-Life Picture Agency, ©Time, Inc. 89 National Trust for Historic Preservation. 90 Dan Guravich; Bruce Roberts, Rapho-Photo Researchers(2). 91 Brian Seed, Black Star(2). 92 C. Thomas Hardin, *Courier Journal & Times*— Billy Davis, *Courier Journal & Times*. 93 Tony Triolo, *Sports Illustrated*, ©Time, Inc.—Bill Strode, *Courier Journal & Times*; Ford Reid, Image, Inc. 94 Nathan Benn. 94-95 Bruce Roberts, Rapho-Photo Researchers. 95 Maldwin Hamlin, Memphis Chamber of Commerce—Dan McCoy, Black Star. 96-97 Richard Meek(3). 98 Hanson Carroll. 99 Mike Mauney, Black Star—Thomas Nebbia; Michael Abramson, Black Star. 100 Burk Uzzle, Magnum(2). 101 Guy Gillette—J. Alex Langley, DPI. 102 Allen Green(2)—Dennis Brack, Black Star—Allen Green. 103 Allen Green. 104 Nathan Benn; David A. Harvey. 104-105 Bruce Roberts, Rapho-Photo Researchers. 105 Ken Heyman. 106 Robert Lightfoot(2); Robert Lightfoot, Van Cleve. 107 Robert Lightfoot, Van Cleve. 108 Robert Lightfoot, Van Cleve; Robert Lightfoot—Robert Lightfoot, Van Cleve. 109 Bruce Roberts,

Rapho-Photo Researchers—M. A. Geissinger, Photo Researchers; Jerry Cooke, Photo Researchers. 110 Frederick Myers, Van Cleve— Steve Wall, Black Star. 110-111 Lee Friedlander. 112 Leo Touchet, Magnum(3). 113 Lee Battaglia. 114-115 Leo Touchet, Magnum(6).

Creative Americans.
Supplementary picture research supplied by Rosemary Eakins and Ann Novotny, Research Reports, New York. 116 Fred Ward, Black Star. 116-117 George Tames, *The New York Times*. 117 Heinz Kluetmeier, Time-Life Picture Agency, ©Time, Inc.—John Zimmerman, FPG; Michael Abramson, Black Star. 118 George Ballis—Jim Holland, Black Star— Jon Brenneis. 119 Don Carl Steffen, Rapho-Photo Researchers. 120 Bruce Davidson, Magnum—Jill Kramentz; Declan Haun, Black Star. 121 Leonard McCombe, Time-Life Picture Agency, ©Time, Inc.—Ralph Crane, *Fortune*, ©Time, Inc.; John Launois, Black Star. 122 Henri Cartier-Bresson, Magnum—Ken Regan, Camera 5. 123 Martha Swope; Herbert Migdoll—Steve Schapiro, Black Star; Marc & Evelyn Bernheim, Woodfin Camp. 124 Jill Kramentz —Jill Kramentz, *People*, ©Time, Inc.; Jill Kramentz—Burton Berinsky, *Time*, ©Time, Inc.; Jill Kramentz. 125 Dominique Berretty, Black Star.

Chapter Three.
126 Rick Smolan; Paul Conklin(4)— Richard Lawrence Stack, Black Star. 128 Guy Gillette. 129 Ralph Crane, Time-Life Picture Agency, ©Time, Inc. 130 Nancy Crampton. 131 Hiroyuki Matsumoto, Black Star(2). 132 Carlo Bavagnoli— Nancy Butler. 133 Retta Richards. 134 Ed Cooper. 135 Margaret Durrance(2). 136-137 Edgar J. Cheatham(2). 138 John Neubauer— (top) Edgar J. Cheatham. 139 *Adventure Road* 140 Bill Weems. 141

Dennis Brack, Black Star. 142 Bill Weems—Schreider. 144 Joe Bilbao, Photo Researchers. 145 Bob Nadler, DPI—DPI. 146-147 Dan Wynn(5). 148 Herb Goro; Hiroyuki Matsumoto, Black Star. 148-149 Guy Gillette. 149 Dan Wynn; Guy Gillette. 150 Hiroyuki Matsumoto, Black Star. 150-151 Lizabeth Corlett, DPI. 151 Joel Peter Witkin—Guy Gillette. 152 Nancy Carlinsky. 152-153 Guy Gillette. 153 Nancy Carlinsky— Herb Goro. 154, 154-155 Dan Wynn. 155 William Katz, Photo Researchers—Dan Wynn. 156-157 Marcia Kay Keegan(5). 158-159 Herb Goro. 159 Herb Goro—Dan Wynn; Herb Goro. 160 Guy Gillette—Lida Moser, DPI. 161 Herb Goro(2). 162-163 Suzanne Szasz. 163 Jonathan Rawle. 164-165 Bob Adler(4). 166 Linda Bartlett—Gulf-Reston Corp. 167 The Rouse Co.—Elliot Erwitt, Magnum; The Rouse Co. 168 National 4-H Foundation— Richard Meek. 168-169 Bill Weems. 169 John Neubauer. 170 Paul Conklin. 171 Bill Weems— Richard Meek. 172-173 Dennis Brack, Black Star. 172 Bill Weems; Paul Conklin. 173 John Neubauer— Paul Conklin. 174 Bill Weems— Jill Durrance. 174-175, 175 Bill Weems. 176-177 Bill Weems(4).

Chapter Four.
178 David A. Harvey; EPA/ Documerica, Ken Heyman; Guy Gillette; Ted Spiegel, Black Star; Ken Heyman— Grant Heilman. 180 Alan Pitcairn. 180-181 EPA/ Documerica, Charles O'Rear. 182 Louis Goldman, Rapho-Photo Researchers—James P. Barry. 183 Bill Strode, Black Star; James P. Barry. 184 Bob Coyle. 185 Buck Miller—Bob Coyle(3). 186 Jerry Souter, Van Cleve. 187 (top) Library of Congress—Charles Harbutt, Magnum. 188-189 James Sugar(3). 190 Georg Gerster, Rapho-Photo Researchers. 191 Paul Conklin—Walter H. Moll, Photo Researchers; Larry

Nicholson. **192** Nelson Morris, Photo Researchers. **193** Gerald Brimacombe, Black Star—J. Alex Langley, DPI. **194** Martin Rogers. **195** Peter de-Krassel, Photo Researchers. **196** Fred J. Maroon, Photo Researchers—Nathan Benn. **197** Margaret Durrance. **198** Farrell Grehan, Photo Researchers. **199** Martin Rogers; Farrell Grehan, Photo Researchers. **200** John Launois, Black Star(2)—Harry Seawell, Black Star. **201** John Launois, Black Star. **202** Chesapeake & Ohio Railroad; (top) United States Steel Corp. **202-203** James Stanfield, Black Star. **204** Robert Madden(2). **204-205, 205** Lee Battaglia(3). **206** James P. Barry; Louis Renault, Photo Researchers. **206-207, 207** James Stanfield, Black Star(2). **208** EPA/Documerica, Ken Heyman. **209** Ken Heyman(2). **210-211** Ken Heyman(5). **212-213** Ken Heyman(4). **214-215** EPA/Documerica, Ken Heyman(3). **216** EPA/Documerica, Ken Heyman(3). **216-217** Ken Heyman. **217** EPA/Documerica, Ken Heyman. **218-223** EPA/Documerica, Ken Heyman(all). **224-225** Grant Heilman(5). **226** David A. Harvey. **227** Roy Zalesky, Black Star; Richard Meek(2). **228-229** James Sugar(5). **230** James Stanfield, Black Star(2). **231** Roger Malloch, Magnum.

Young Americans.
232-233 Larry Morris, *The Washington Post*. **233** Suzanne Szasz(2). **234** Jim Holland, Black Star—EPA/Documerica, Ken Heyman—Edward Lettau, DPI. **235** Margaret Durrance; (top) James Sugar—Paul Seaman—Margaret Durrance. **236** Jonathan Blair, Black Star(2). **237** Hiroyuki Matsumoto, Black Star—Jonathan Blair, Black Star—Bob Coyle. **238** Nathan Benn. **238-239** Ted Streshinsky. **239** Ted Streshinsky; VOSCAR, the Maine Photographer. **240-241** Vocational Industrial Clubs of America(5). **242** Ken Heyman—Bill Ray—James Sugar(3). **243** Grey Villet, Time-Life Picture Agency, ©Time, Inc.—Paul Conklin. **244-245** Charles O'Rear(4).

Chapter Five.
246 Jonathan Blair, Black Star—John Lewis Stage(3). **248-249** Ted Streshinsky. **250** David Muench. **251** James Katzel. **252-253** Jill Durrance(3). **254** Joern Gerdts, Photo Researchers. **255** Bruce McAllister, Black Star. **256** David Muench. **257** Larry Nicholson, Photo Researchers. **258-259** Robert Phillips. **259** John Chvilicek, FPG; Yale Joel. **260-261** William Albert Allard(2). **262-263** Duane Howell, *The Denver Post*(2). **264-265** William Albert Allard(2). **266** William Albert Allard—Martin Weaver, Woodfin Camp. **266-267** Martin Weaver, Woodfin Camp. **267** William Albert Allard. **268-269** Earl Scott, Photo Researchers. **268, 269** William Albert Allard(3). **270** Ernst Haas, Magnum—William Albert Allard(3). **270-271** David Muench. **271** Paul Conklin; William Albert Allard; Gerald Brimacombe, Black Star. **272-273** John C. Russell(3). **273** (top) Jonathan Rawle, Stock, Boston—Fred Lindholm—Margaret Durrance. **274** Gerald Brimacombe, Black Star—Lawrence Schiller, Time-Life Picture Agency, ©Time, Inc. **275** Richard Meek—Margaret Durrance. **276** Paul Fusco, Magnum; J. R. Eyerman—Alan Clifton, Black Star. **277** Josef Muench—J. R. Eyerman. **278** Morton Beebe—Jim Amos, Photo Researchers; Morton Beebe. **279** Herb & Dorothy McLaughlin. **280-281** Carlo Bavagnoli(3).

Chapter Six.
282 David Muench; Paul Conklin; Judith Gersten; Leo Choplin, Black Star; Bob Adelman, Magnum—David Muench. **284** David Muench. **285** Gerald Brimacombe, Black Star. **286** Richard Noble, Time-Life Books. **287** David Muench(2). **288-289** Ken Heyman(3). **290-291** Ed Cooper(2). **292** Paul E. LeFebvre. **293** David Muench. **294** Ralph Crane, Time-Life Books. **294-295** Ken Heyman. **296-297** John Lewis Stage. **297** Henri Cartier-Bresson, Magnum. **298-299** Del E. Webb Development Co.(2). **300-301** Bert Brandt. **301** James Sugar. **302** John Zimmerman, *Fortune*, ©Time, Inc.—Shel Hershorn, Black Star(2); Yoichi Okamoto. **303** Bert Brandt(2). **304** Ralph Crane, Time-Life Picture Agency, ©Time, Inc.—John Lewis Stage(2). **305** John Lewis Stage(3). **306** Hans Namuth, Photo Researchers(2). **307** Bruce McAllister, Black Star—Hans Namuth, Photo Researchers. **308** Shel Hershorn, Black Star; (top) Texas Highway Dept.—Dennis Brack, Black Star. **309** Brian Seed, Black Star. **310** Josef Muench(2). **310-311** David Muench. **312-313** Josef Muench(7). **314** Paul Conklin—Susanne Anderson(2). **315** Ken Heyman—Paolo Koch, Rapho-Photo Researchers.

Chapter Seven.
316 Maria Ealand(2)—Paul Seaman; Maria Ealand—Bob & Ira Spring; Maria Ealand—Josef Muench; Christopher Springmann ©1975—Maria Ealand; Christopher Springmann ©1975. **316-317** Cole Weston. **318** Gerald Brimacombe, Black Star; Jonathan Blair, Black Star. **319** San Francisco Visitors Bureau, Sandor Balatoni. **320** Sam Abell(2). **321** John Launois, Black Star. **322** Roy Wallace Hankey—David Muench. **323** Christopher Springmann ©1975. **324** Jon Brenneis. **325** David Muench. **326** J. R. Eyerman. **326-327** Co Rentmeester, Time-Life Picture Agency, ©Time, Inc. **327** John Loengard, Time-Life Picture Agency, ©Time, Inc.—Paul Fusco, Magnum. **328** John Brenneis, *Fortune*, ©Time, Inc.; Roger Marshutz. **328-329** General Atomic Co. **329** Roger Marshutz(2). **330** Teresa Zabala, *The New York Times*—Michael Philip Manheim ©1974—Maria Ealand. **330-331** Maria Ealand. **331** Donald H. Timm—Maria Ealand. **332** Morton Beebe—Ted Streshinsky. **333** Ted Streshinsky(3). **334-335** Christopher Springmann ©1975(5). **336** Joern Gerdts, Photo Researchers; Christopher Springmann ©1975. **336-337** Ray Atkeson. **337** Norman Hurst ©1973. **338-339** Christopher Springmann ©1975(4). **340** Ray Atkeson(2). **341** Joern Gerdts, Time-Life Books. **340-341** Ted Spiegel, Black Star. **342** Robert Goodman. **343** David Muench(2). **344** John Lewis Stage—Paul Seaman. **345** Paul Seaman. **346** Paul Seaman. **347** *Honolulu Star-Bulletin*(2). **348** Robert Goodman, Black Star. **349** David Muench; (top) Robert Goodman, Black Star—Paul Seaman. **350** Morton Beebe, DPI—Paul Seaman. **350-351, 351** Paul Seaman(3). **352** Robert Goodman. **352-353, 353** David Muench. **354** James Siers. **354-355** Robert Goodman, Black Star. **355** Robert Goodman(2). **356** Ted Streshinsky—Robert Goodman, Black Star. **356-357** Farrell Grehan, Photo Researchers. **357** Robert Goodman, Black Star. **358** John Lewis Stage, Photo Researchers; Bob & Ira Spring. **358-359** Morton Beebe, DPI. **359** Bob & Ira Spring; Joe Rychetnik, Photo Researchers; Bob & Ira Spring; Propix, Monkmeyer; Bob & Ira Spring—Bob & Ira Spring. **360** Joe Rychetnik, Photo Researchers. **360-361, 361** Bob & Ira Spring(2)—J. R. Eyerman. **362** Galen Rowell—Joe Rychetnik, Photo Researchers. **363** Steve McCutcheon. **364-365** Joe Rychetnik, Photo Researchers(3). **366-374** John Metzger(all). **375** Dave Johnston.

Index

381